IMAGES
of America

BRUNSWICK

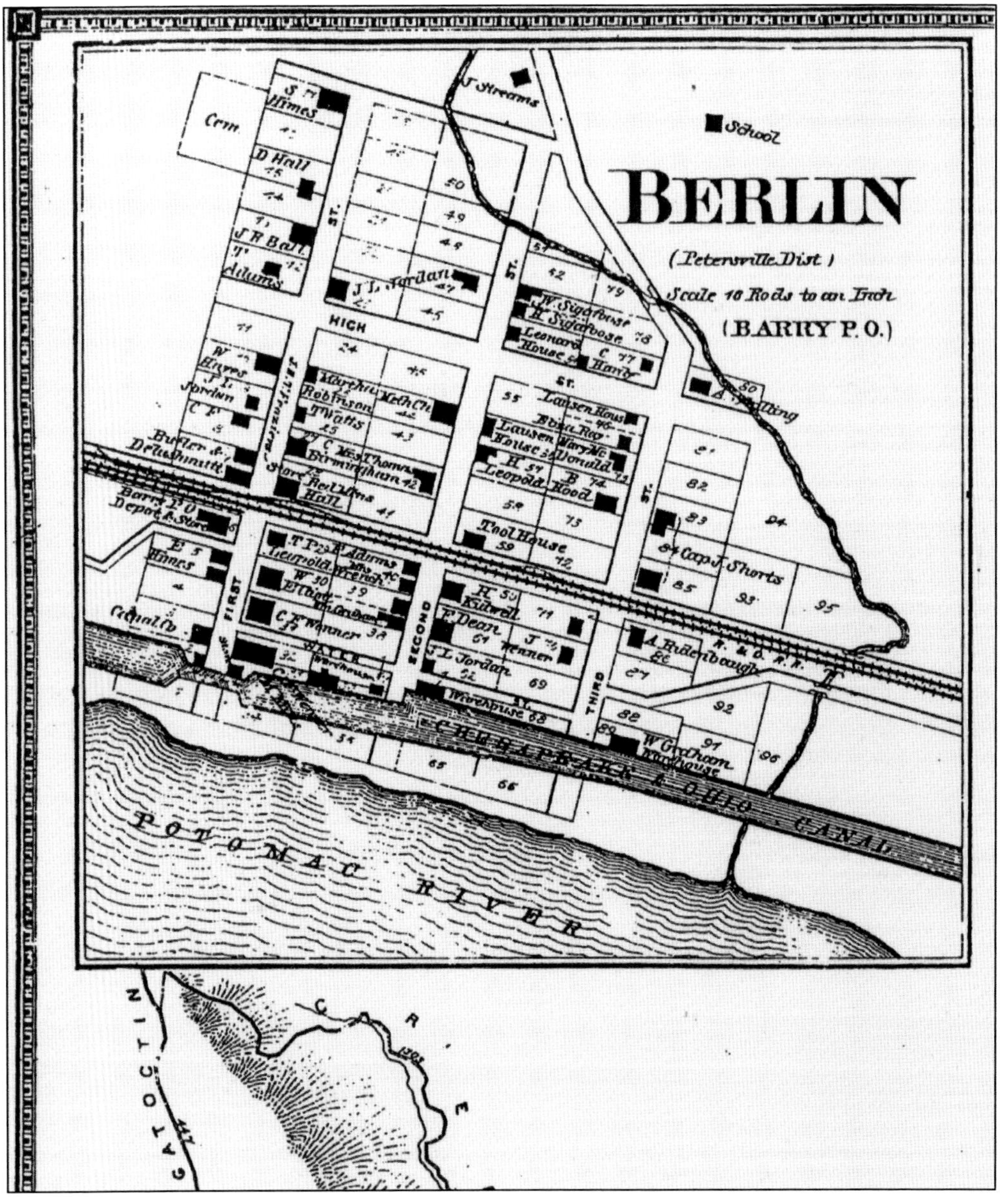

This map shows the layout of Brunswick when it was still known as Berlin. Various lots are identified by owner name, and the Baltimore and Ohio (B&O) Railroad tracks are shown running right through town. The Chesapeake and Ohio (C&O) Canal and the Potomac River are also included. Note the map title indicates the town is in the Petersville District and the Barry Post Office. (Courtesy C&O Canal National Historical Park Headquarters.)

On the Cover: This photograph of the Smith and Carlisle General Store on South Maple Avenue was taken in 1907. Pictured are, from left to right, ? Smith, ? Carlisle, Luther B. Darr (store clerk), G. E. Magaha (store bookkeeper), and Dr. ? Watson (dentist). (Courtesy Brunswick History Commission.)

IMAGES
of America

BRUNSWICK

Mary H. Rubin

ARCADIA
PUBLISHING

ISBN 978-0-7385-5273-6

Published by Arcadia Publishing
Charleston, South Carolina

Printed in the United States of America

Library of Congress Control Number: 2007924180

For all general information contact Arcadia Publishing at:
Telephone 843-853-2070
Fax 843-853-0044
E-mail sales@arcadiapublishing.com
For customer service and orders:
Toll-Free 1-888-313-2665

Visit us on the Internet at www.arcadiapublishing.com

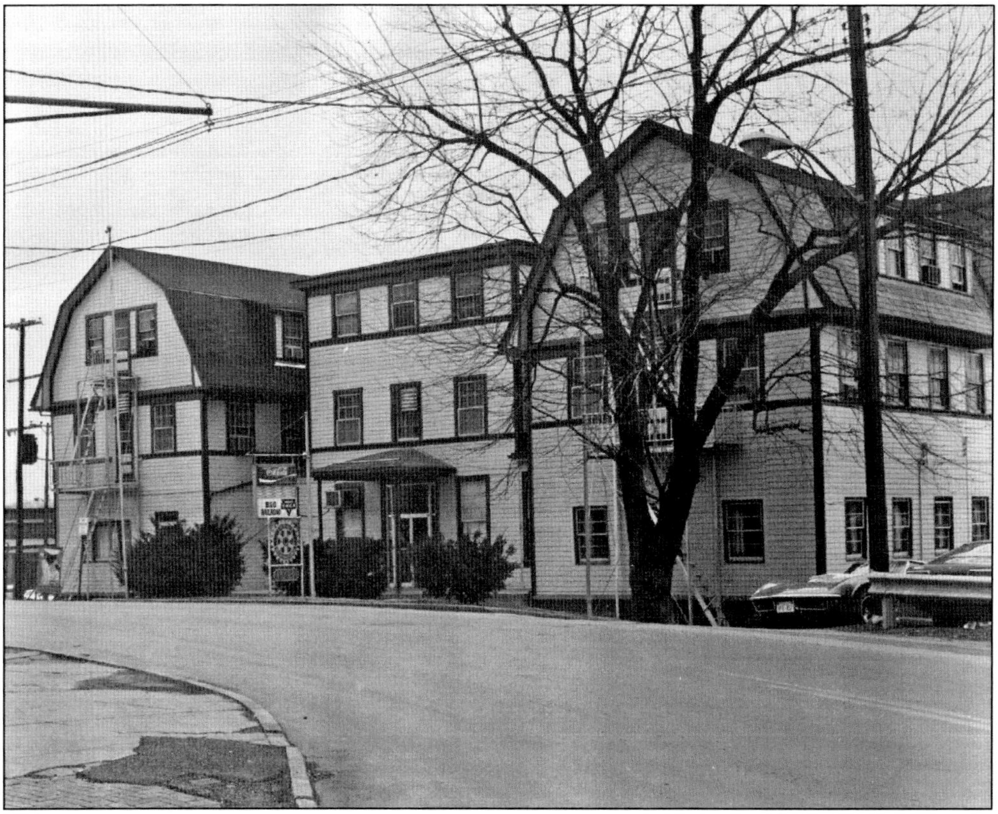

This photograph shows the B&O Railroad YMCA. The YMCA served as a focal point for local railroaders and the greater Brunswick community for many years. (Courtesy Brunswick History Commission.)

Contents

ACKNOWLEDGMENTS

The author wishes to gratefully acknowledge all the help provided by the Brunswick History Commission, in particular Wendell Stewart. His generosity in opening the commission's collection to me made this title possible. The C&O Canal National Historical Park also generously provided a number of the images in this title to help document the canal's role in Brunswick's history. The author would also like to thank Kay Rubin for her always-willing assistance in helping to gather and research information. Also thanks to everyone in the community for their support of my efforts to bring our region's history back to life.

Introduction

Just six miles by towpath from historic Harpers Ferry, West Virginia, Brunswick, Maryland, is rich in history. The town's name itself serves as a lesson in history. Though it was incorporated as Brunswick in 1890, the town's roots reach back to its original settlement in 1728 when it was known as Coxson Rest. This plot of land was located where Lock 30 of the Chesapeake and Ohio (C&O) Canal now stands and was built by an Indian trader, Abraham Pennington, who ran a trading post and a ferry across the Potomac River. This spot along the river grew as a major crossing point for those heading to Virginia. The Highland Indian Trail was a direct north-south route through this region and ran as far as Florida.

Some of the other names given to what was to become Brunswick, each with their own story to tell, include Eel Pot, Buffalo Wallows, Tankerville, and Hawkins' Merry-Peep-O-Day. Arguably the most well-known, previous name was Berlin, so named for the large number of German immigrants in the area at the time. The name caused great confusion for the U.S. Postal Service because there was already a "Berlin, Maryland" located on the state's eastern shore. To avoid postal problems, the town began operating under the post office name of Barry. In 1890, the Baltimore and Ohio (B&O) Railroad was making its presence known in town, and a railroad official was asked to suggest a fancier name for the community, and "Brunswick" was born.

When exploring downtown Brunswick today, it is hard to picture it as the thriving town it used to be. In the days before suburban sprawl, people not only lived in town, but also shopped there, met friends and family for social events, and traveled to points far and near on the train. In short, town was where the action was! Today only commuter and freight trains stop in Brunswick, but at one time, excursion trains left Brunswick for Hagerstown and to one of the most popular parks of its day, Pen Mar Park, on the border of Maryland and Pennsylvania. The five-and-ten store was once a treasure trove to all who entered—you name it and it could be found. The counters, walls, and ceiling were stuffed with merchandise of every kind. Russell Baker writes in his biography, *Growing Up*, that coming across the river from Virginia to Brunswick was like coming to paradise, and a trip to the movie house or an ice cream soda at the drugstore was a dream come true. The canal was a thriving, living thing, and trains rumbled by endlessly. In fact, the kind of activity that one only associates today with large towns was once the commonplace way of life in Brunswick, as was true of other small communities throughout Maryland and, indeed, the rest of the country.

Today the town sits on the now-quiet banks of the C&O Canal, and the train whistles don't sound the way they used to, but this community continues to draw visitors seeking history, outdoor recreation, and small-town charm. Join author Mary Rubin in a look back at Brunswick as seen through photographs of days gone by. Images from the Brunswick History Commission and the C&O Canal National Historical Park Headquarters bring the area back to life and illustrate the vital role it played in the growth of our nation.

One

The Early Years

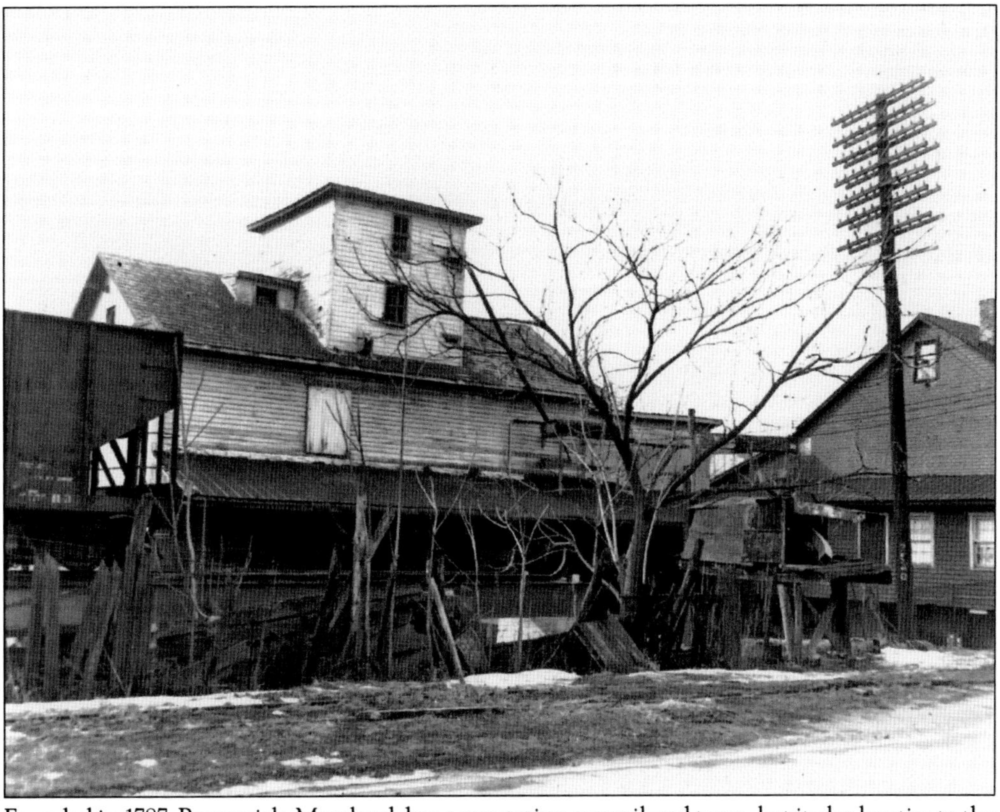

Founded in 1787, Brunswick, Maryland, has a reputation as a railroad town, but it also has ties to the C&O Canal. The town was located at Milepost 55 along the canal, and ferry service was the original mode of crossing the Potomac River prior to the bridge service used now. This 1964 photograph shows a dilapidated mill from the old canal days. Note the rail tracks in front of the mill and the hopper car to the left. (Courtesy U.S. Department of the Interior, National Park Service.)

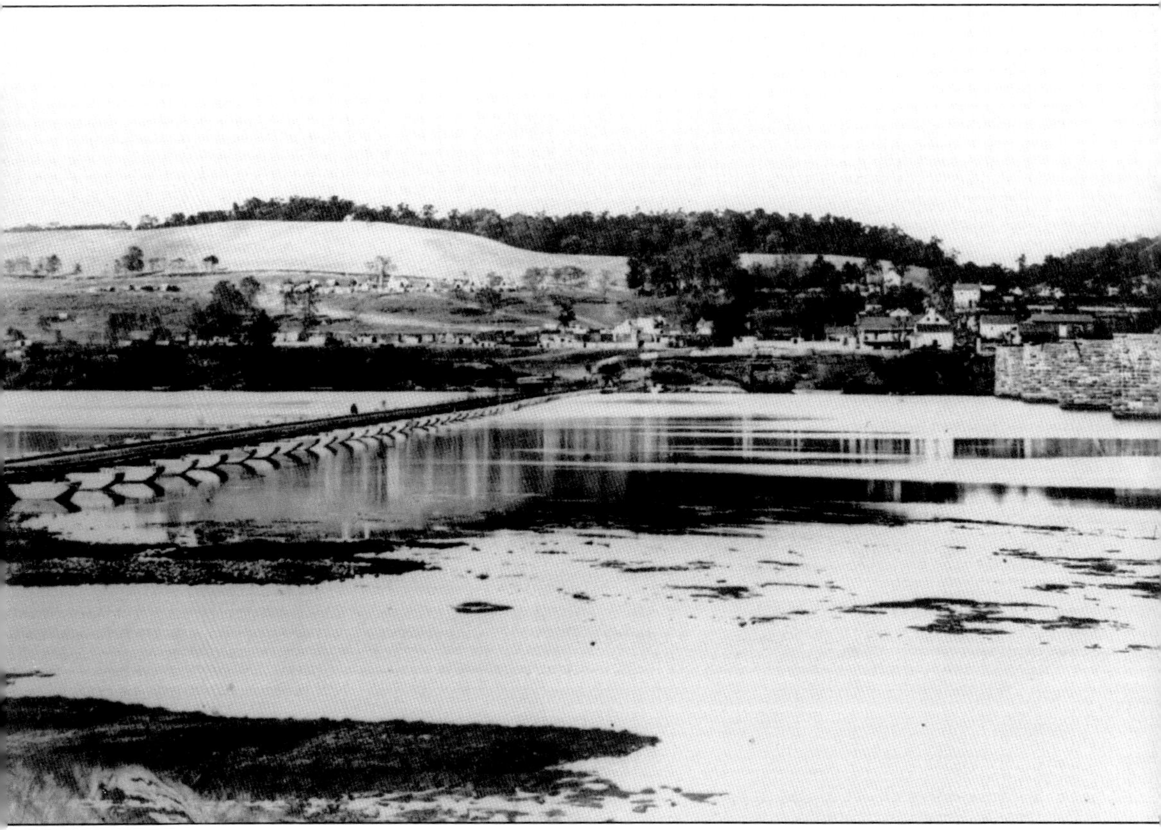

Here is a close-up view of the pontoon bridge across the Potomac River at Berlin (Brunswick), Maryland, in October 1862. The bridge was built on pontoons that floated on the surface of the water rather than traditional bridge pilings driven into the riverbed. The Civil War was already in progress, and troops would use this bridge to cross the river in the days to come. In November 1862, the pontoons were removed and transported to Fredericksburg, Virginia, for use in crossing the Rappahannock River. (Courtesy C&O Canal National Historical Park Headquarters.)

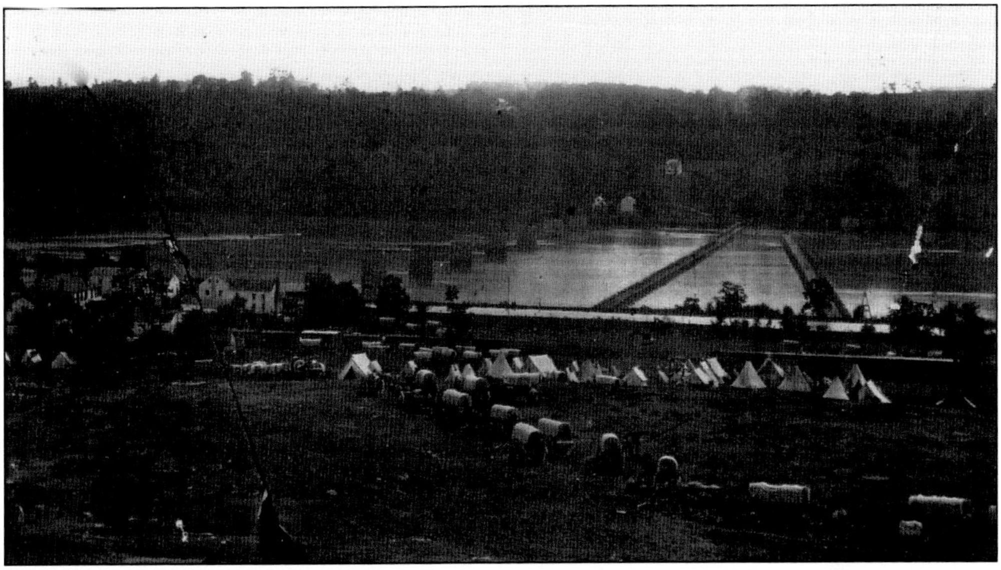

Known at the time as Berlin, the town of Brunswick, Maryland, played a role during the Civil War. This July 1863 photograph shows a segment of the Army of the Potomac crossing the river. Earlier bridges that had been constructed across the river had been destroyed during the war. Note the covered wagons with the tent encampment behind it. Buildings belonging to the town of Berlin are to the left. (Courtesy C&O Canal National Historical Park Headquarters.)

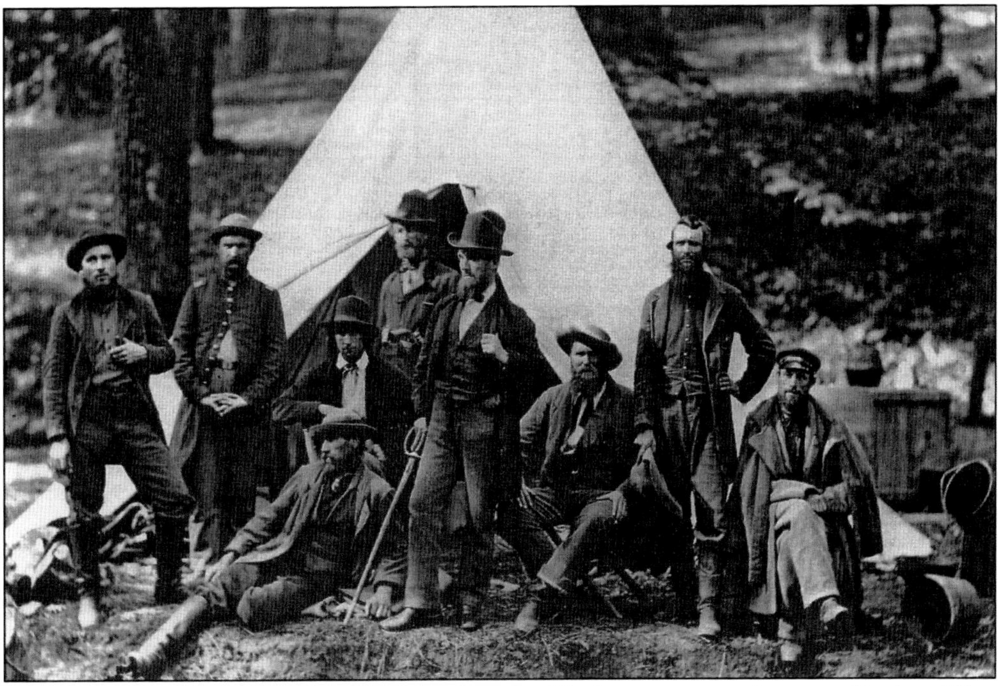

Taken around 1862, this photograph shows a group of Pinkerton men in the area of Berlin. Allan Pinkerton started his national detective agency in 1850 and founded the United States' first Secret Service. During the Civil War, Pinkerton served as Gen. George B. McClellan's chief of secret services and was instrumental in foiling an attempt on Pres. Abraham Lincoln's life. (Courtesy C&O Canal National Historical Park Headquarters.)

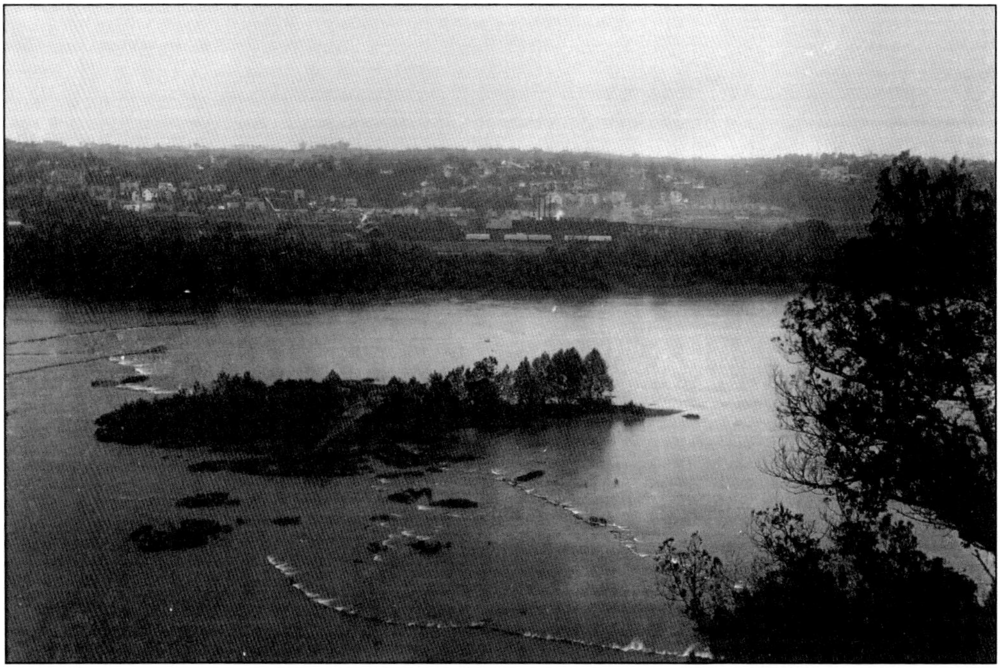

This image shows Brunswick as seen from across the river on the Virginia hills. The island that appears in the middle of the photograph is no longer there. The four smokestacks in the middle of the photograph are from the steam plant at the railroad shop. (Courtesy Brunswick History Commission.)

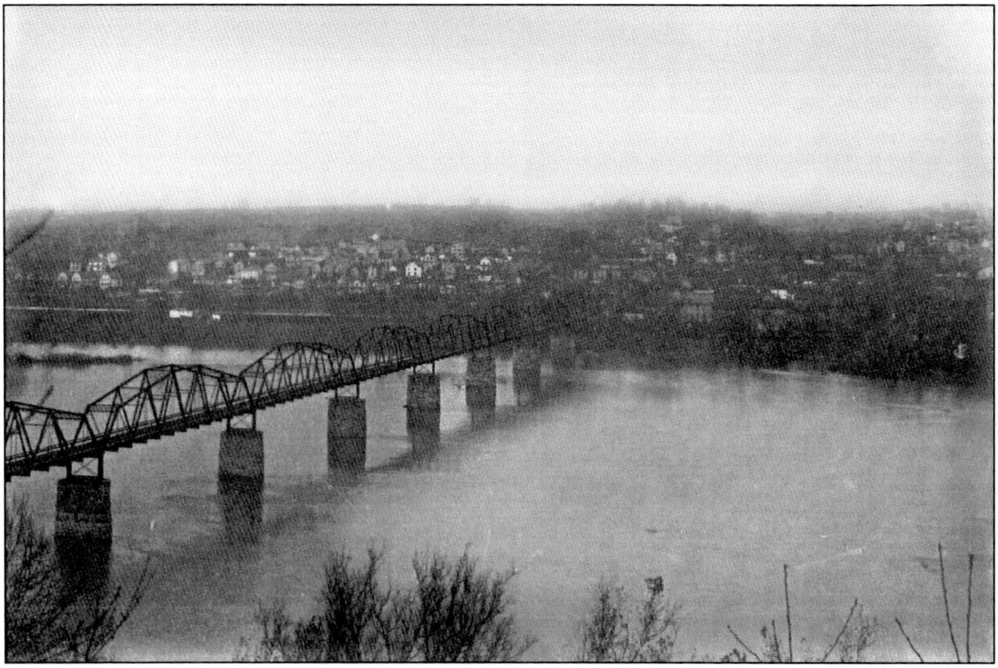

Here is another image, taken c. 1900, showing Brunswick from the Virginia side of the river. Note the old metal bridge with its wooden-plank flooring crossing the Potomac River. A new cement bridge replaced the metal bridge in 1955. (Courtesy Brunswick History Commission.)

Two

COMMERCE AND INDUSTRY

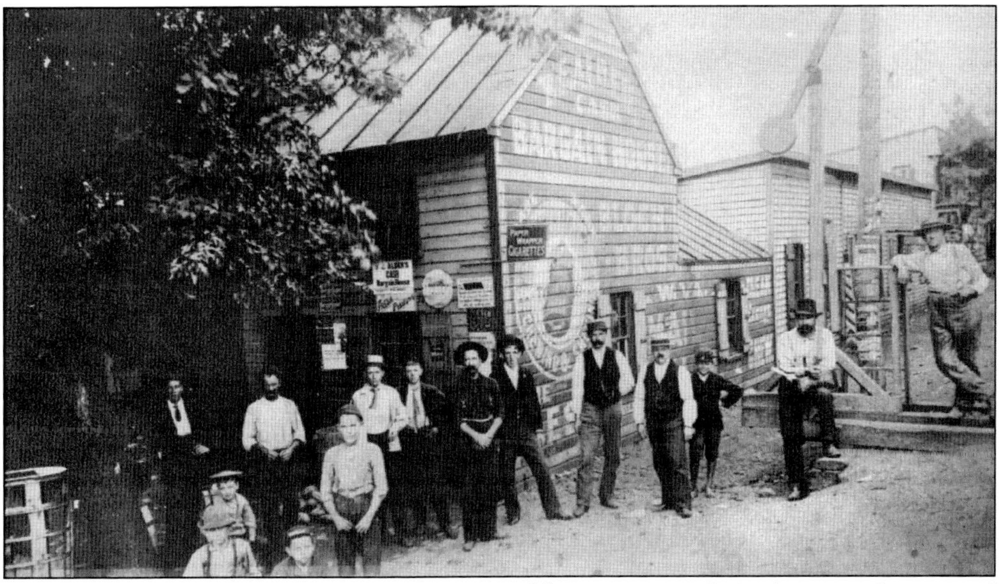

This photograph shows Frank Alder's store on Middle Street *c.* 1895. At this time, the east and west tracks of the B&O Railroad were both at the location of the present-day westbound tracks. Alder's general store also carried jewelry and confections. Jewelry, railroad watches in particular, later became a specialty. A 1924 directory lists the store's location as 5 West Potomac Street and notifies the reader that the store is under new ownership: "J. E. Moore, successor to F. E. Alder, Railroad watches a specialty." Pictured are, from left to right, the following: (first row) four unidentified youths; (second row) unidentified, Ben House, unidentified, G. Berry, Lawson House, unidentified, Webb Hawes, Frank Alder, Garland Alder, Dick Hawes, and unidentified. Note the advertisement painted on the side of the building, a common practice at the time. (Courtesy Brunswick History Commission.)

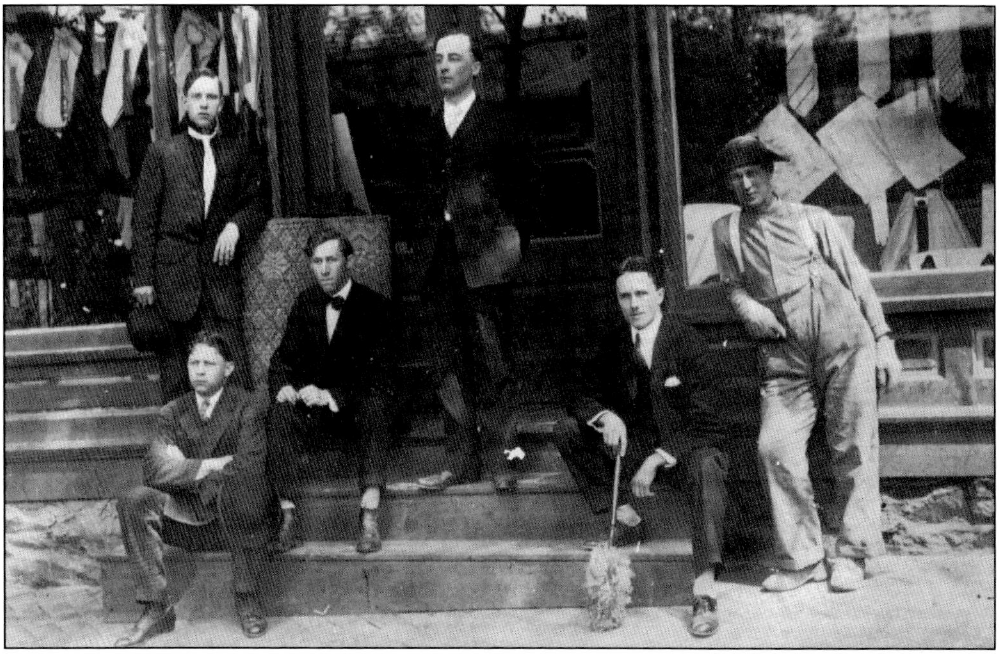

This 1896 image shows the Jones and Robinson Store on East Potomac Street. The store advertised as, "The Leading Store for Ladies' and Gents' Furnishings, Dry Goods, Shoes and Hats our Specialties." The store would later become Barnett's store and then Walt Ambrose's barbershop. In the photograph are, from left to right, (seated) unidentified, Brooke Stewart, and Alonza Stewart; (standing) two unidentified and Bob Stewart. (Courtesy Brunswick History Commission.)

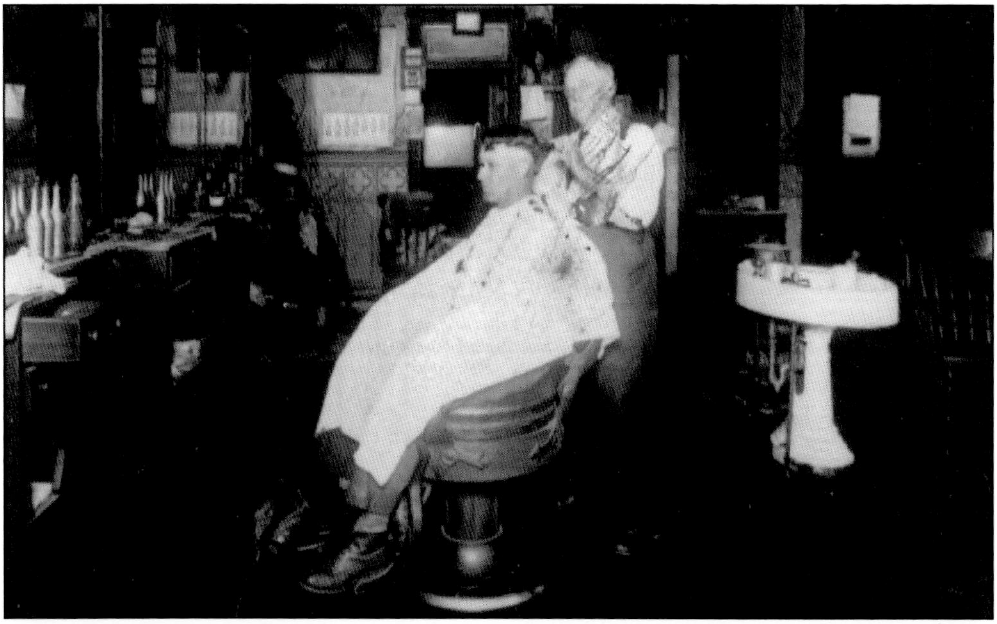

Here is Elias Flynn cutting hair at his barbershop, one of many in town, located at the railroad tracks and Maple Avenue. The American Legion parking lot is on this location now. The last barbershop owner, Kenneth Harshman, retired in 1989 and brought in the town's first female barber, Karen Poole, to take over. (Courtesy Brunswick History Commission.)

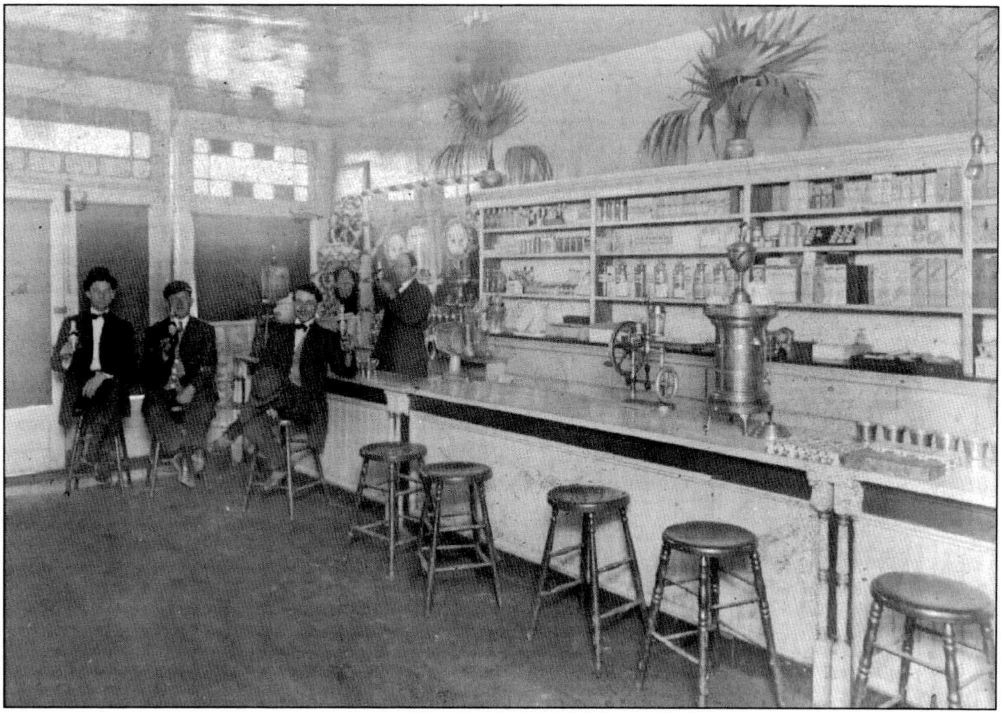

Taken *c.* 1908, this photograph shows the interior of the soda fountain at 5 East Potomac Street. Pictured are, from left to right, Ed Darr, Pres Orrison, Guy Dinges, and John Brady (owner). The Darr brothers, Ed and Lucas, bought the business in 1914. Operated as Darr's Confectionery, the business became Darr's Tavern after the repeal of Prohibition in the 1930s. (Courtesy Brunswick History Commission.)

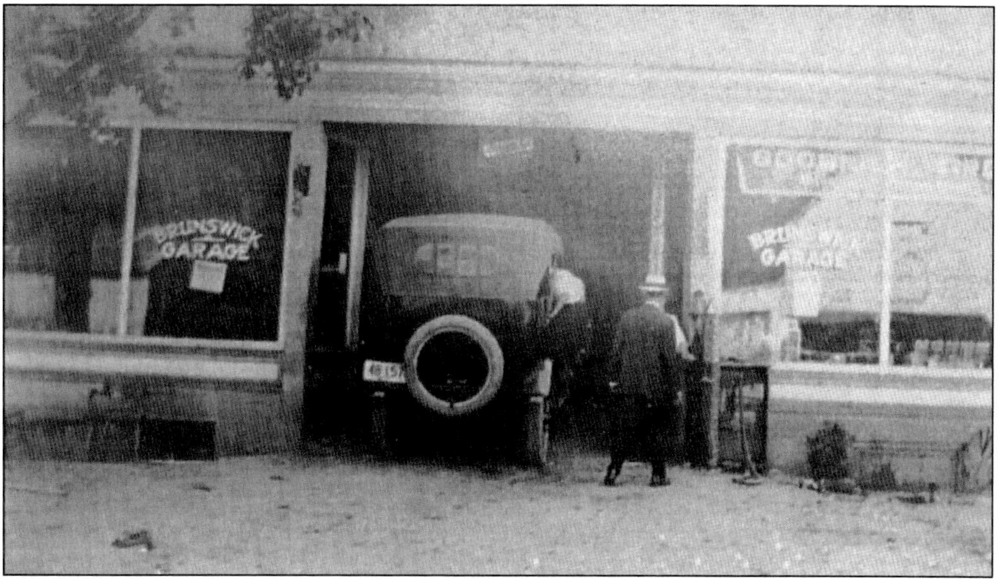

Here is an old image of the Brunswick Garage located at the intersection of A Street, Maple Avenue, and Petersville Road. The old car in the garage's entrance evokes a sense of days gone by when compared to today's modern service bays. (Courtesy Brunswick History Commission.)

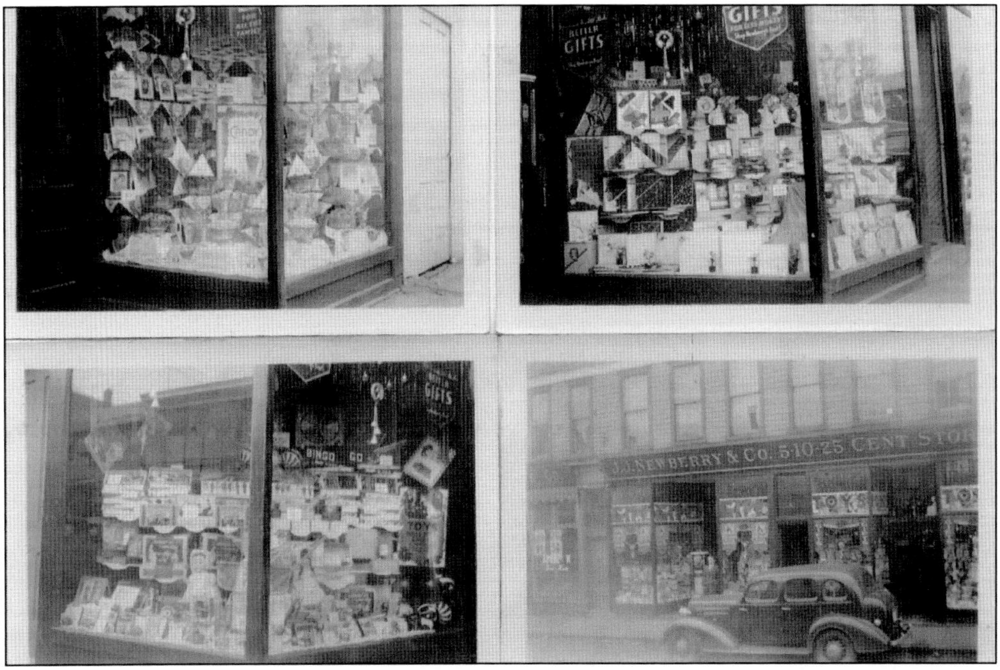

This collage of photographs shows the windows of the J. J. Newberry Company five-and-dime store decorated for Christmas during the mid- to late 1930s. Wendell Stewart, the stock boy, was responsible for the attractive window dressing—the company goal was to fill the windows as tightly as possible with merchandise. (Courtesy Brunswick History Commission.)

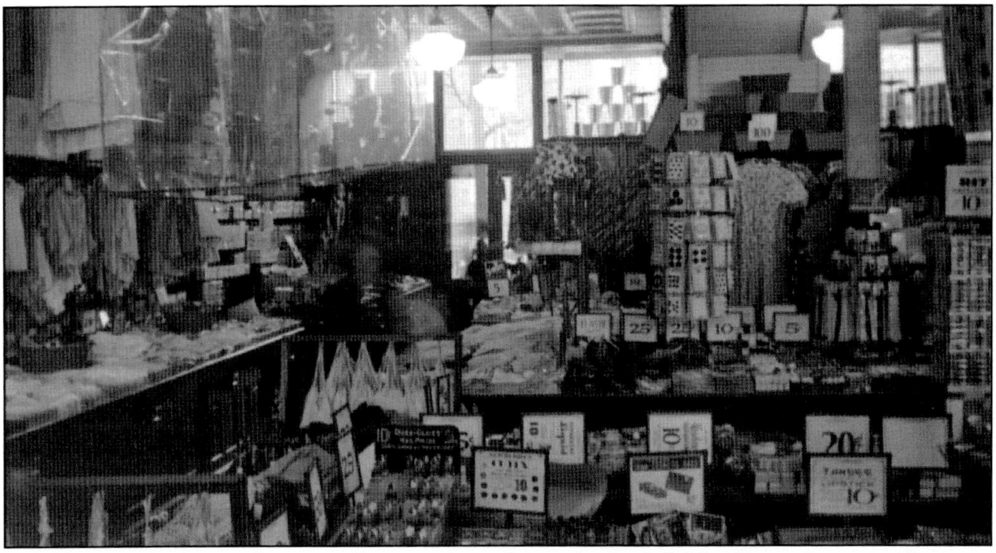

What a treasure trove of items to browse through inside the J. J. Newberry Company store on West Potomac Street. Taken in the mid- to late 1930s, this photograph shows the store crammed with merchandise on counters, shelves, and even hanging from the ceilings. Wendell Stewart, the stock boy at the store, was also responsible for regularly escorting store clerks to the bank with money from the registers. On Saturday nights, the store was so packed with customers it was hard to turn around. Today Wendell is active with the Brunswick Historical Commission. (Courtesy Brunswick History Commission.)

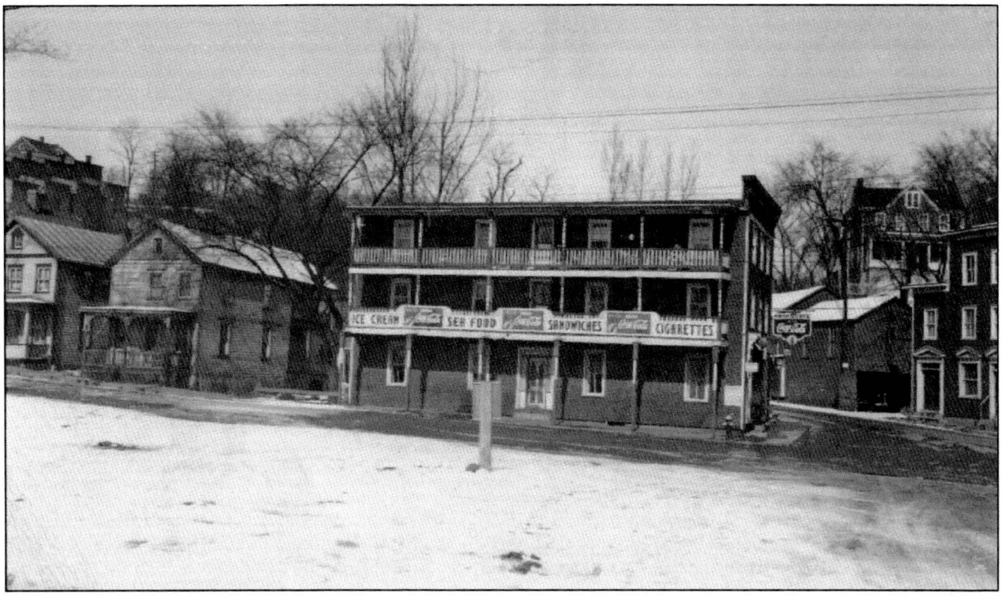

This photograph was taken sometime prior to 1950 and shows Hahn's Café at the corner of West B Street and Petersville Road. Operated by Bessie and Harry Hahn, the café was open daily for more than 20 years. The popular eatery, constructed from wood salvaged from houses that had been between the railroad tracks, was torn down in 1950 as part of the right-of-way for the new bridge. (Courtesy Brunswick History Commission.)

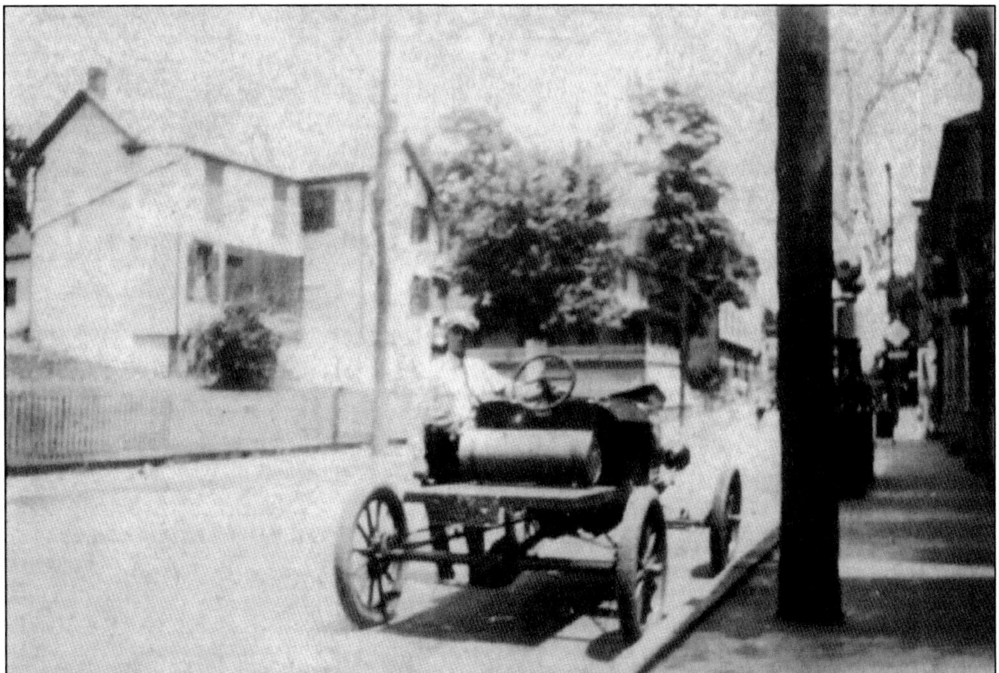

Here is Ralph A. Mulkey outside his service station on West Potomac Street in 1930. He is posed for the photograph next to his Ford car with its large gas tank on the rear. (Courtesy Brunswick History Commission.)

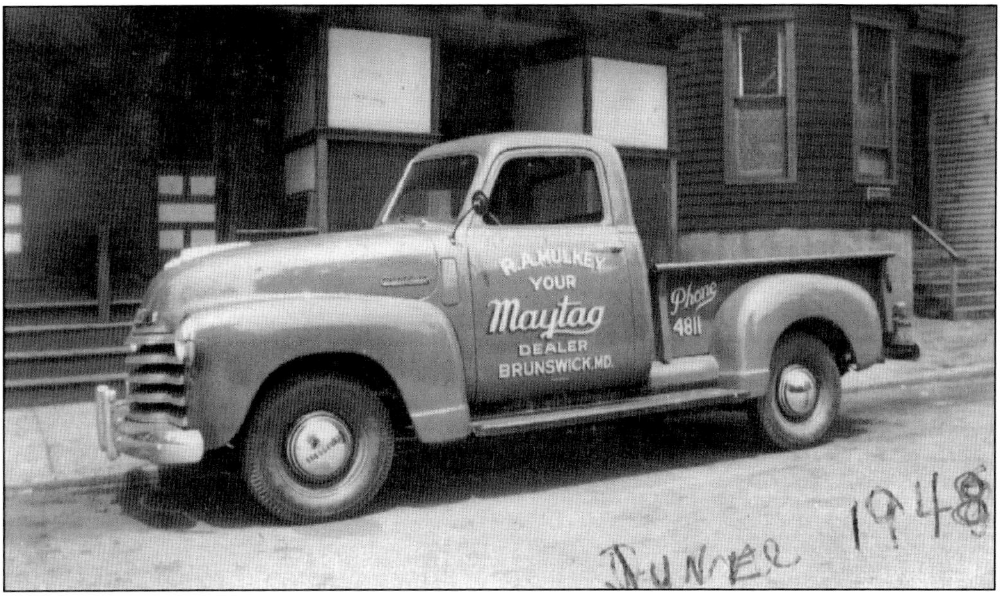

This image shows Ralph Mulkey's pickup truck with its Maytag-dealership paint job in Brunswick in June 1948. Note the telephone number painted on the truck was only four digits long. (Courtesy Brunswick History Commission.)

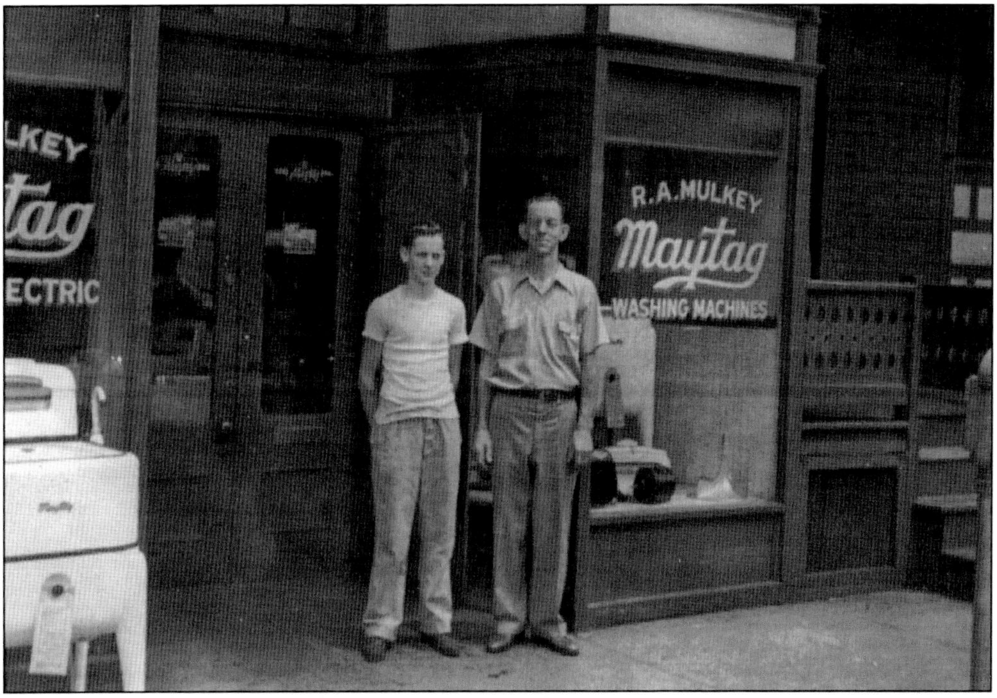

In this photograph, Ralph Mulkey (right) and John Brady are standing outside Mulkey's Maytag store. Look at that old wringer-style washing machine on display on the left. (Courtesy Brunswick History Commission.)

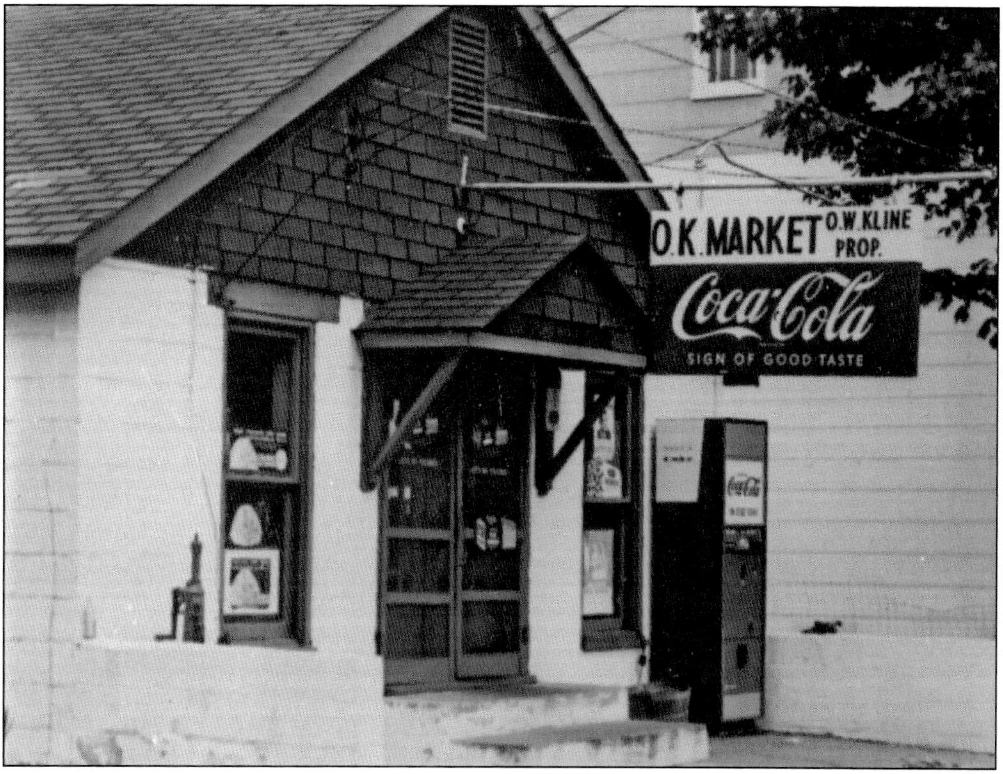

This photograph shows the outside of the O. K. Market on North Maple Avenue. Owen W. Kline was the proprietor, and as the signs state, he stocked Coca-Cola. Note the outside vending machine that probably dispensed the soda in their trademark glass bottles. (Courtesy Brunswick History Commission.)

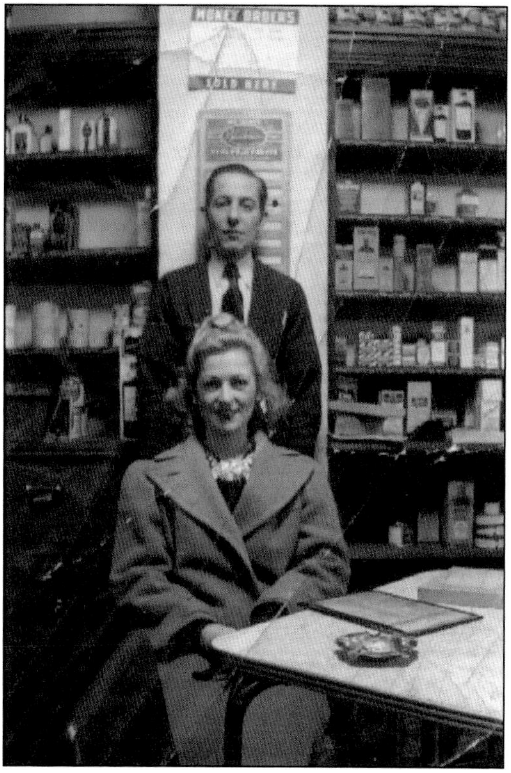

Here is an interior view of Barnett's drugstore on West Potomac Street *c.* 1943. Doc Barnett is in the photograph with Ruth Lee Howie. A sign on the wall indicated that money orders could also be purchased at the store. (Courtesy Brunswick History Commission.)

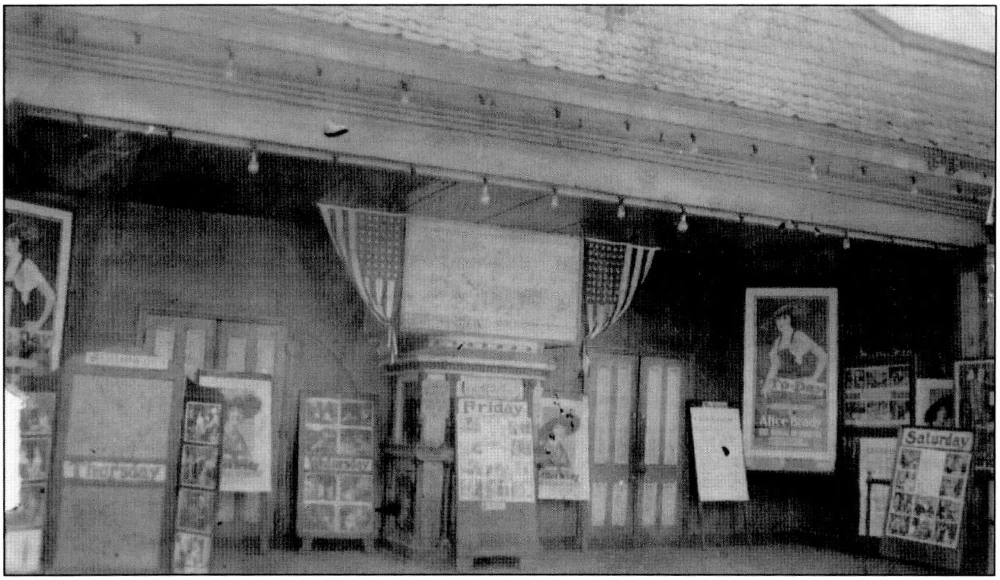

The Imperial Theatre, built on West Potomac Street in the years preceding World War I, served the entertainment needs of Brunswick for almost 50 years, and admission never cost more than 50¢. In the years before "talking" movies, sound was added to films via a pianist. The hoofbeats and gunshots were imitated for Western films, and smoke was sometimes blown into the theater to help create the desired mood. The theater closed in 1962 and was purchased with the intention of opening a club for teenagers, but the building collapsed during renovations. (Courtesy Brunswick History Commission.)

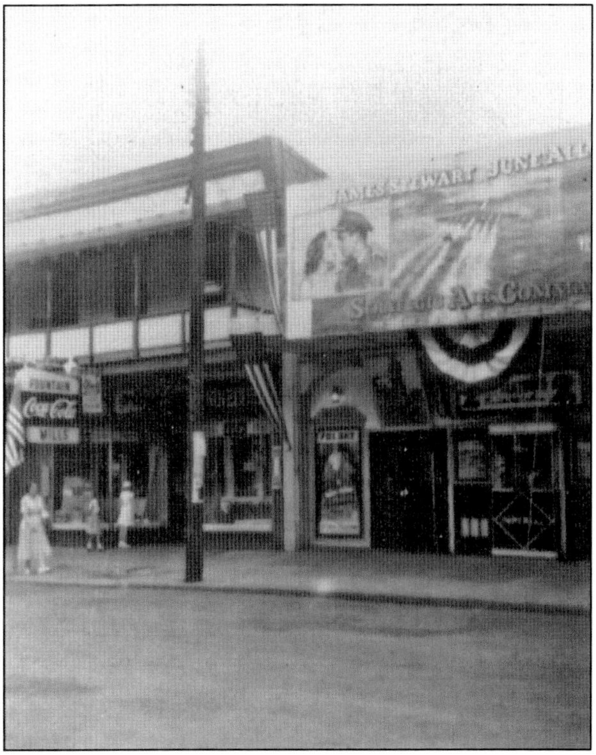

This photograph shows the Imperial Theatre during the World War II years. Note the advertisement for the movie *Strategic Air Command* with James Stewart and June Allyson. The left side of the photograph shows the Mills Soda Fountain and Candy Store. (Courtesy Brunswick History Commission.)

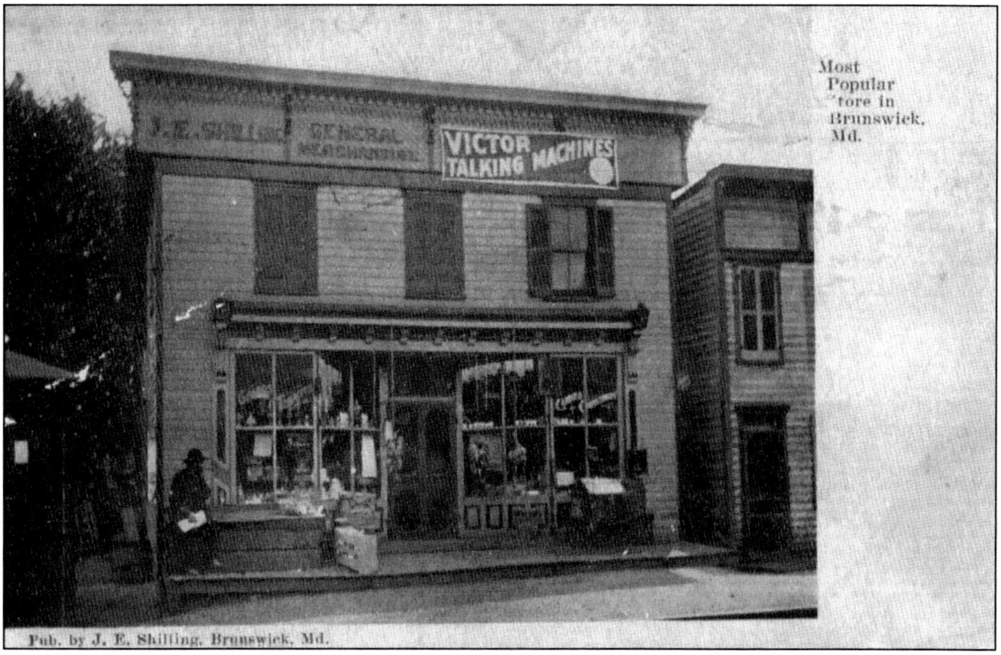

This postcard shows the J. E. Shilling general store opposite the B&O Station in 1902. The postcard bills the business as the "Most Popular Store in Brunswick, MD." Notice the large hanging advertisement for Victor Talking Machines. (Courtesy Brunswick History Commission.)

Here is an interesting set of tokens that were once used in exchange for goods at Brunswick merchants. The tokens indicate they serve as "checks" good for their value (25¢, 50¢, and $2 tokens are shown) in merchandise with a blank line to fill in the name of the store. (Courtesy Brunswick History Commission.)

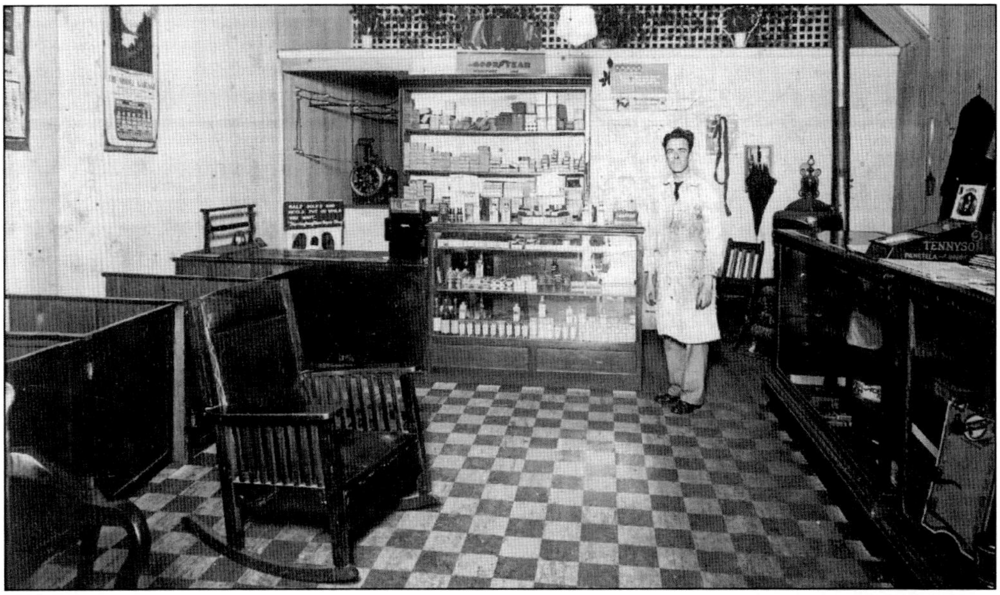

This photograph was taken inside the Harrington Shoe Repair Shop in the Swank Building on West Potomac Street. William Eugene Harrington was the shop's proprietor. Note the old stove in the back right corner. William's father, George, had started the business and gained a reputation for quality work. The shoe shop was a favorite gathering place, especially for retired railroaders. (Courtesy Brunswick History Commission.)

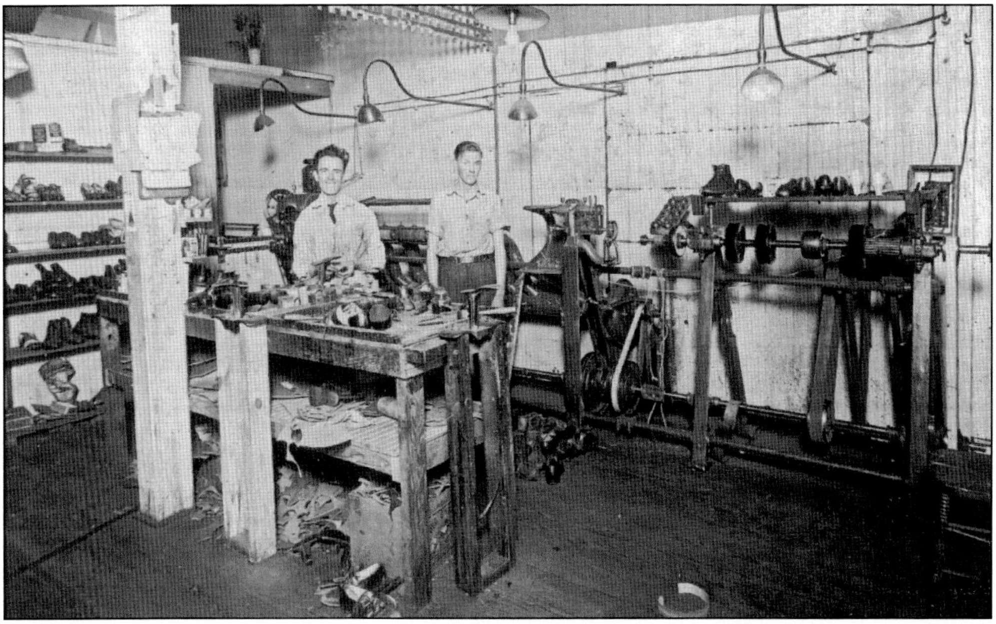

Here is another image from the Harrington Shoe Repair Shop. Donald Earl Harrington (right) is pictured next to his brother William. Donald operated his own shoe repair shop in Berkeley Springs, West Virginia, but returned to Brunswick after his brother died in 1964 to take over the family business. Note some of the machinery used in the trade—when Bill took over from his father, he was able to take advantage of new machinery that made the work much easier. (Courtesy Brunswick History Commission.)

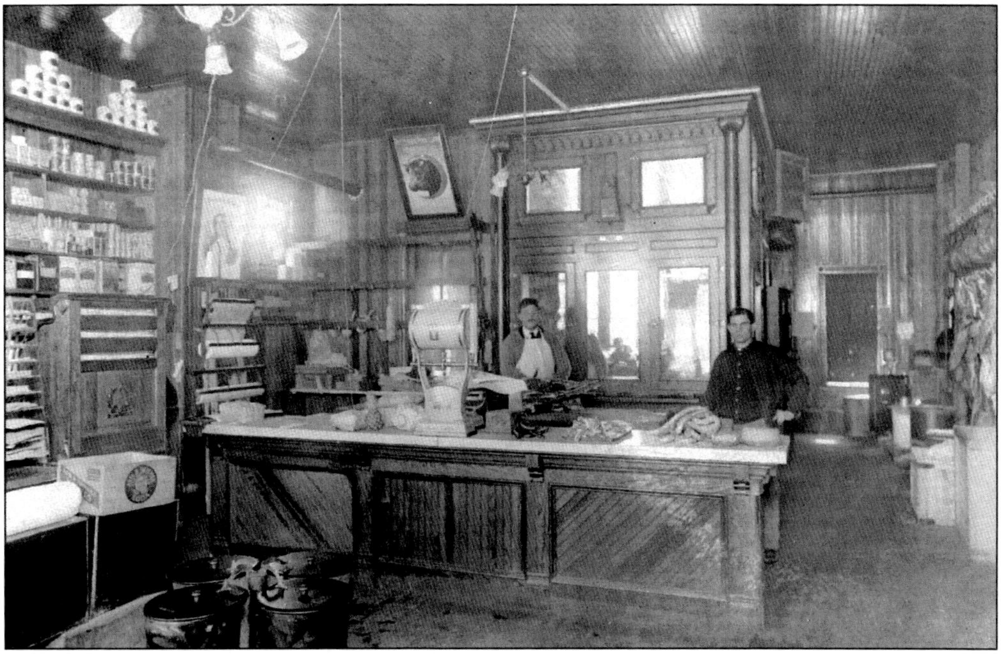

This photograph shows the inside of Hemp's Meats and Groceries in the 200 block of West Potomac Street. Hemp is the man with the moustache in this c. 1920 photograph. The building later became Roelke and Dixon Grocery and then Bill Harrington's shoe repair shop and home of the *Nicodemus News*. Note the vats of pickles in the forefront of the photograph and the neat stacks of merchandise on the shelves. (Courtesy Brunswick History Commission.)

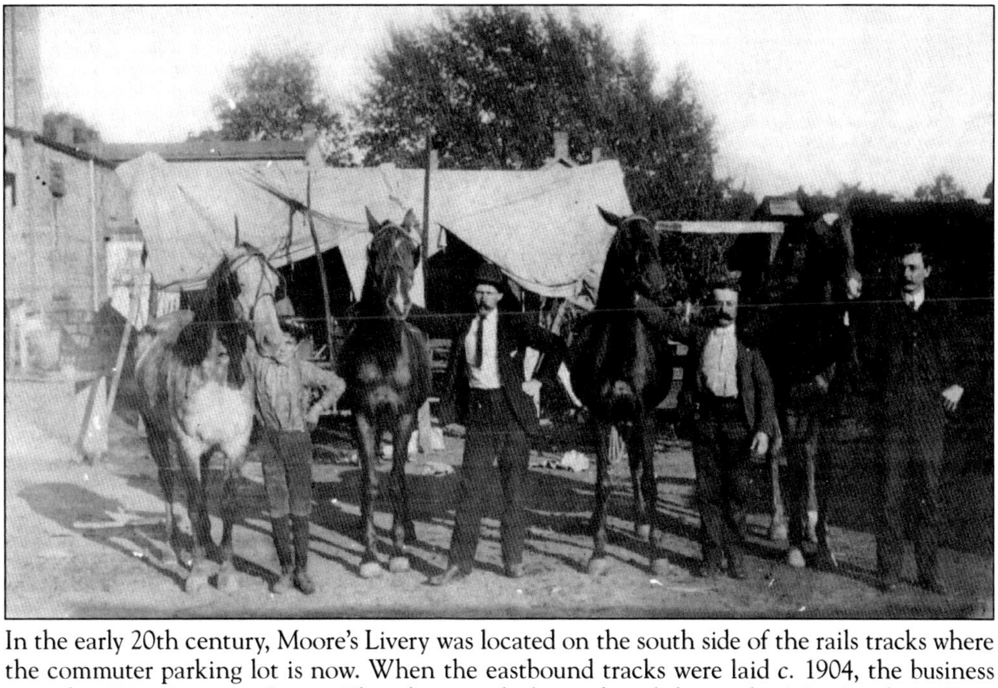

In the early 20th century, Moore's Livery was located on the south side of the rails tracks where the commuter parking lot is now. When the eastbound tracks were laid c. 1904, the business moved to West Potomac Street. This photograph shows, from left to right, Mac Sigafoose, E. L. Bell, Raleigh Moore, and Clarence Mohler. (Courtesy Brunswick History Commission.)

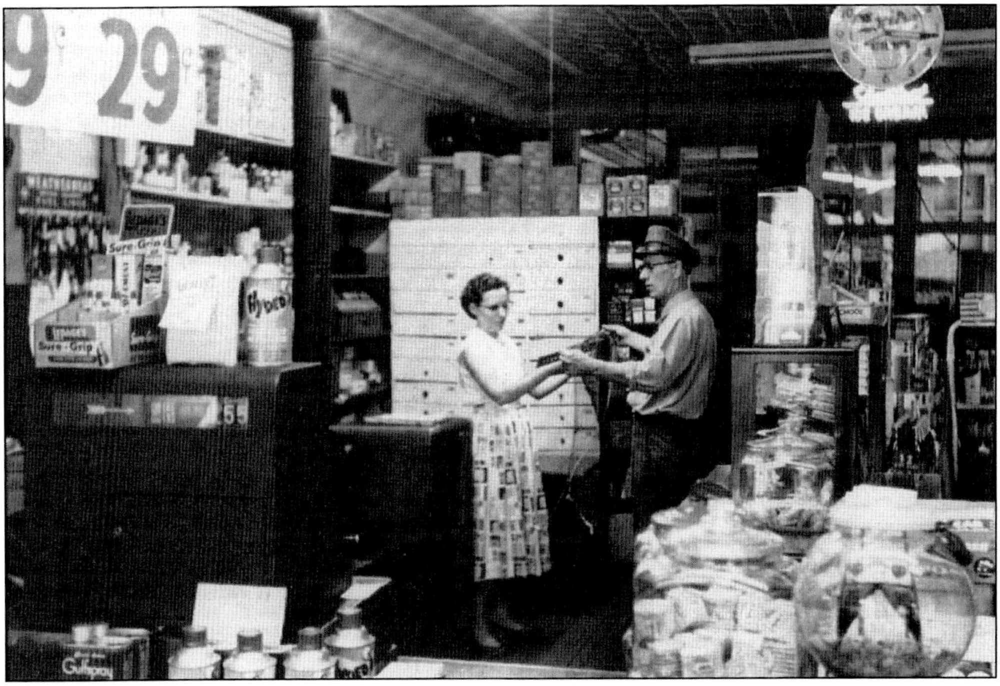

This photograph shows Virginia Lee Koogle and Hugh Cage inside Cage Brothers Garage on East Potomac Street. The garage was in business at this location from the 1930s through the 1950s. Cage's was one of a number of garage/service stations that were located in Brunswick over the years. The first reference to a filling station in town records was on June 2, 1914, when A. Kaplon was given approval to open a station on West Potomac Street. (Courtesy Brunswick History Commission.)

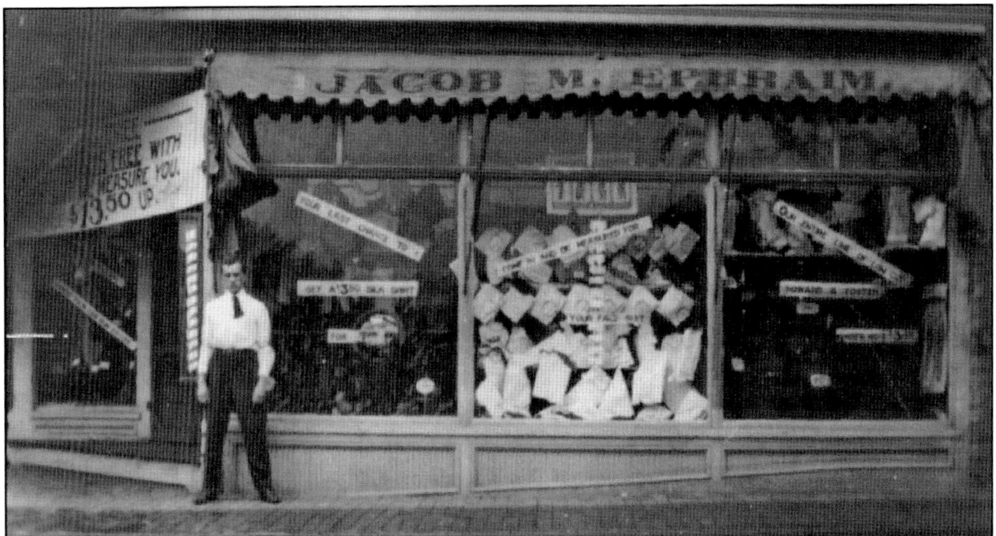

This image shows Jacob M. Ephraim's clothing store on Potomac Street. A fire destroyed the store at 2:00 a.m. December 27, 1917. Note the sign hanging over the entrance announcing free trousers with every suit purchase. Prices began at $13.50 in those days. (Courtesy Brunswick History Commission.)

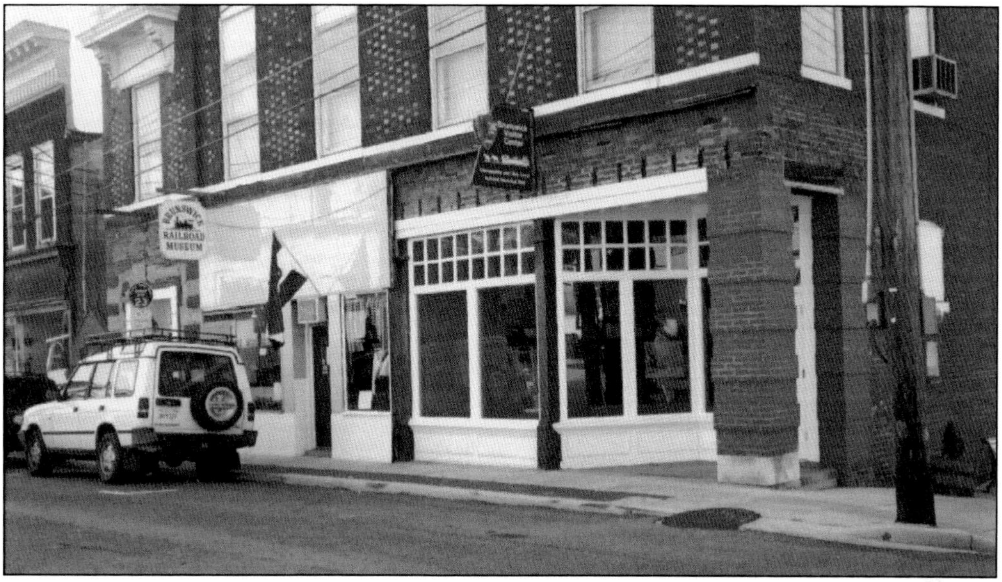

This photograph shows the corner of Maryland Avenue and West Potomac Street, the home of the Brunswick Railroad Museum and the National Park Service's Brunswick Visitor Center for the Chesapeake and Ohio Canal. Both museums are popular attractions and play a role in the town's annual Brunswick Railroad Days each fall. (Courtesy Brunswick History Commission.)

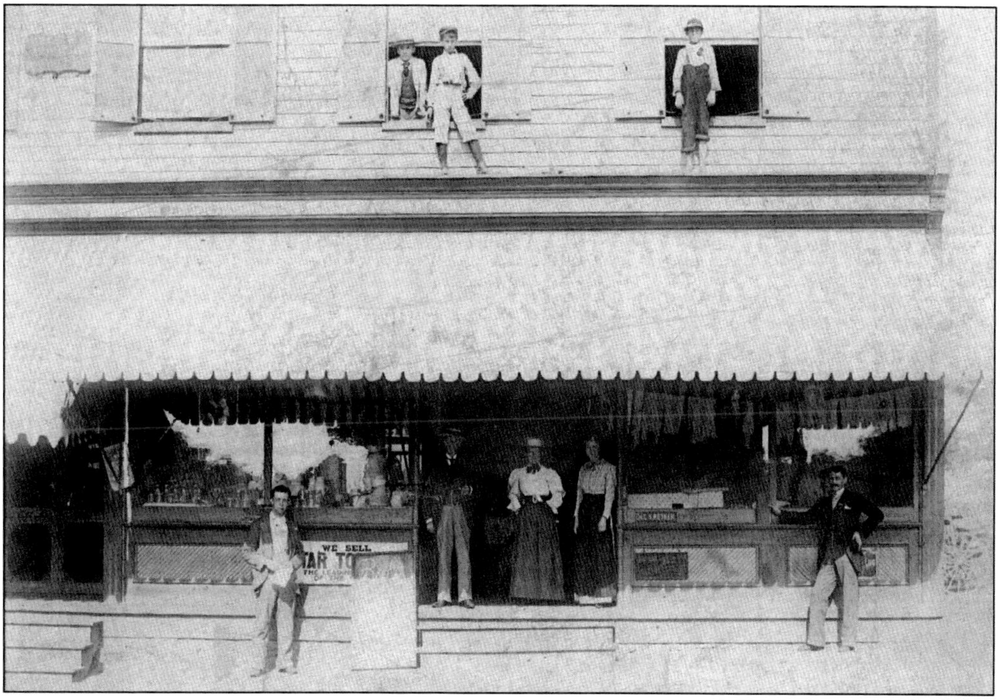

This image shows the Gross General Store when it was located on South Maryland Avenue. The store, like many other general stores across the country, was a treasure trove of merchandise. Ladies' corsets, large wheels of cheese, suspenders, radios, and glassware were just a few of the items to be found. The cool basement served as storage for perishable items such as butter and fish, while the attic stored all manner of out-of-season items. (Courtesy Brunswick History Commission.)

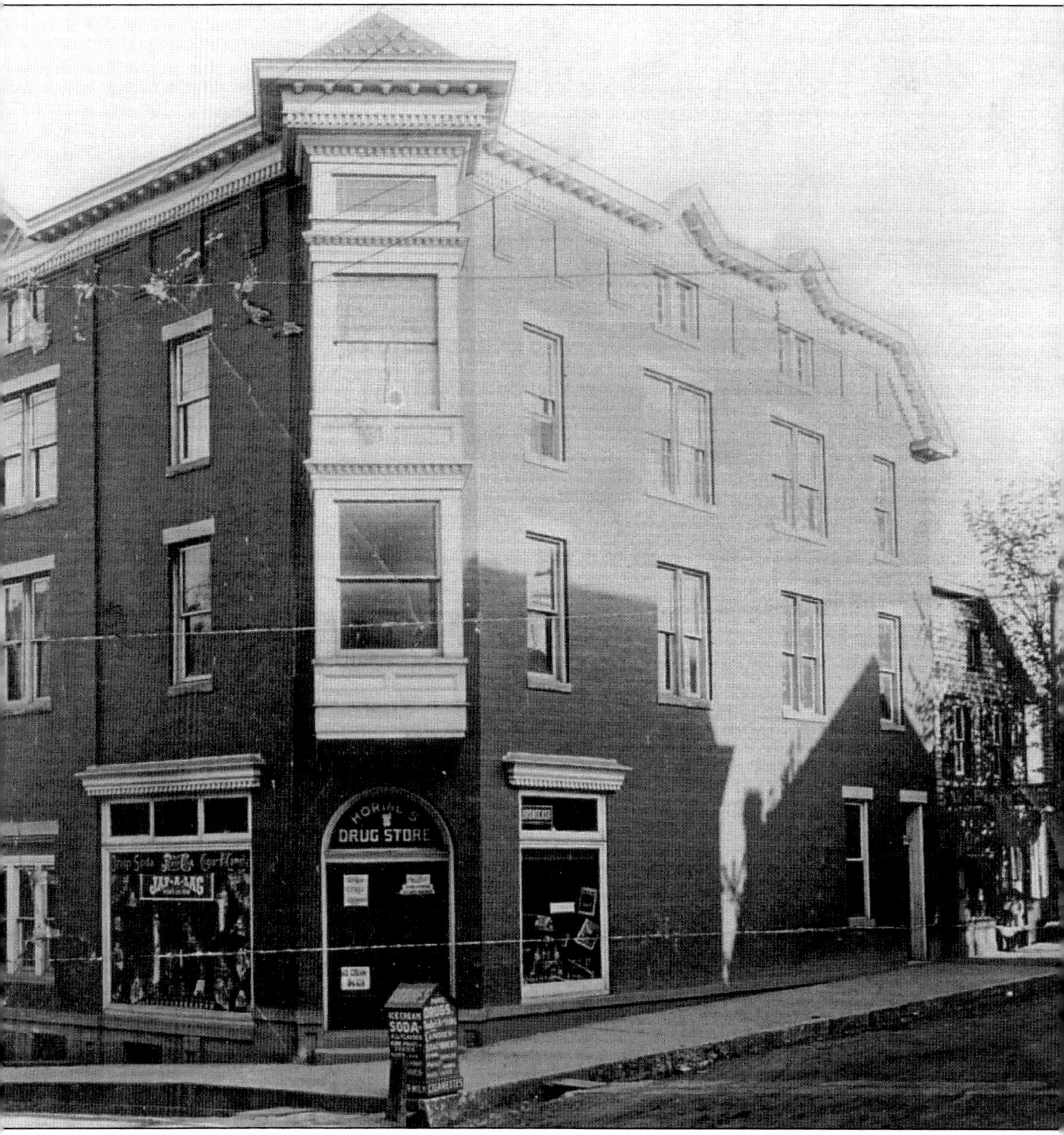

This photograph shows Horine's Drug Store on the corner of Potomac Street and Maple Avenue. The building to the rear was used as a stable for Dr. Arlington G. Horine's horse and buggy. Horine built this building in 1905, and it included an office for him, apartments upstairs for his son and daughter, and a drugstore and soda fountain on the first floor. Horine's corner was once the bus stop for buses that ran south to Winchester or north to Frederick where riders could connect with the Blue Ridge intercity bus line. The Book Crossing bookstore is located in this building today. (Courtesy Brunswick History Commission.)

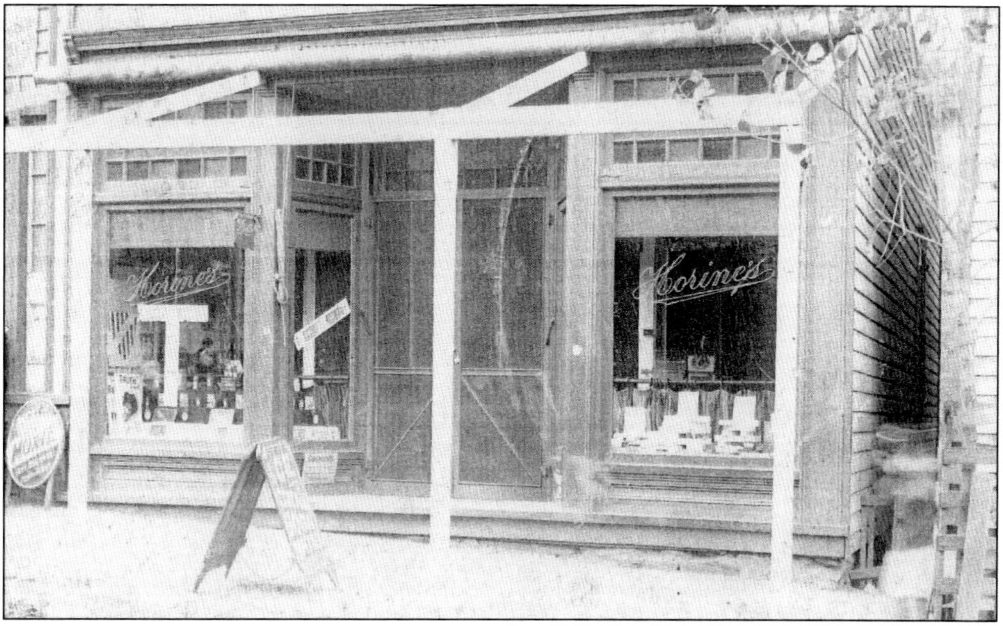

Here is Dr. Arlington G. Horine's original store prior to 1900 located on Railroad Street next to the westbound train tracks. Dr. Horine opened his drugstore in 1890 and later moved the business to the corner of Maple Avenue and Potomac Street. Dr. Horine served as surgeon for the B&O Railroad from 1891 to 1903 and treated 1,200 accident cases during this time period. Note the sign advertising the popular Moxie drink on the left. (Courtesy Brunswick History Commission.)

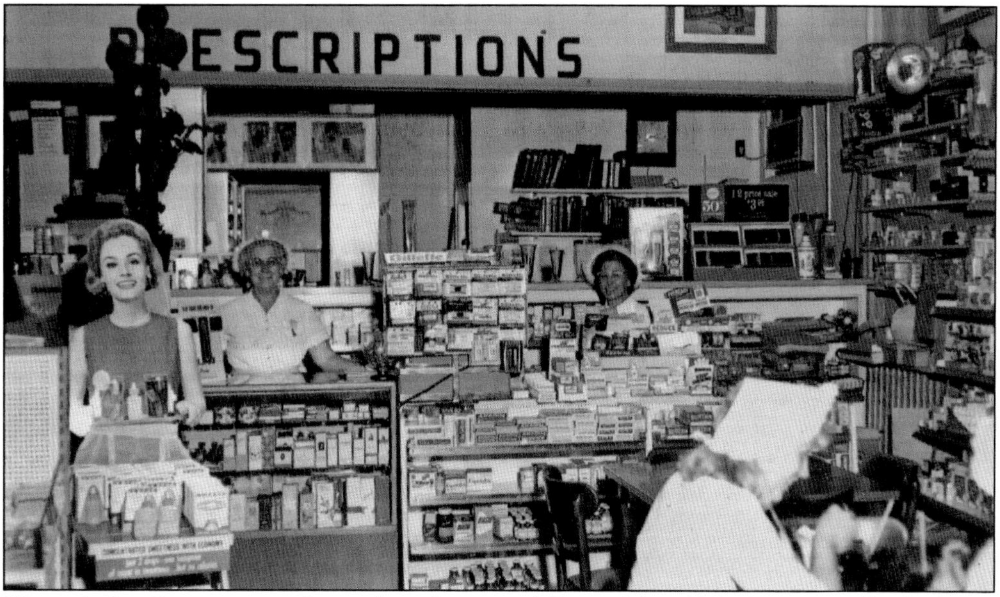

Watson's Cut Rate store was located on the ground floor of the old Red Men's Hall, which was built in 1904 on the southwest corner of West Potomac Street and South Maryland Avenue. Pearl K. Taylor is shown behind the counter on the left. There have been various occupants of this space over the years, including the Bank of Brunswick, the Brunswick Post Office, Prescription Arts Pharmacy, Brunswick Office Supply, and Lost Control Antiques. (Courtesy Brunswick History Commission.)

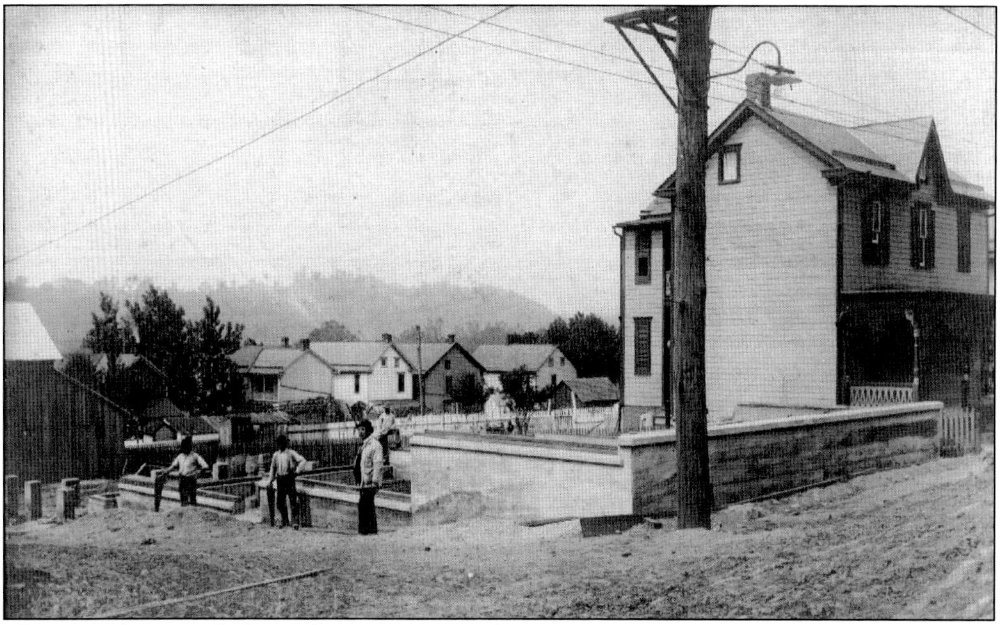

This 1907 photograph shows the construction of Harry George's hardware store on the southwest corner of Potomac Street and Delaware Avenue. Previously a partner in the Swank and George hardware store, Harry George built this store after buying out George Swank. Houses on Walnut Street can be seen in the background and a dirt road in the foreground. (Courtesy Brunswick History Commission.)

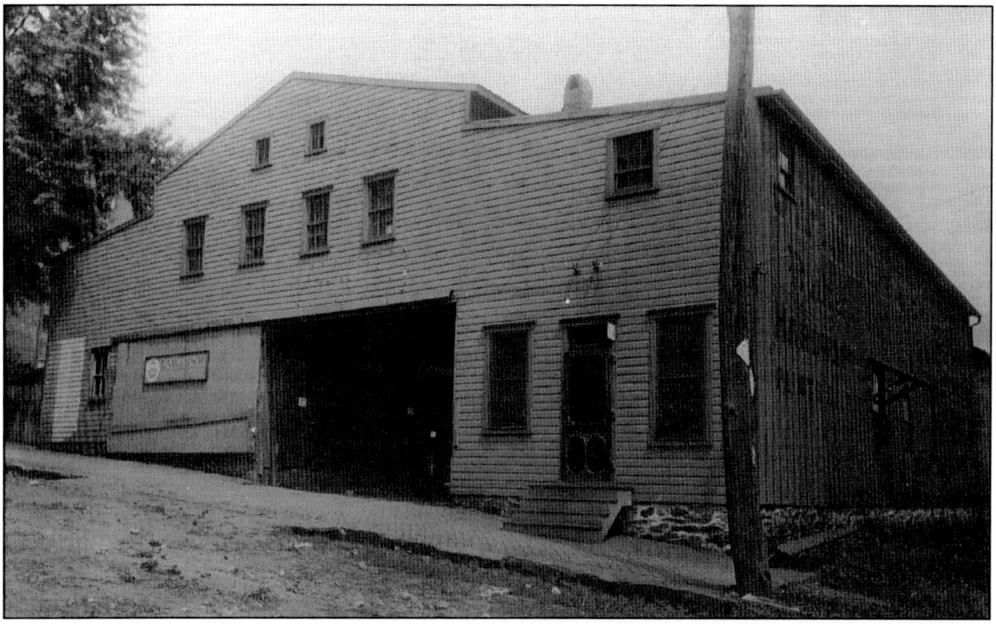

This image shows J. P. Karn's lumberyard, J. P Karn and Brother. Jeremiah Karn was born in nearby Burkittsville and first practiced his carpentry and building trade with the B&O Railroad and the C&O Canal companies. He opened the Brunswick lumberyard with his brother in 1892. The slope of the dirt road in front of the building provides a hint of the hills that Brunswick is built upon. (Courtesy Brunswick History Commission.)

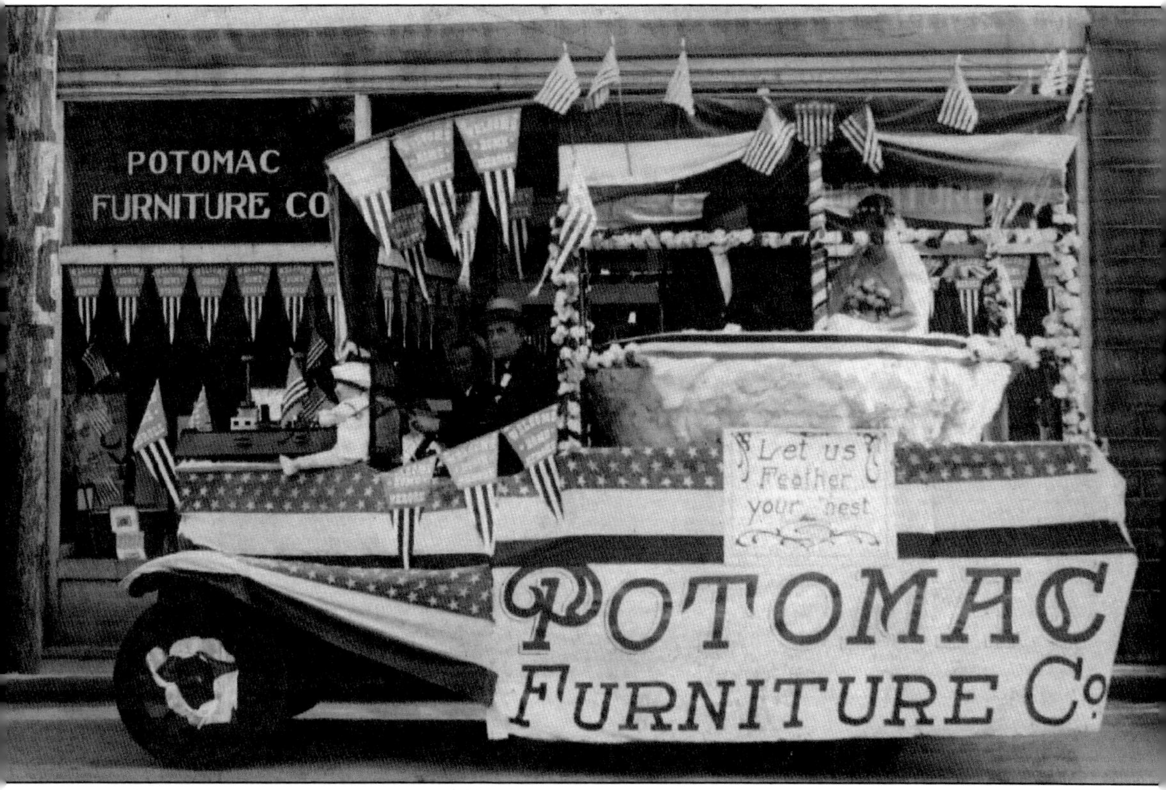

Decked out in patriotic red-white-and-blue bunting and flags, the Potomac Furniture Company shows off this parade float, parked in front of the store at 310 West Potomac Street. Bessie Cummings is seated on the float, and the driver is unidentified. The furniture store was opened by Theodore Siehler in 1913 and was owned by him until he died in 1981. His daughter, Joann Siehler Durst, continued to run the store until it closed in 1984. During the store's 71 years of operation, Brunswick residents didn't need to leave town to purchase brand-name furniture. When the store first opened, Polan Katz ran an umbrella factory on the second floor of the building and employed 40 people. (Courtesy Brunswick History Commission.)

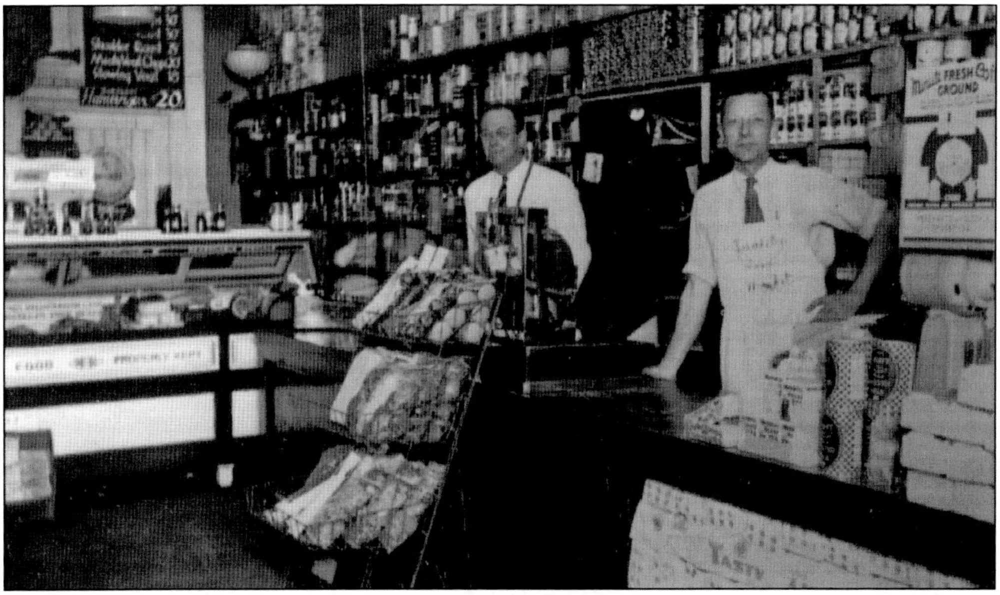

This image shows the interior of the Quality Food Market at 1 East Potomac Street. Pictured are ? Hemp (left) and Ed Darr. Note the merchandise stacked on the shelves behind the counter—this photograph dates from the days when shoppers handed the clerk a list and the clerks picked the merchandise off the shelves and packed it up for the customer. (Courtesy Brunswick History Commission.)

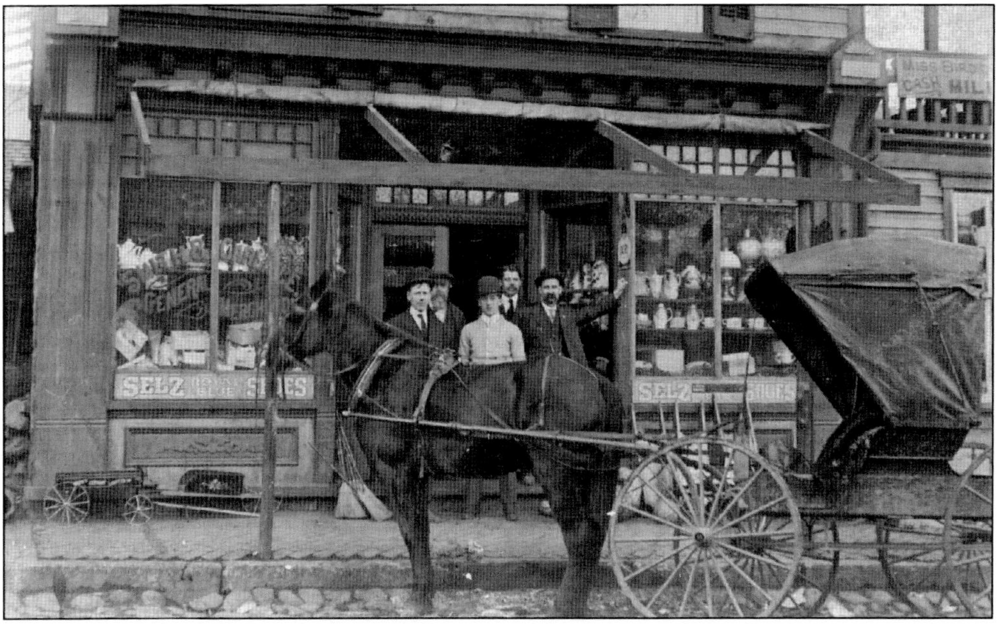

This photograph of the Smith and Carlisle General Store on South Maple Avenue was taken in 1907. Note the sign in the upper right advertising Miss Birdie's Millinery. Pictured from left to right are ? Smith, ? Carlisle, Luther B. Darr (store clerk), G. E. Magaha (store bookkeeper) and Dr. ? Watson (dentist). Dr. Watson's dentist office was located there at one time. The general store was, in later years, Nelson's Restaurant, the Silver Rail Diner, and My Sister's Place. (Courtesy Brunswick History Commission.)

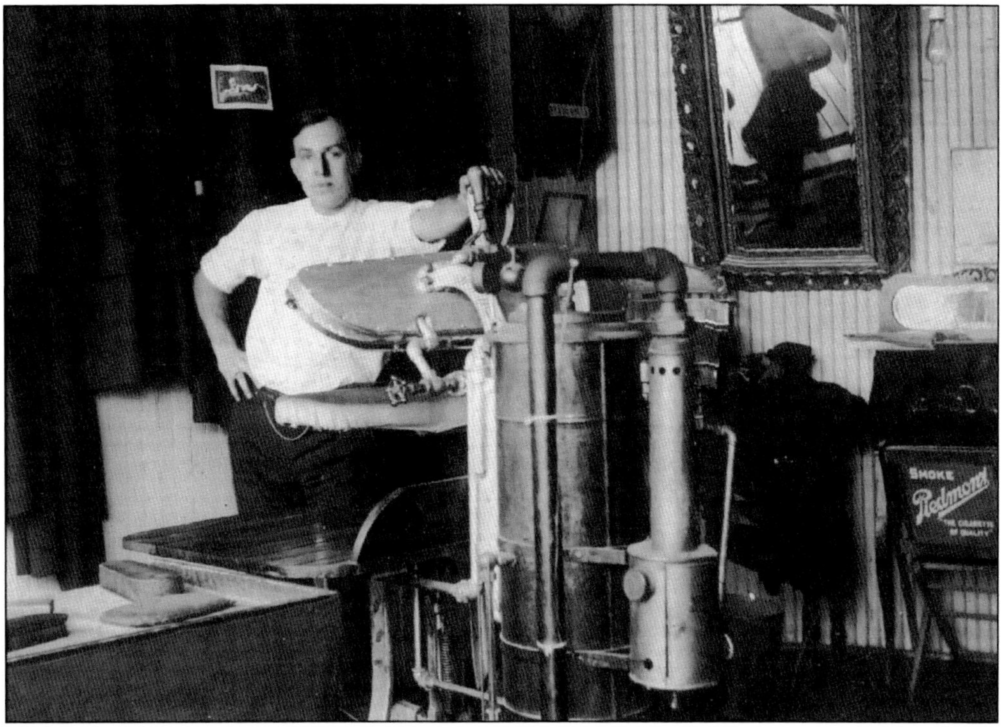

Charles A. Barger Jr. of Barger Dry Cleaning operated the first modern steam press in Brunswick. Located in a small building on East Potomac Street, this October 29, 1918, photograph shows Barger with his press. Note the advertisement on the right for Piedmont cigarettes. (Courtesy Brunswick History Commission.)

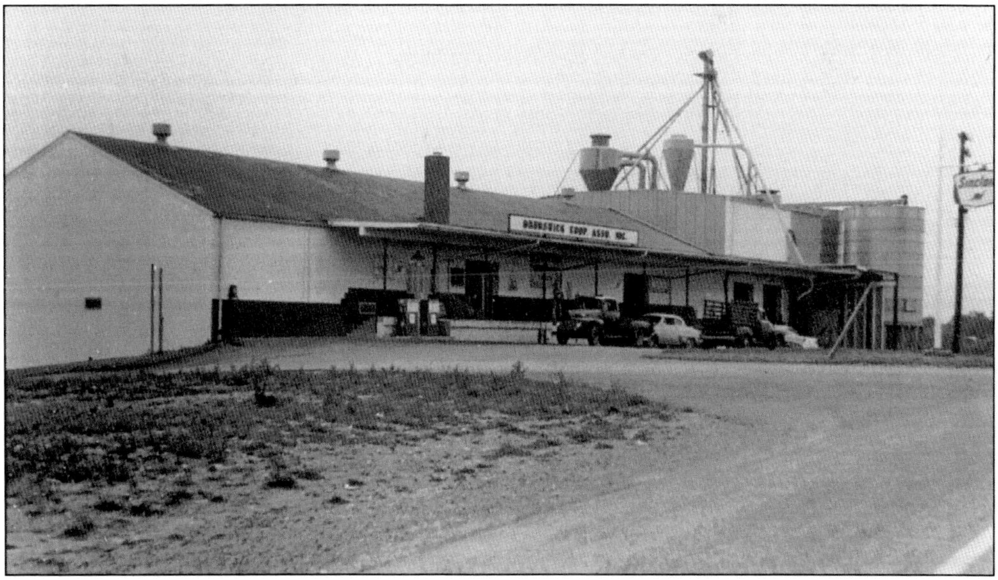

This image shows the Brunswick Co-Op Association. The cooperative began in 1926 in the mill building by the canal. When the Brunswick cooperative moved to Souder Road in 1962, the old mill was abandoned, and it was destroyed by a fire in April 1972. (Courtesy Brunswick History Commission.)

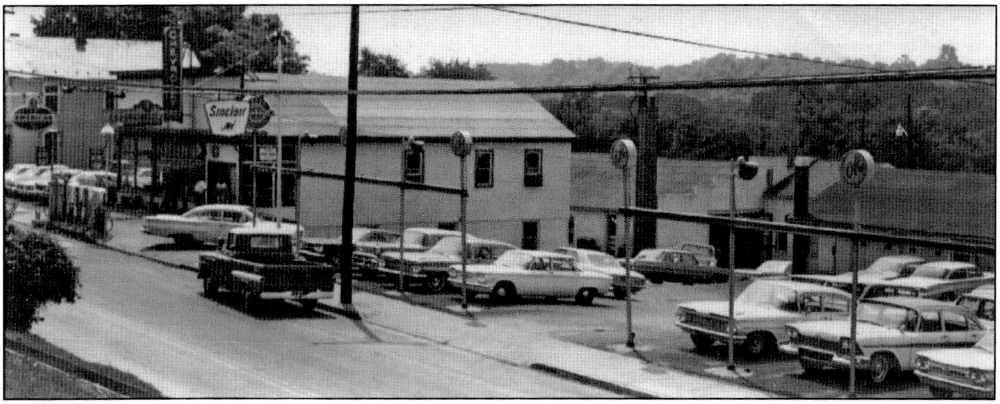

This image shows the sales lot of Litten Chevrolet at 600 West Potomac Street during the 1930s. Gasoline was available at the sign of the green dinosaur (for Sinclair-brand gas) or the sign of the flame (for American-brand gas). (Courtesy Brunswick History Commission.)

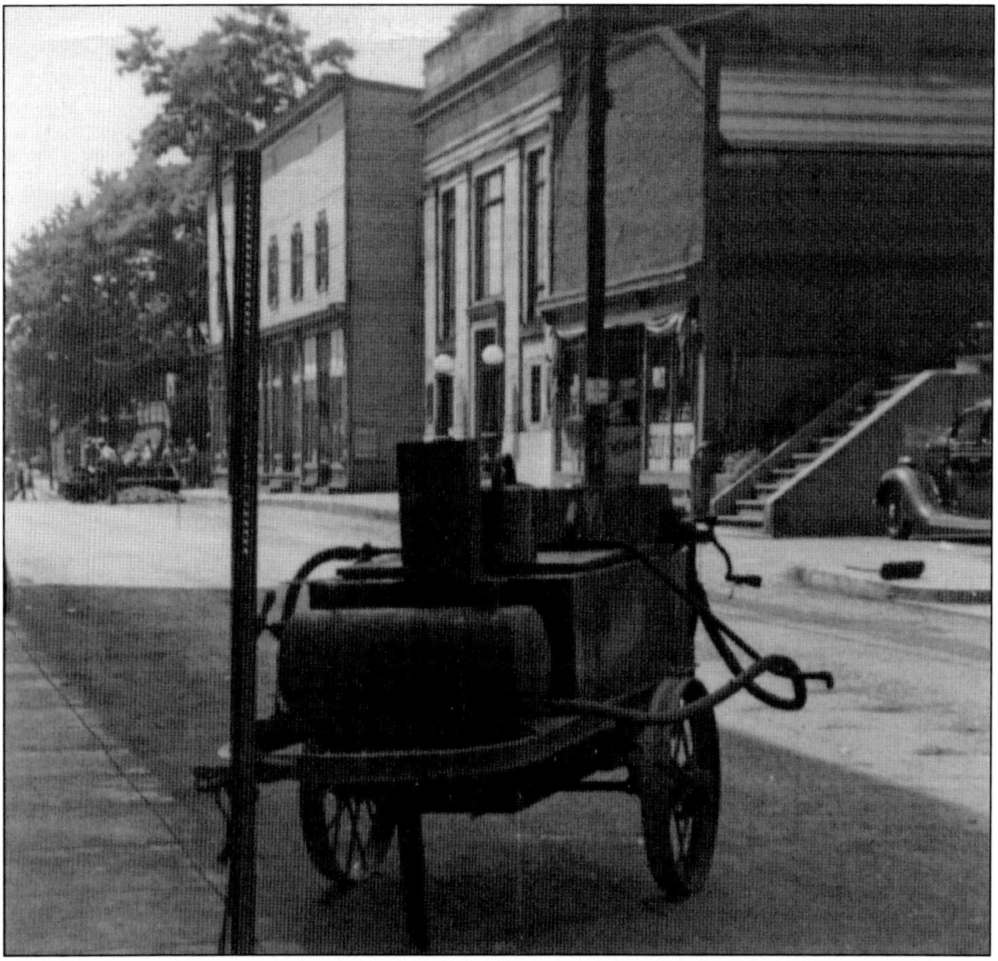

This West Potomac Street scene shows a tar machine used to heat tar for patching roads. More road equipment can be seen in the background farther down the street. Also in the background are White's Grocery, F&M Bank, and Swank's Hardware. (Courtesy Brunswick History Commission.)

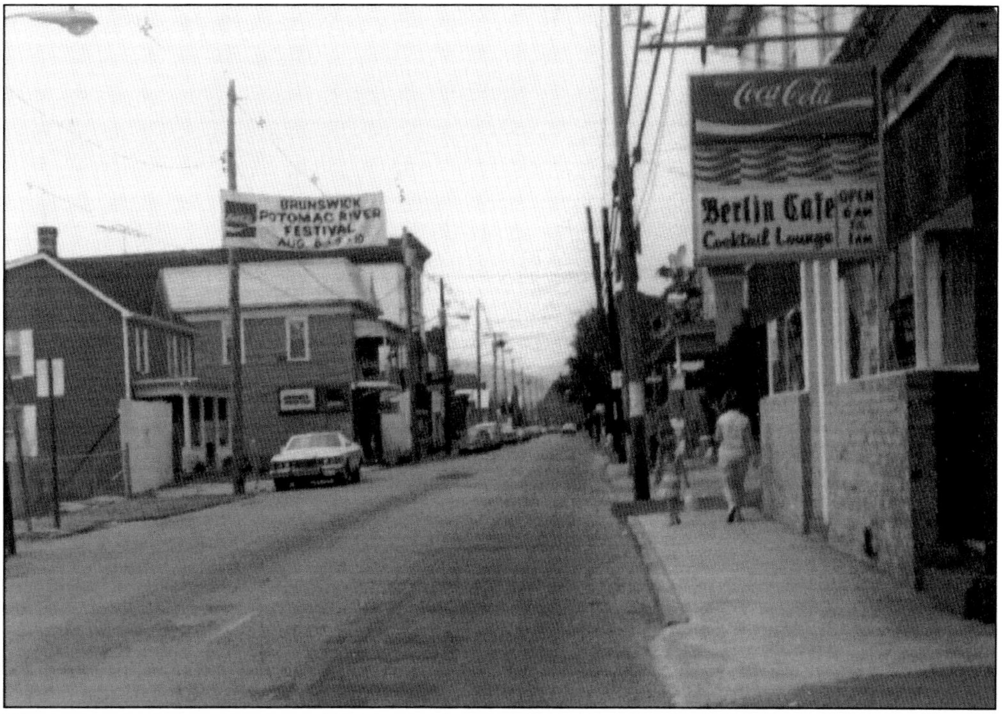

This street scene shows an establishment that gives a nod to Brunswick's past with its name, the Berlin Café and Cocktail Lounge. Strung across the street is a banner advertising Brunswick's Potomac River Festival. (Courtesy Brunswick History Commission.)

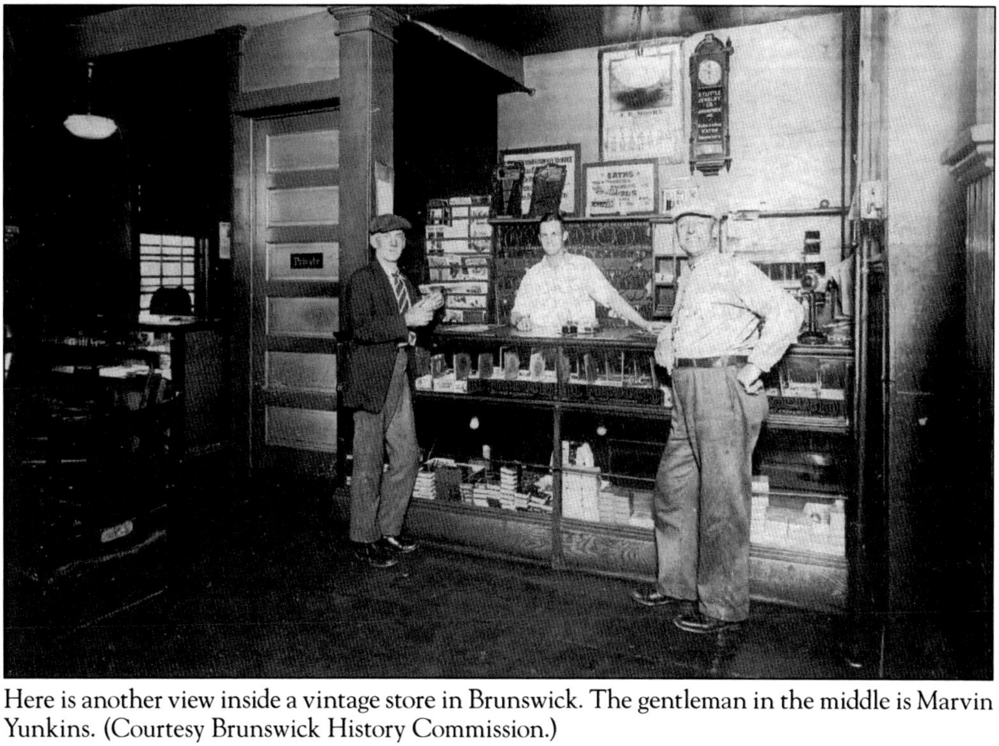

Here is another view inside a vintage store in Brunswick. The gentleman in the middle is Marvin Yunkins. (Courtesy Brunswick History Commission.)

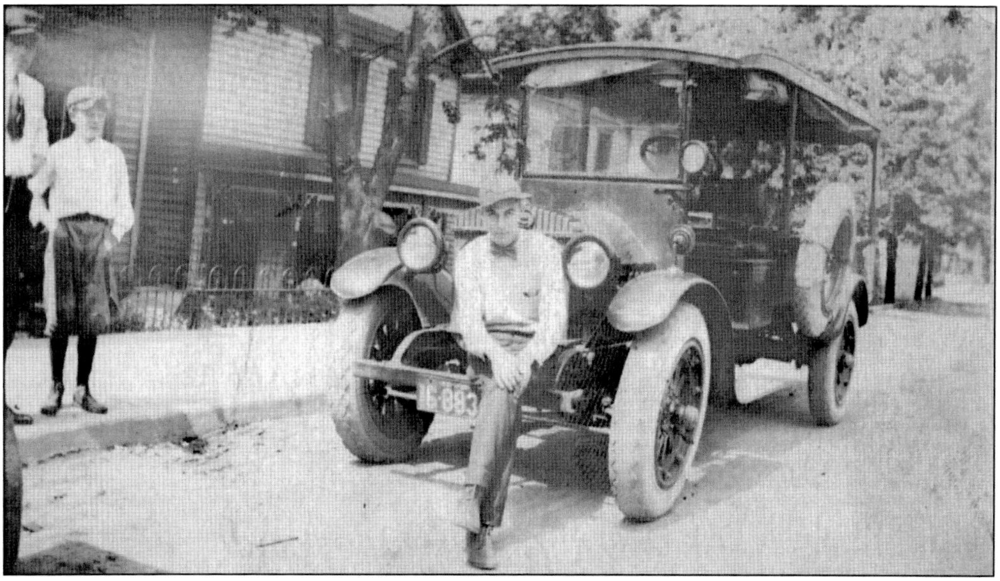

Ralph Fry ran a neighborhood grocery store at 326 West Potomac Street. This early photograph shows him outside his west-end store. (Courtesy Brunswick History Commission.)

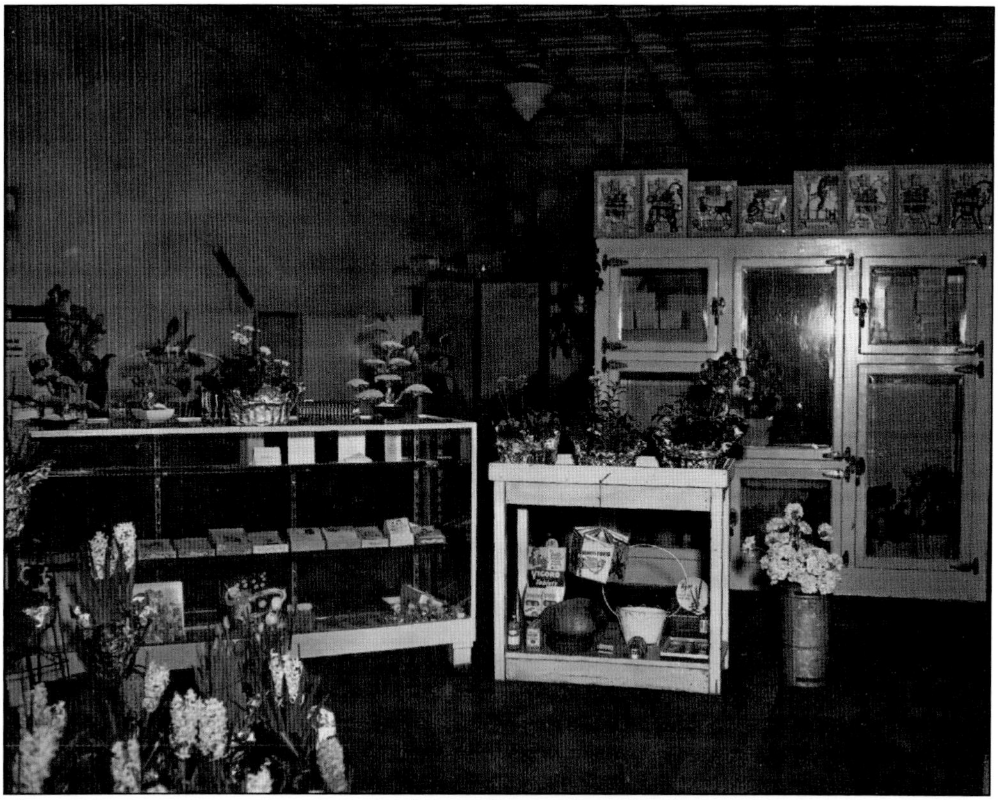

This image shows the inside of E. Donald Darr's flower shop. The florist trade flourished, resulting in several moves throughout town to house the growing business. Note the high, tiled ceilings and refrigerated storage. (Courtesy Brunswick History Commission.)

Three

THE C&O CANAL

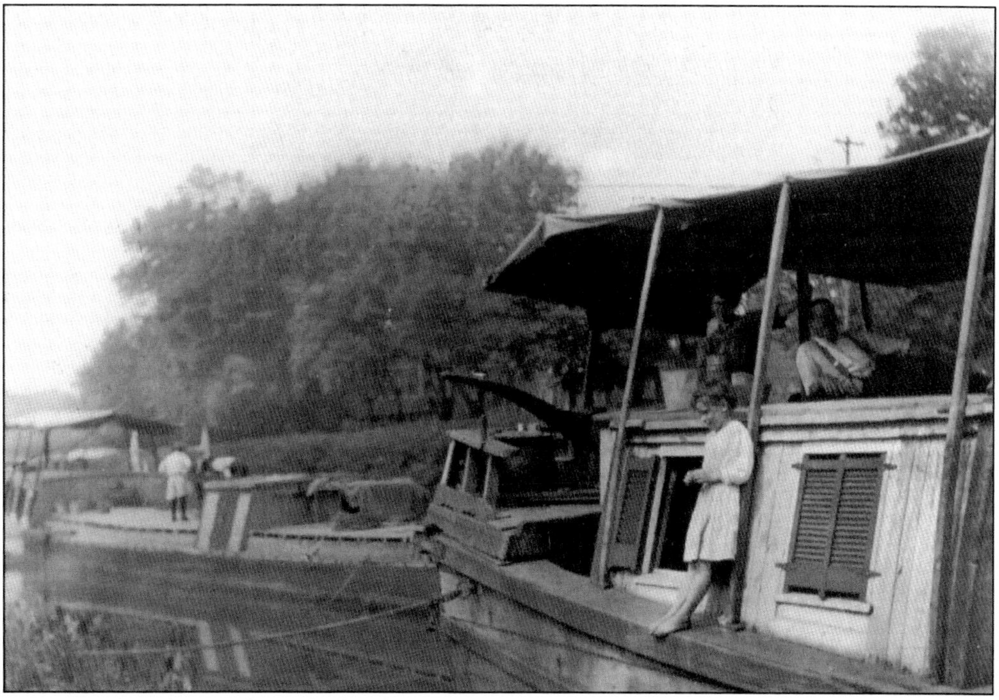

Living on the Chesapeake and Ohio (C&O) Canal was a special way of life. Brunswick is situated near Milepost 55 of the 184.5-mile-long canal that stretches from the tide lock in Georgetown, Virginia, to Cumberland, Maryland. This canal boat is tied to the shore, and the inhabitants are taking a rest from the daily hardships of plying up and down the canal. (Courtesy Brunswick History Commission.)

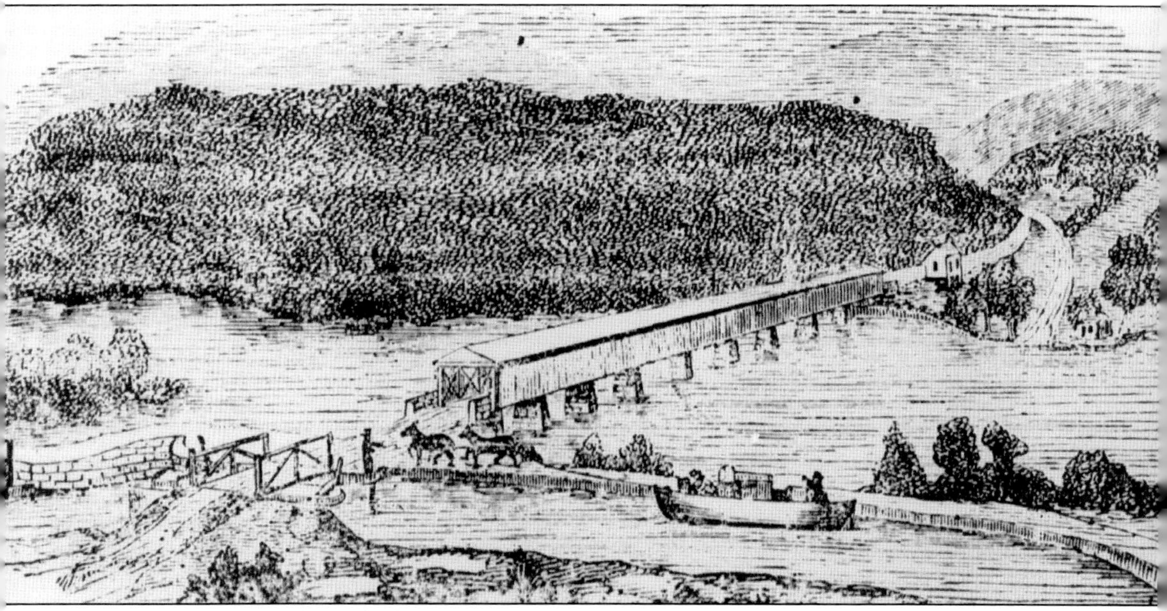

This engraving is from the banner of the *Brunswick Herald and Loudoun County Advertiser*, the town's first weekly newspaper. First appearing in June 1890, the paper was full of local news, such as the train schedule and town council ordinances, as well as advertisements for local businesses. The newspaper ended publication on January 17, 1914. The loss of a local paper was keenly felt by the community and resulted in various other papers coming into existence in succession beginning in September 1914. Today's current paper is *The Brunswick Citizen*, which began in 1973 and covers news not only in Brunswick, but also in the neighboring communities in both Maryland and Virginia, including Point of Rocks, Lovettsville, Jefferson, and Burkittsville. (Courtesy C&O Canal National Historical Park Headquarters.)

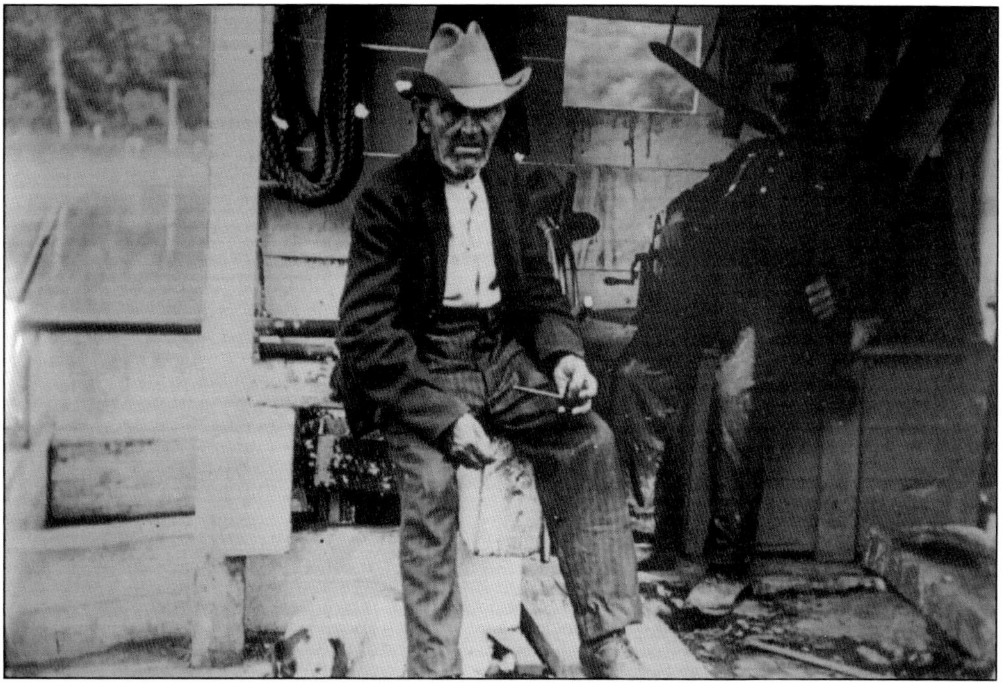

The inside of a canal boat had limited living space, with most of the room being dedicated to cargo, as well as the stable quarters for the all-important canal mules. This image shows two unidentified men inside a canal boat. (Courtesy Brunswick History Commission.)

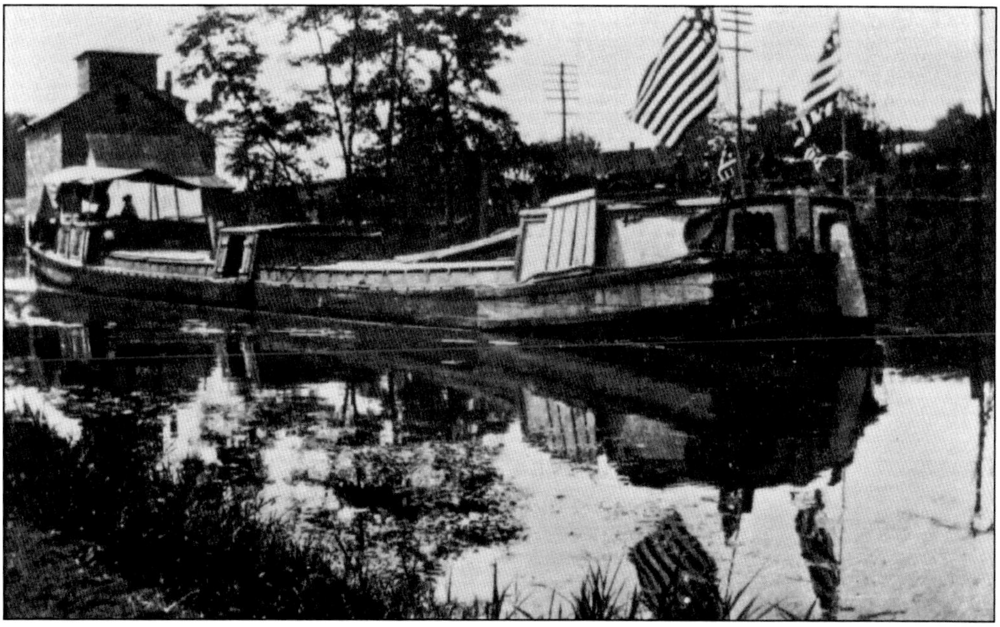

This canal boat, with patriotic flags flying (no 50 stars yet on this old Stars and Stripes), is near the mill in Brunswick, Maryland, *c.* 1909. This was the C&O Canal–boat standard design—note the length of the barge. Boats were generally uniform in size—90 to 95 feet long and 14.5 feet wide. When fully loaded, the boat would draw a depth of about 4.5 feet. (Courtesy C&O Canal National Historical Park Headquarters.)

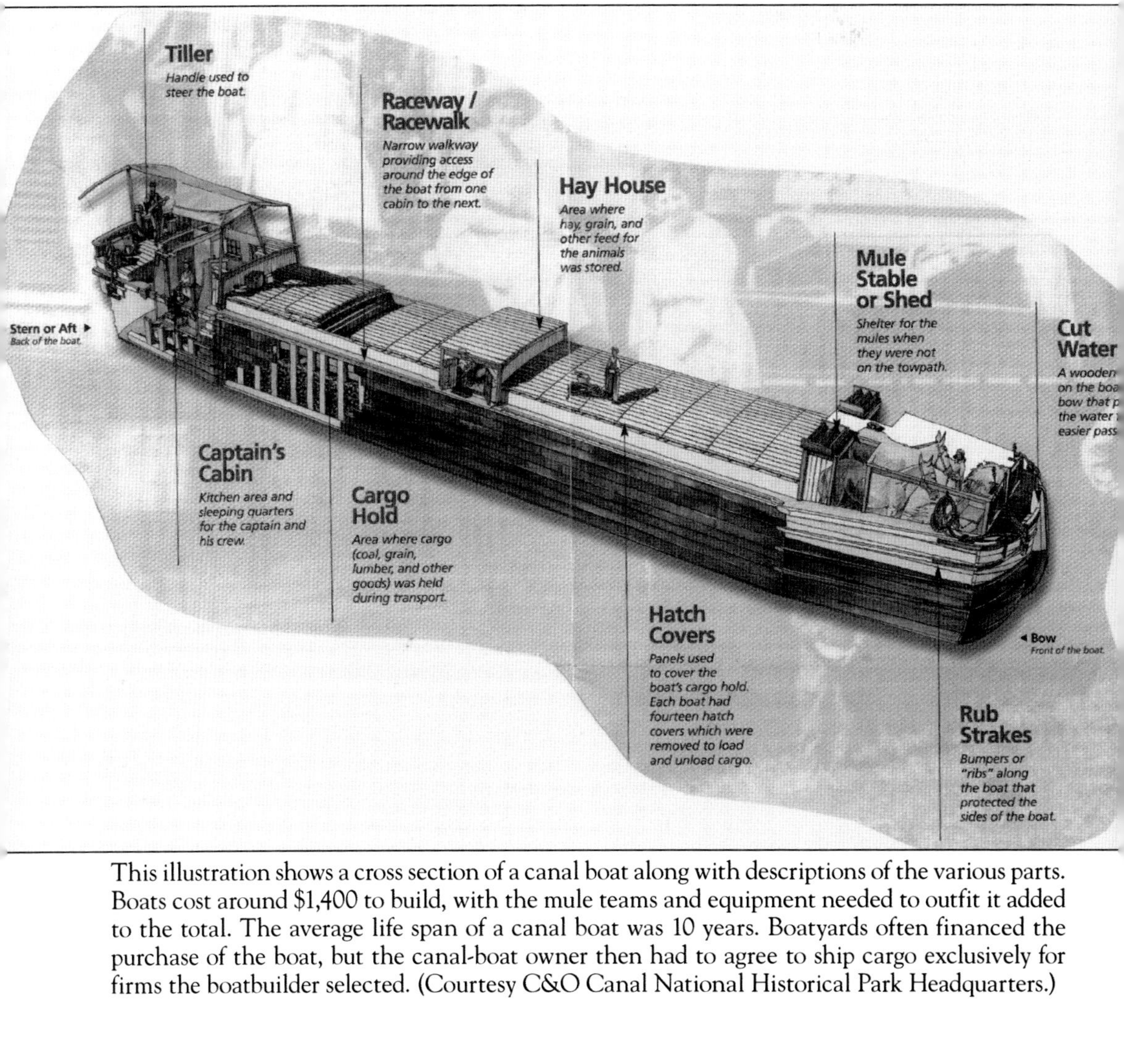

This illustration shows a cross section of a canal boat along with descriptions of the various parts. Boats cost around $1,400 to build, with the mule teams and equipment needed to outfit it added to the total. The average life span of a canal boat was 10 years. Boatyards often financed the purchase of the boat, but the canal-boat owner then had to agree to ship cargo exclusively for firms the boatbuilder selected. (Courtesy C&O Canal National Historical Park Headquarters.)

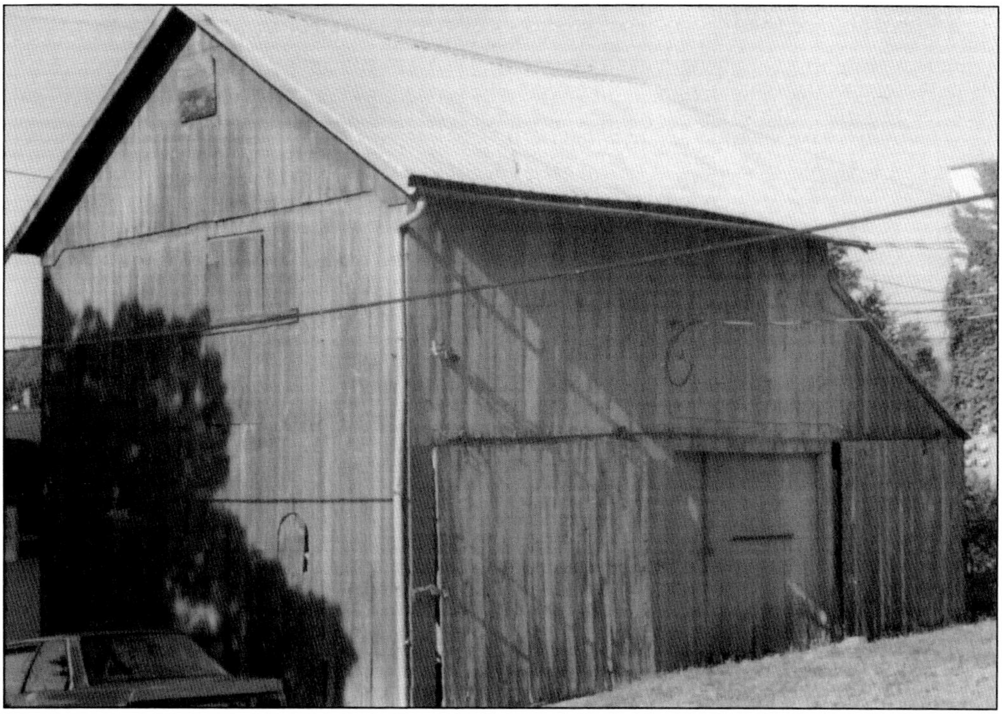

Here is a view of Harry George's stables that housed horses and mules used to haul coal. Delaware Avenue is just behind the stables. (Courtesy Brunswick History Commission.)

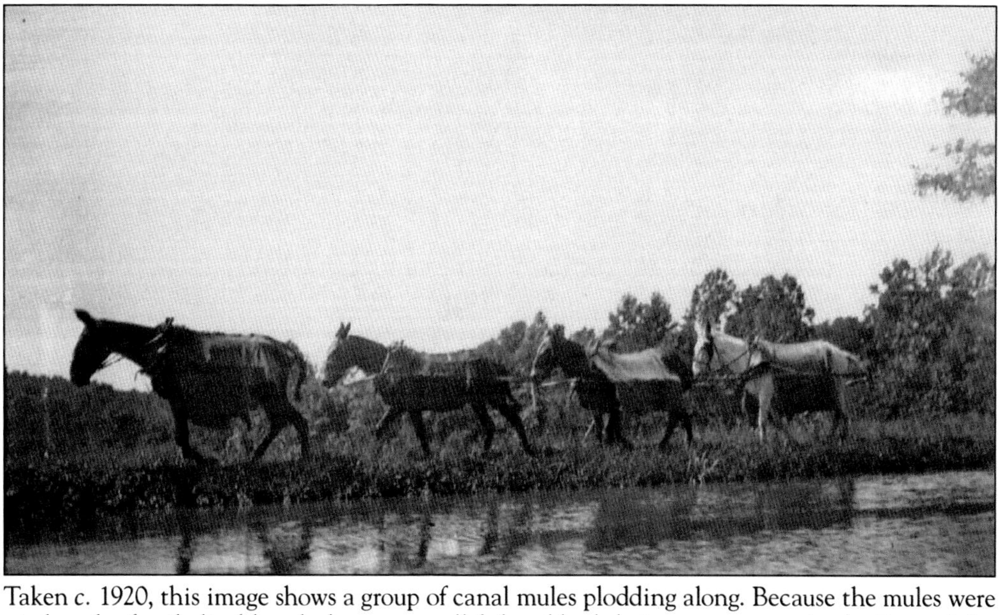

Taken *c.* 1920, this image shows a group of canal mules plodding along. Because the mules were vital to the family livelihood, they were well fed and had their own quarters in the front of the boat for rest periods. Teams worked a rotating shift of six hours on and six hours off and were unhitched and led into their shady stalls during off hours. (Courtesy C&O Canal National Historical Park Headquarters.)

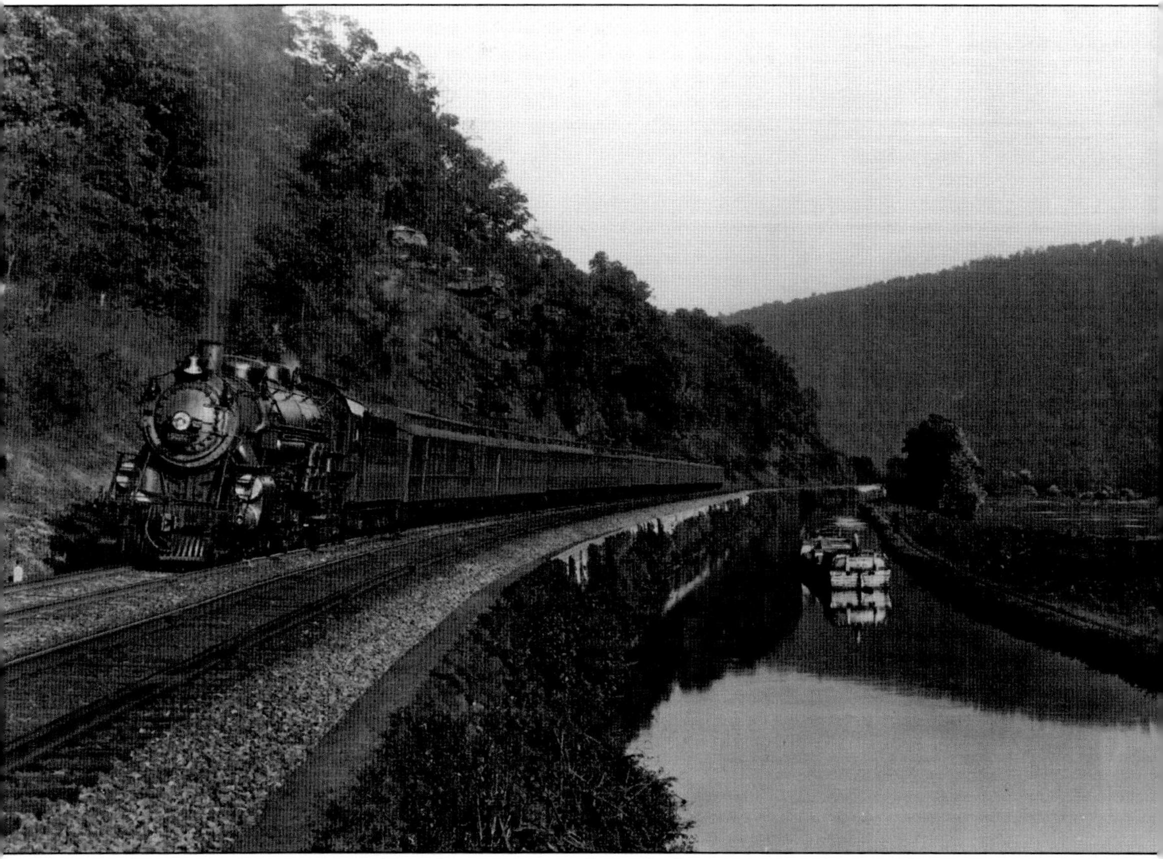

This image shows a scene along the C&O Canal not far from Brunswick at Sandy Hook, Maryland, and depicts the competition of the railroad against the canal. The train steams alongside the C&O Canal as a canal barge progresses at a much slower rate. Some stories report that passing trains would intentionally blow their horns to frighten the mules along the towpath. The coming of the railroad and its promise of quicker, easier delivery of goods spelled the beginning of the end for the canal trade. Taken in 1923, a year prior to the close of canal operations, this photograph shows the Canal Towage No. 49 bound for Washington, D.C., with 120 tons of coal. The train was B&O Railroad's *Capitol Limited* on its way west to Cumberland. The boat's captain was George Bowers, and the mule driver was Lloyd Lemen. Standing on deck is Heaver Eversole. All three men were from Williamsport, Maryland. (Courtesy C&O Canal National Historical Park Headquarters.)

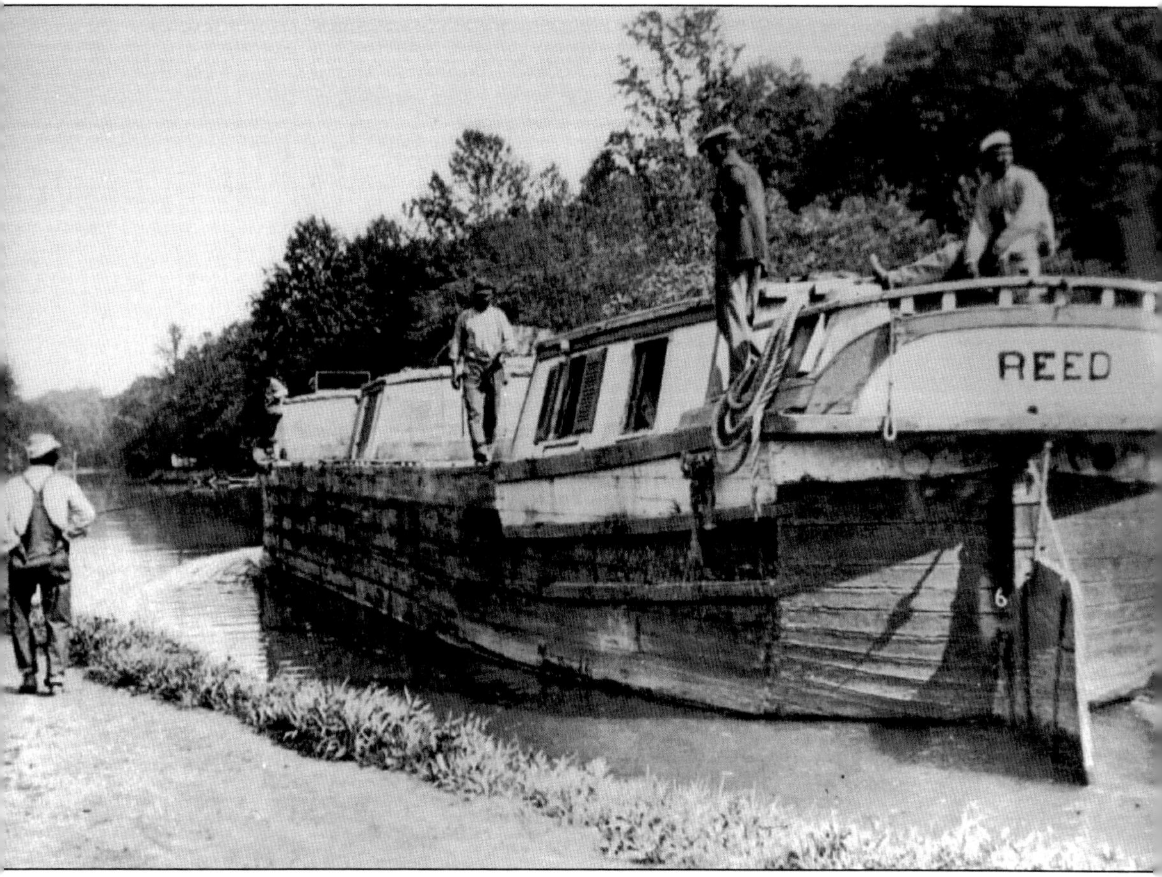

This image shows the *Reed*, a typical canal boat. Note the African American crew onboard. African Americans worked as deckhands on canal boats but were banned from owning their own until after the Civil War. There were African American boat captains during the 1870s, but by the final years of the canal, only one African American canal boat family was still listed. Note that the boat has a special name. Once boatbuilder Canal Towage began supplying the canal boats, the days of each boat having a unique name faded into the past. Instead, the boats began to carry a simple boat number. (Courtesy Brunswick History Commission.)

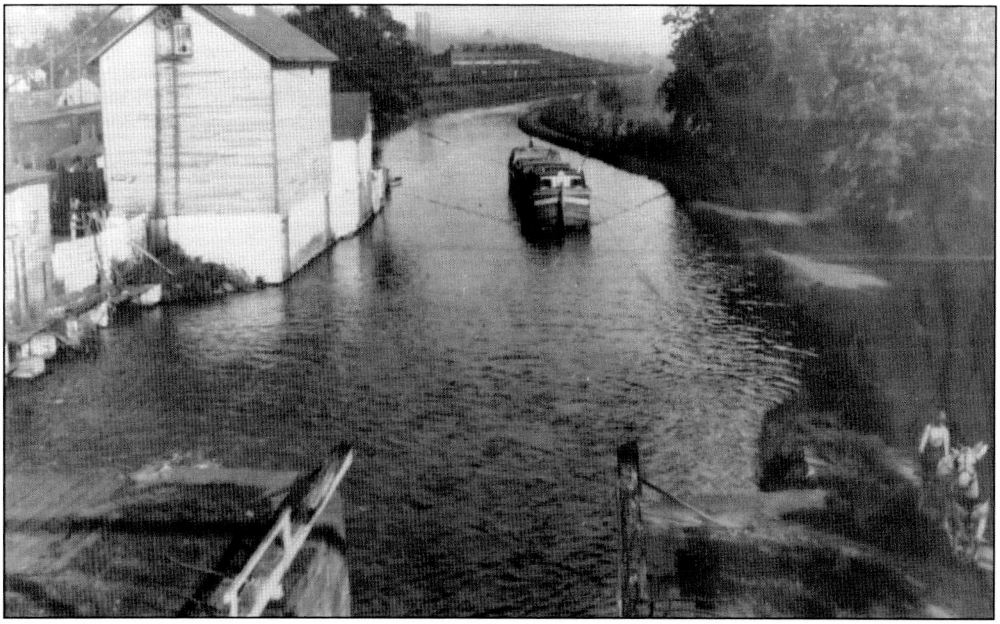

Here is a canal boat approaching Lock 30 in Brunswick, Maryland. The mule and his driver, sometimes called a "hoggee," are at the entrance to the lock in the lower right corner of the photograph. (Courtesy C&O Canal National Historical Park Headquarters.)

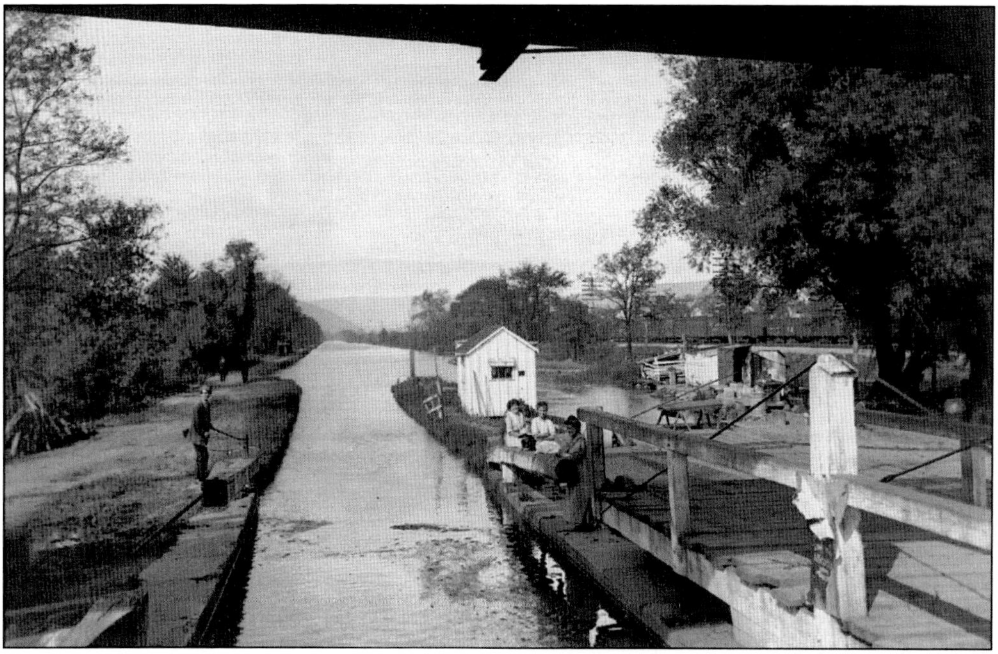

This image is one of many taken by the Consolidation Coal Company c. 1920 documenting the full length of the canal. This photograph shows Lock 30 at Brunswick and was taken from the vantage point of the bridge over the canal. Note the lockkeeper's shanty on the spit of land extending out into the canal. There are chicken and hog pens off to the right. Railcars on the tracks can also be seen through the trees on the far right. Note the people, perhaps the lockkeeper and his family, posed for the photograph. (Courtesy C&O Canal National Historical Park Headquarters.)

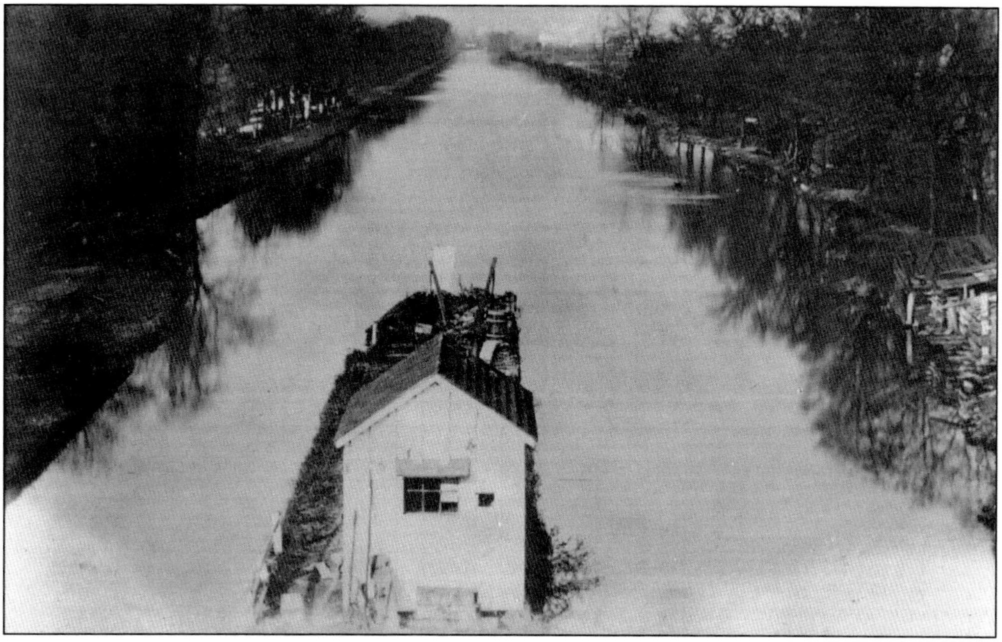

Here is another view of Lock 30 at Brunswick looking downstream from the lockkeeper's wait house in the middle of the canal. Here the lockkeeper would await the call "Hey-ey Lock!" from an approaching boat. The C&O Canal National Historical Park opened its newest visitors' center in downtown Brunswick in 1999. (Courtesy C&O Canal National Historical Park Headquarters.)

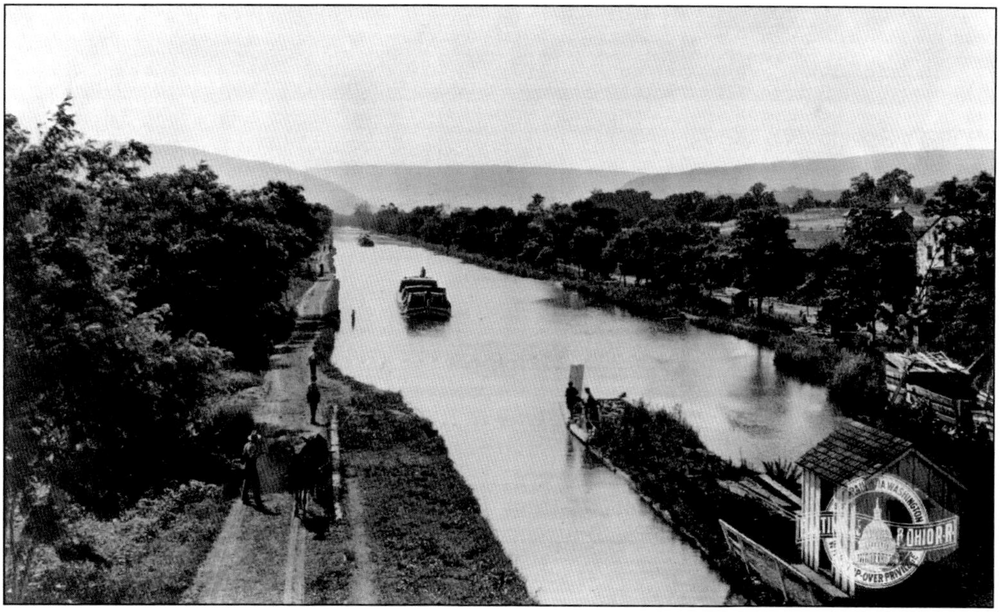

This Baltimore & Ohio (B&O) Railroad photograph shows Lock 30 at Brunswick, Maryland. The canal paralleled the right-of-way of the B&O Railroad for miles between Washington, D.C., and Martinsburg, West Virginia. In this photograph, two boats are approaching the lock from downstream. This image, showing a mule and its driver on the left, provides a good look at how boats traveled along the canal under mule-power. The second boat can be seen farther in the distance. (Courtesy C&O Canal National Historical Park Headquarters.)

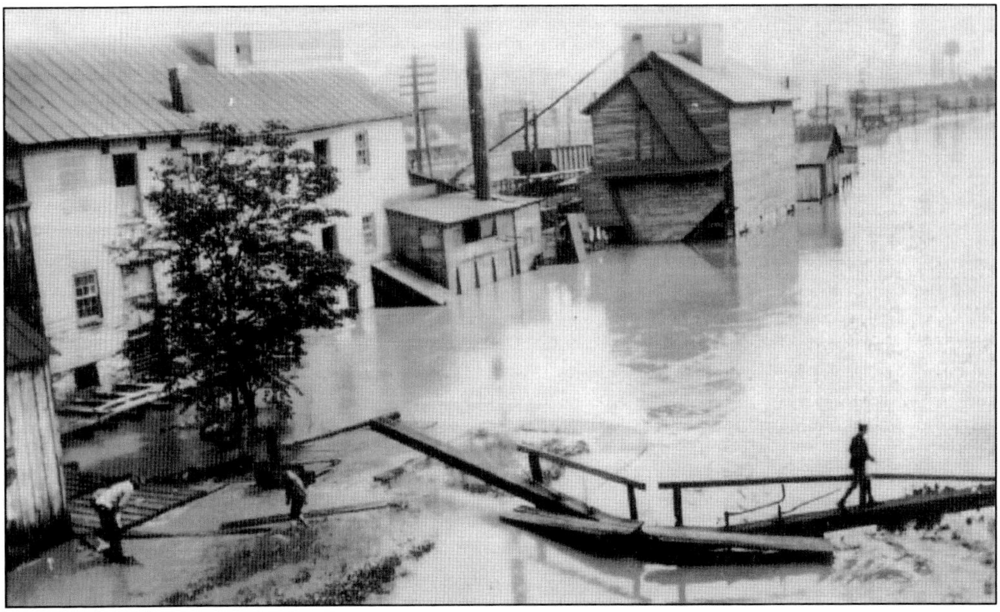

Here is a view of the rear of the mill along the canal during one of the floods that plagued the canal over the years. Note that the water level is over the central gates on the canal lock at the east end. The mill burned down in 1972, and a new mill, the Brunswick Co-Op Association, was opened on Souder Road. (Courtesy Brunswick History Commission.)

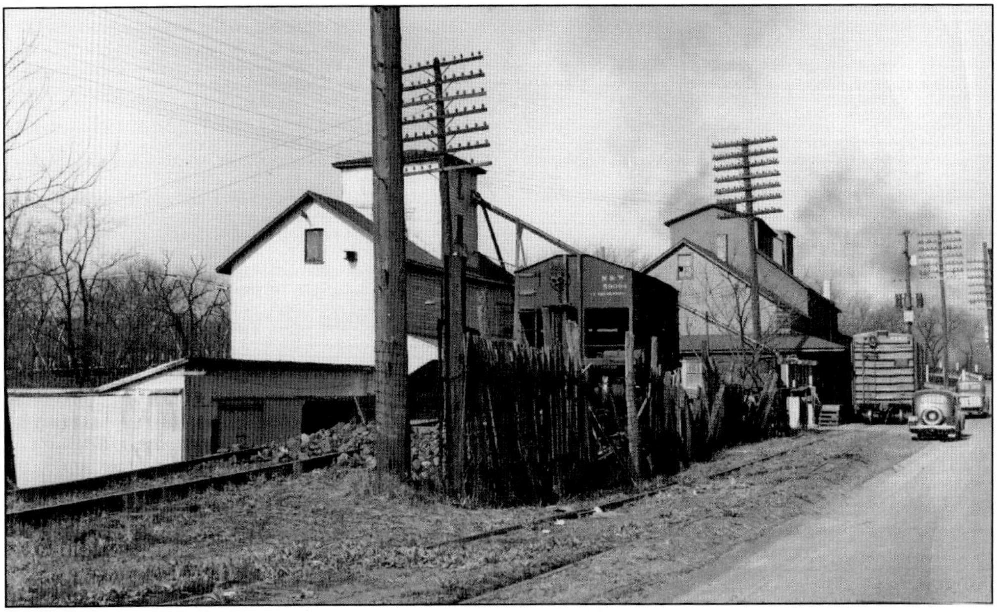

This view of the Brunswick mill was taken in the late 1930s. The old Brunswick Bridge is in the background on the left behind the trees. The ramp to the bridge appears on the far right at the white posts. There is some uncertainty about the exact dates surrounding the establishment of a mill in Berlin, but there is no doubt about the important role it played in the local economy. Originally powered by water from the C&O Canal, the mill had docking facilities for canal barges to load and unload. Steam power was available by the 1920s, when accounts say the mill was producing 100 barrels of flour per day. (Courtesy Brunswick History Commission.)

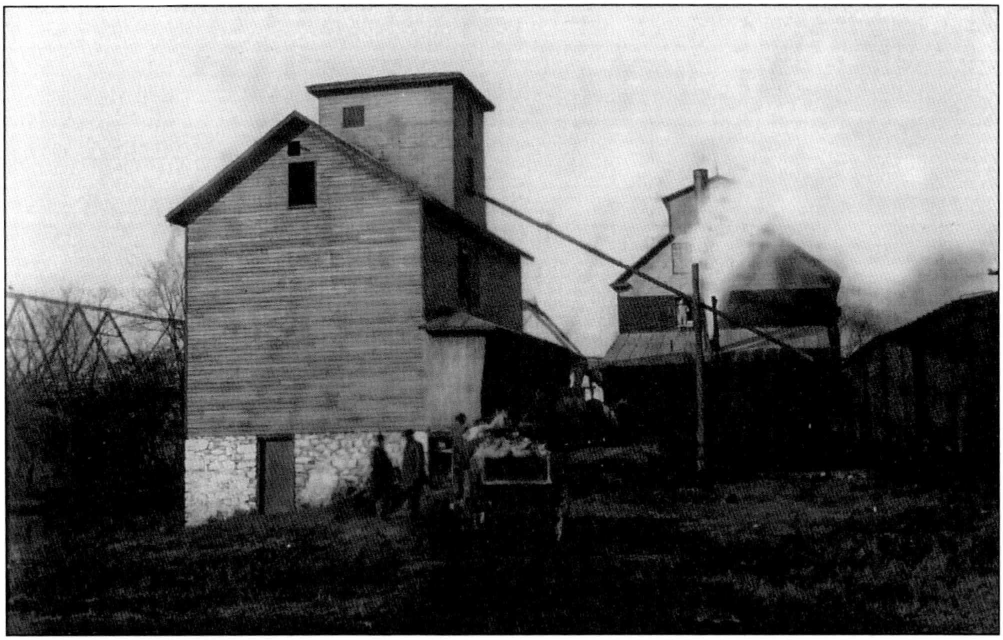

This early 20th century photograph is of the mill located at the end of the bridge in Brunswick along the canal. Water from the canal powered the mill, and the grain was shipped by rail and, locally, by horse and wagon. (Courtesy Brunswick History Commission.)

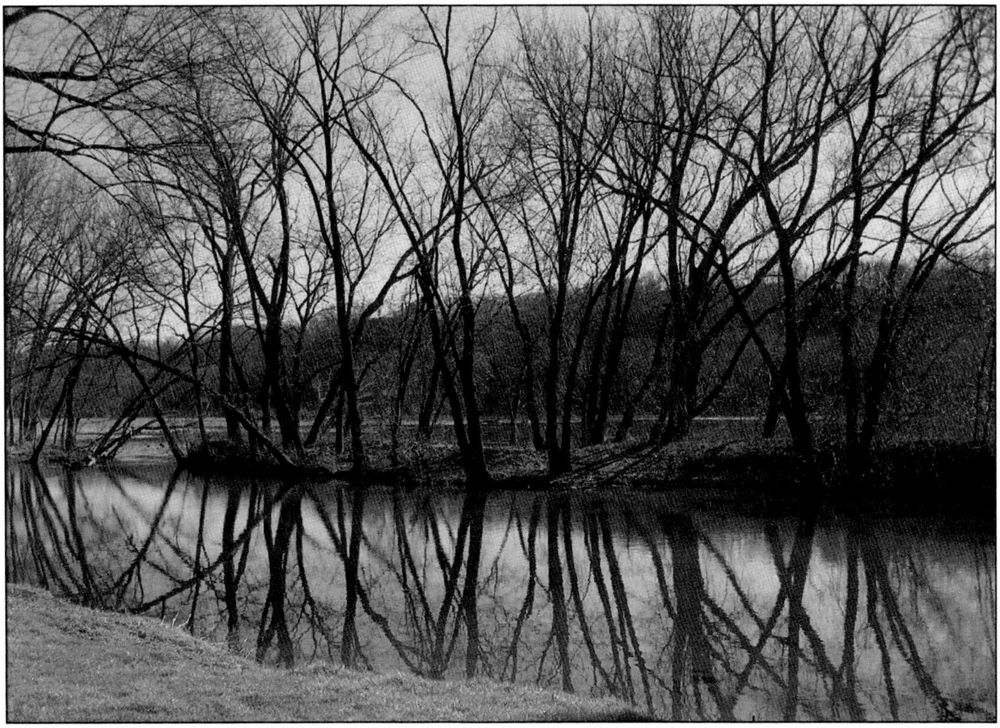

This quiet scene shows the outlet to the Potomac River from the boat ramp under the Brunswick Bridge. The old canal lock is to the left of the vantage point of this photograph. (Courtesy Mary H. Rubin.)

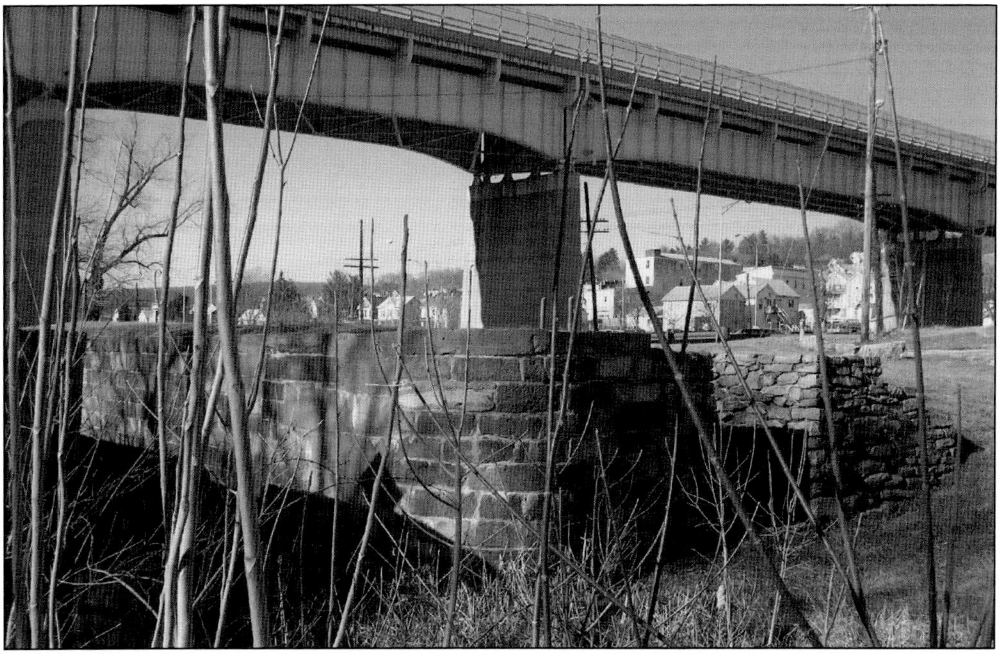

This image shows the empty and deteriorating Lock 30 of the C&O Canal. The new bridge over the river can be seen above. During the Great Depression, the canal towpath was no longer in use and it became a hobo jungle of men coming and going on the freight trains that stopped in Brunswick. Knowing times were hard for everyone, the B&O Railroad was, apparently, not as harsh as other rail lines in pulling transients off their trains. Girls were warned not to go down to the towpath out of concern for their safety. (Courtesy Mary H. Rubin.)

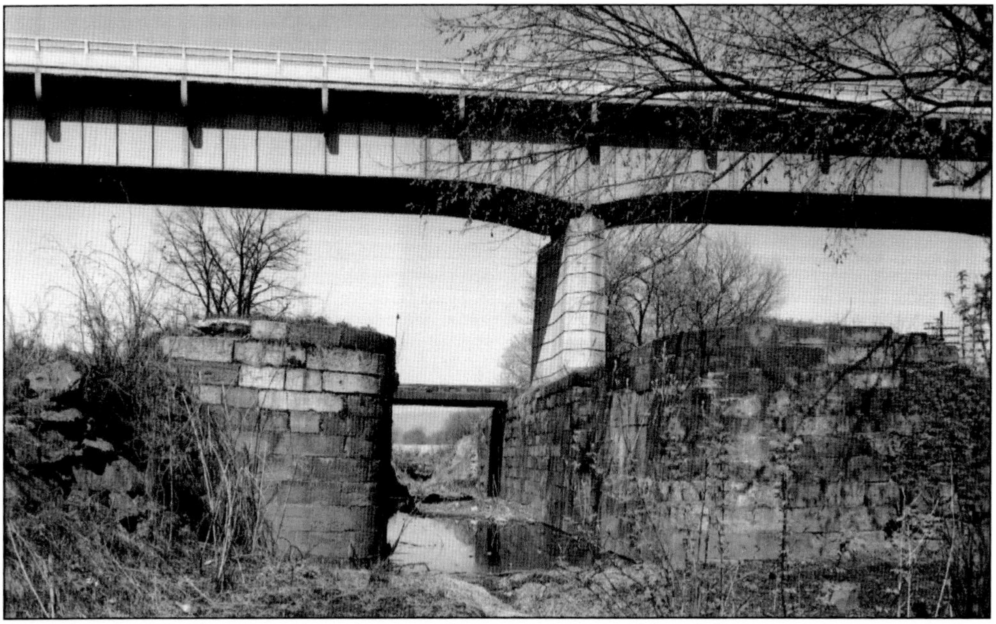

This photograph shows just how far into disrepair the canal has fallen over the years. Taken sometime after 1955, this image shows old Lock 30 where it sits under the new bridge. (Courtesy C&O Canal National Historical Park Headquarters.)

Four

The B&O Railroad

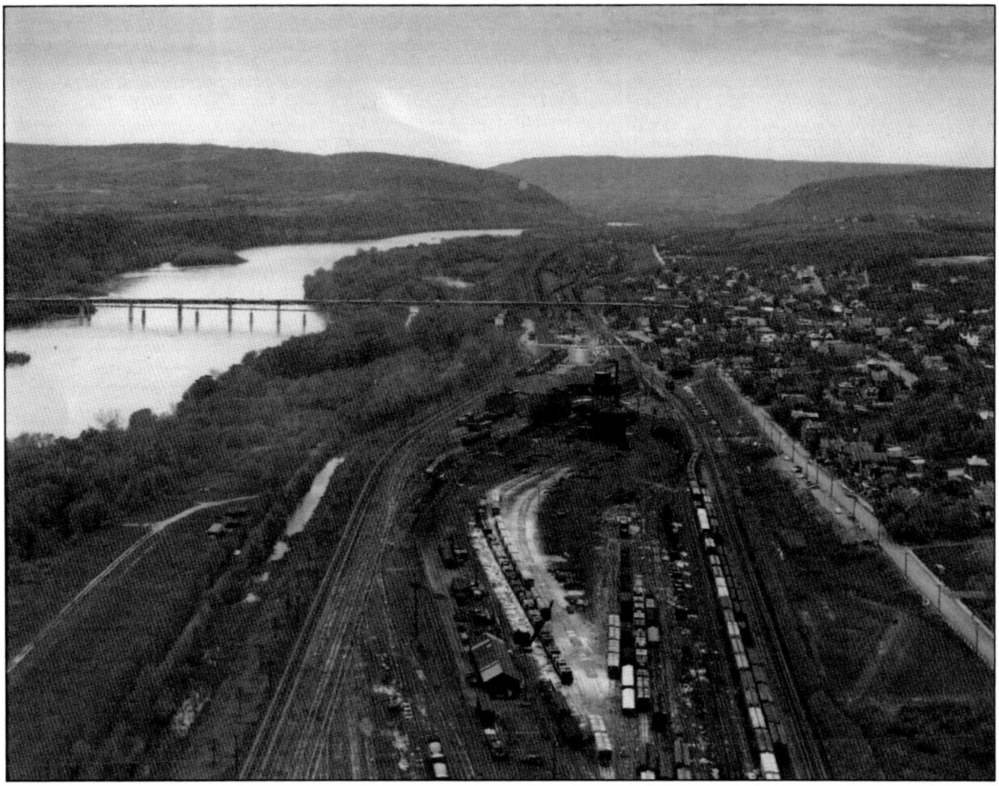

Here is an aerial view of Brunswick showing the Baltimore and Ohio Railroad yard in 1955. Both the old and new Potomac River bridges can be seen straddling the river. (Courtesy C&O Canal National Historical Park Headquarters, Abbie Rowe Collection.)

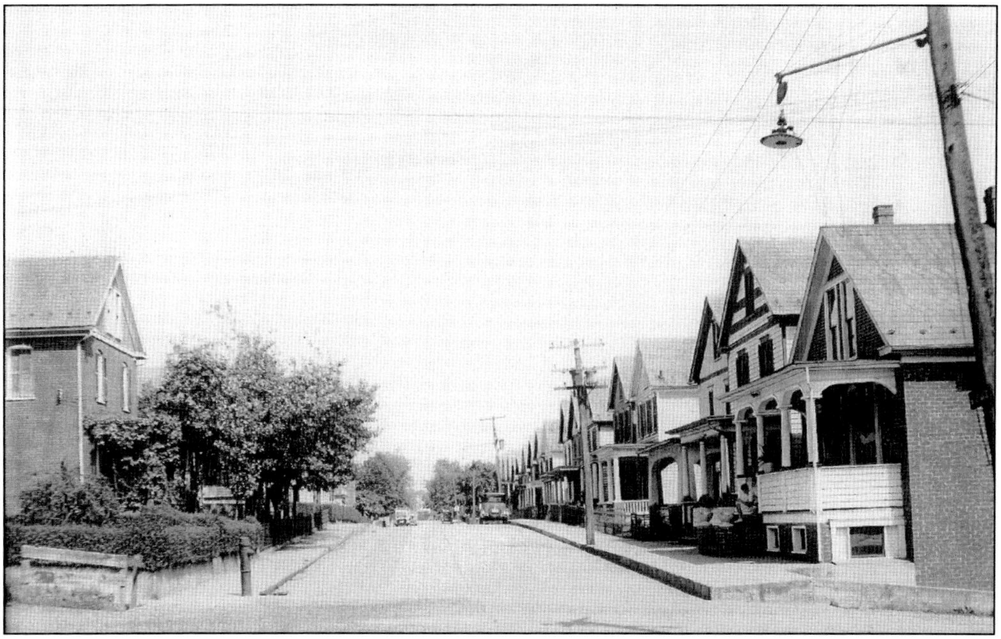

A good argument can be made that without the B&O Railroad there may not have been a Brunswick. The westbound yards were opened May 10, 1891, and during the next dozen years, business expanded so rapidly that a new eastbound classification yard was constructed. This photograph, taken in the early 20th century, shows the 500 block of Brunswick Street. Note the row of nearly identical houses built by the railroad as company homes for workers. (Courtesy Brunswick History Commission.)

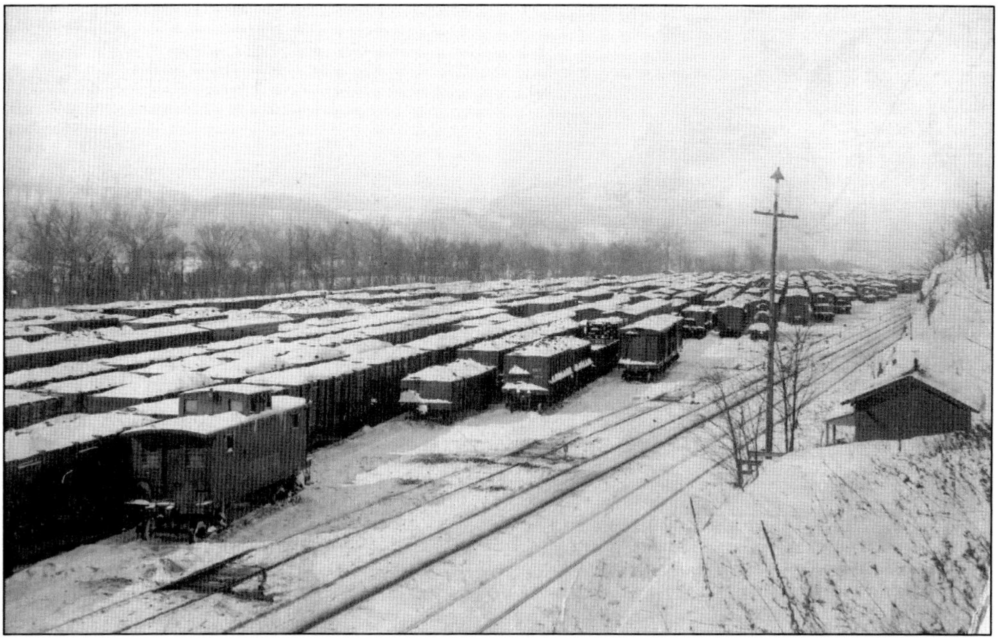

If anyone had any doubts about the huge rail operations taking place at Brunswick, this February 17, 1899, photograph of the snow-covered railcars at the east end of the Brunswick yard should be enough to convince them. (Courtesy Brunswick History Commission.)

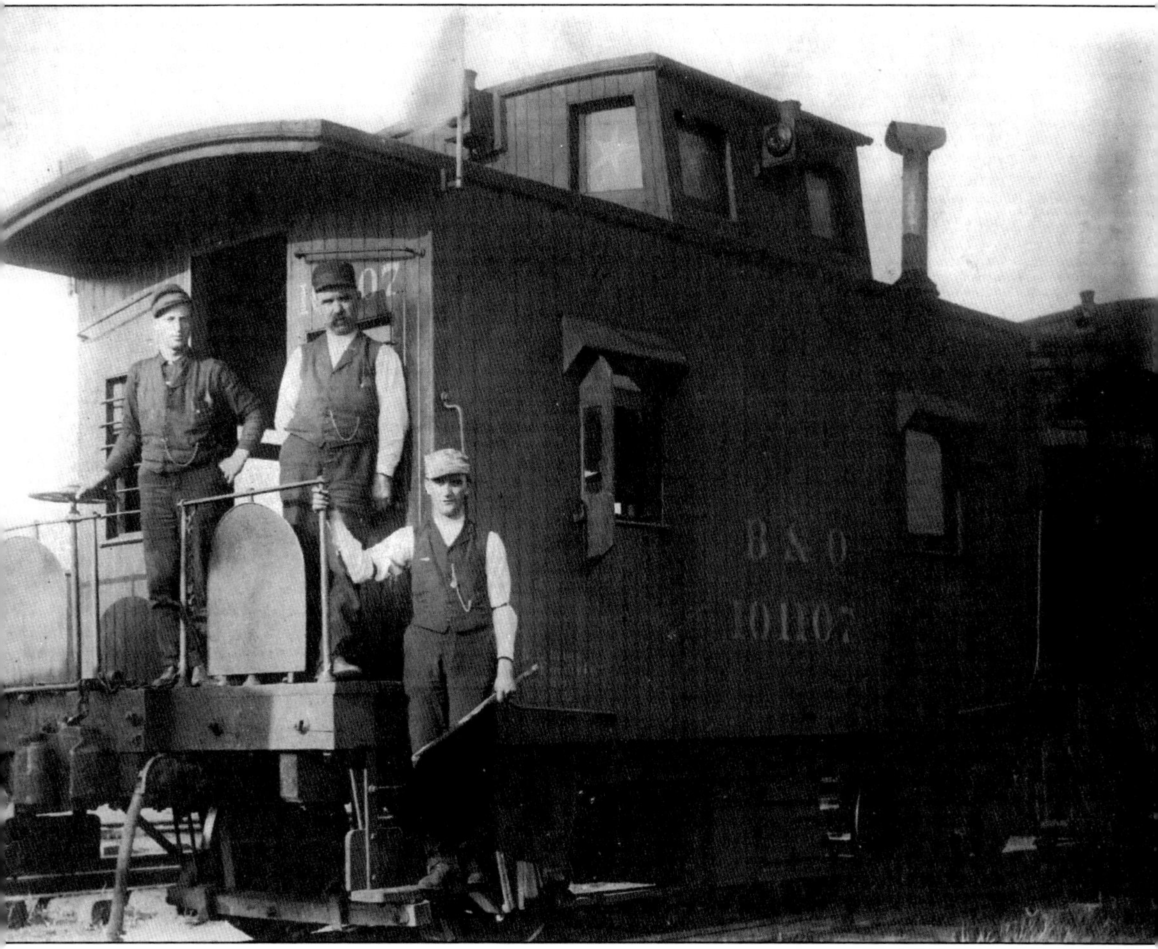

Here is B&O caboose No. 101107 with Dollie Shewbridge (brakeman), Charles Woodcock (conductor), and Ben Myers (flagman). Note the spark board in the window used to deflect cinders and dirt. The board was removed and stored inside when the caboose was not running. (Courtesy Brunswick History Commission.)

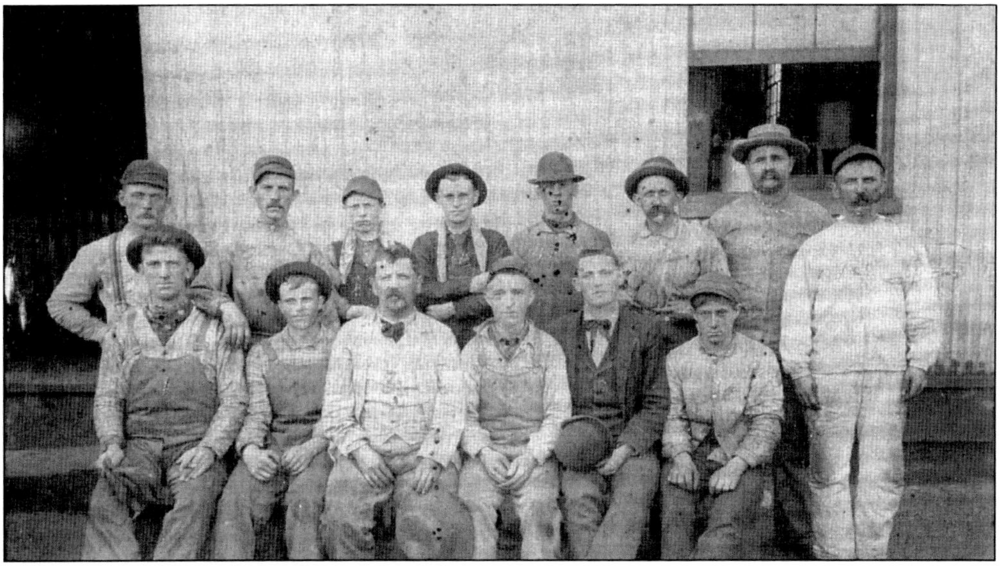

This photograph, taken in the late 1890s, shows the following railroad shop men from left to right: (first row) Crockett Bingham, Jim Carey, Fork Shewbridge, Charles Gosnell, Tom Corbett, and W. W. Shewbridge; (second row) Bill Clipp, John Dunn, William Neal, C. H. "Judy" Bond, W. W. Utterback, T. Hardy, A. R. "Jumbo" Spitzer, and E. Shewbridge. (Courtesy Brunswick History Commission.)

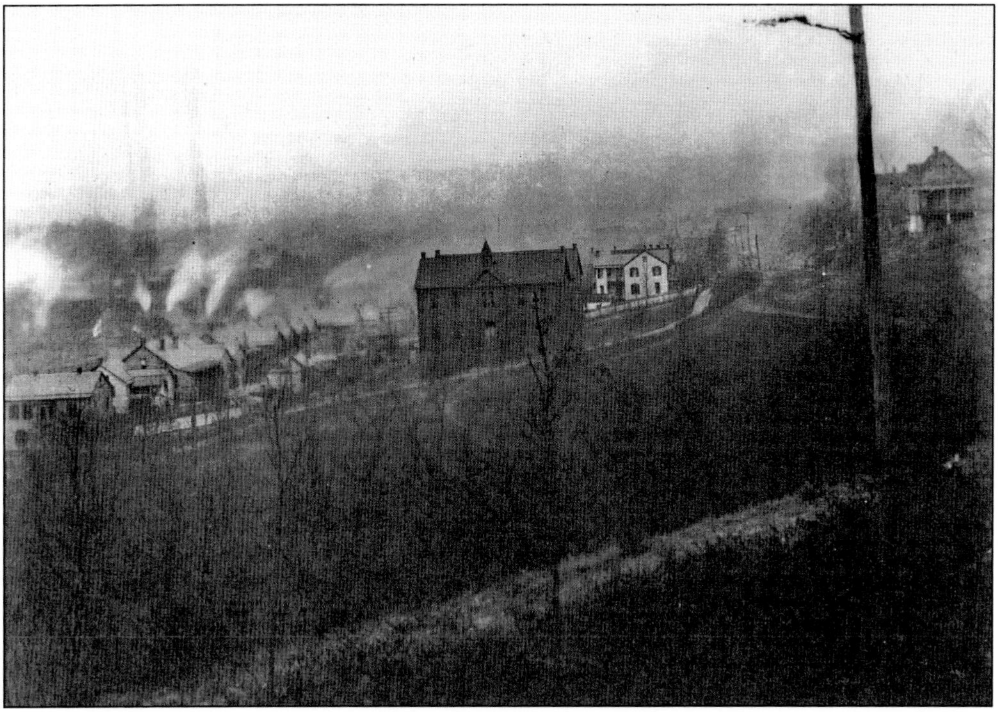

This early-20th-century image shows Brunswick Elementary School in the center and the Westall House in the lower left. The Westall House was once used by both the elementary and high schools. Each visible smoke plume in the photograph represents an engine on the Brunswick tracks, an incredible sight. (Courtesy Brunswick History Commission.)

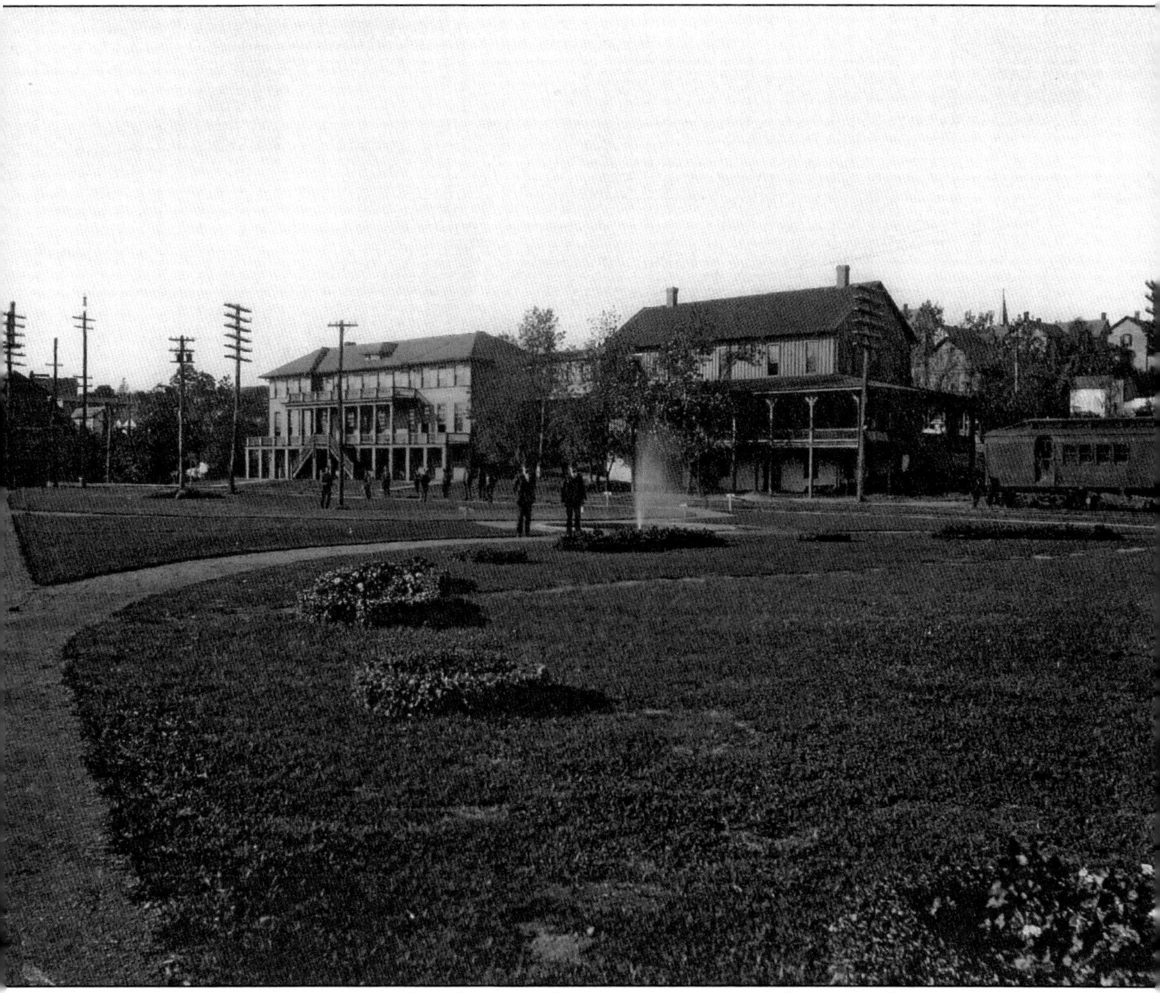

Taken in the early 20th century, this photograph shows the original YMCA building on the left and the B&O hospital building on the right. The westbound tower for the railroad is also on the left, while a mail car is on the tracks to the right. The flowers and fountain in the foreground belong to the B&O Railroad Park, which once existed near Potomac Street. (Courtesy Brunswick History Commission.)

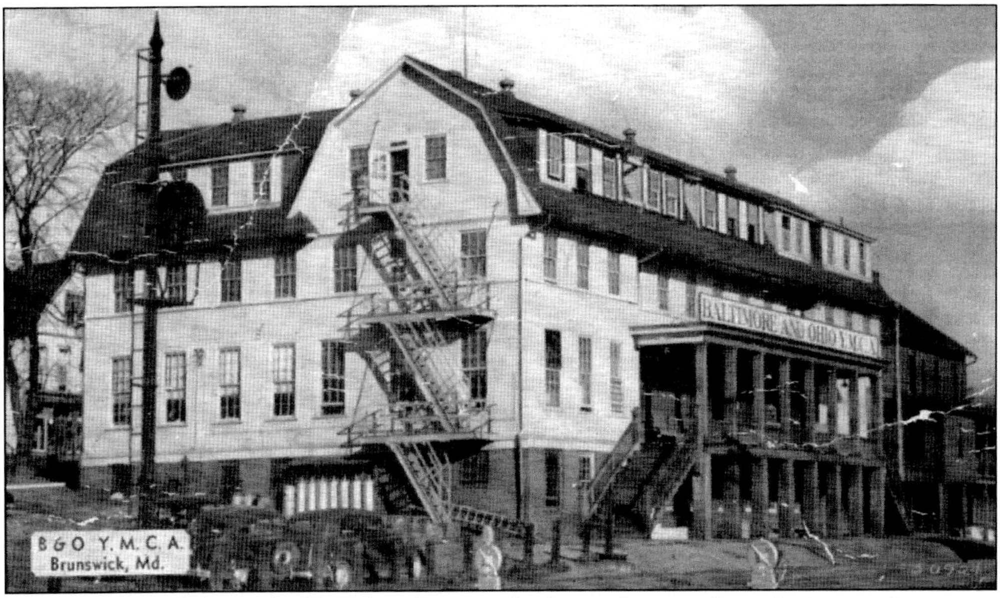

This old postcard shows the YMCA in Brunswick. As can be seen from the image, the correct name was actually the Baltimore and Ohio YMCA, and it was created by the railroad as a place for train crews to stay and to have something to eat between trips. The YMCA did not limit itself to the train crews, opening its doors to the community for meetings, social events, and even bowling. A tragic fire destroyed the YMCA on November 8, 1980. (Courtesy Brunswick History Commission.)

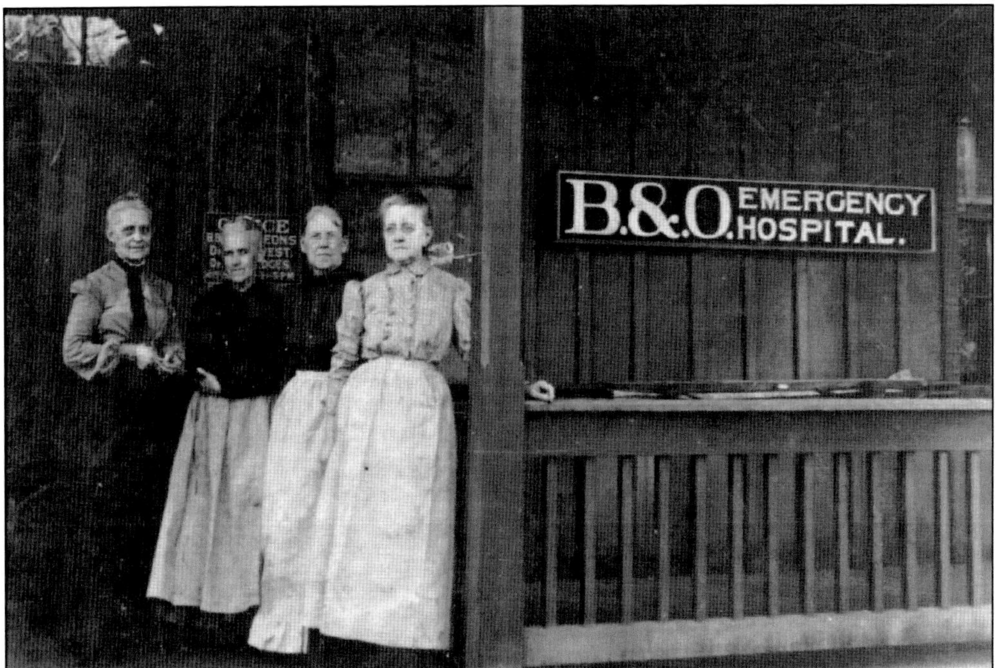

The B&O Railroad took care of its employees. In this image, women are working at the B&O Emergency Hospital. Pictured are, from left to right, unidentified, Sara Jane Kercheval Cole, unidentified, and Leona Nicodemus. (Courtesy Brunswick History Commission.)

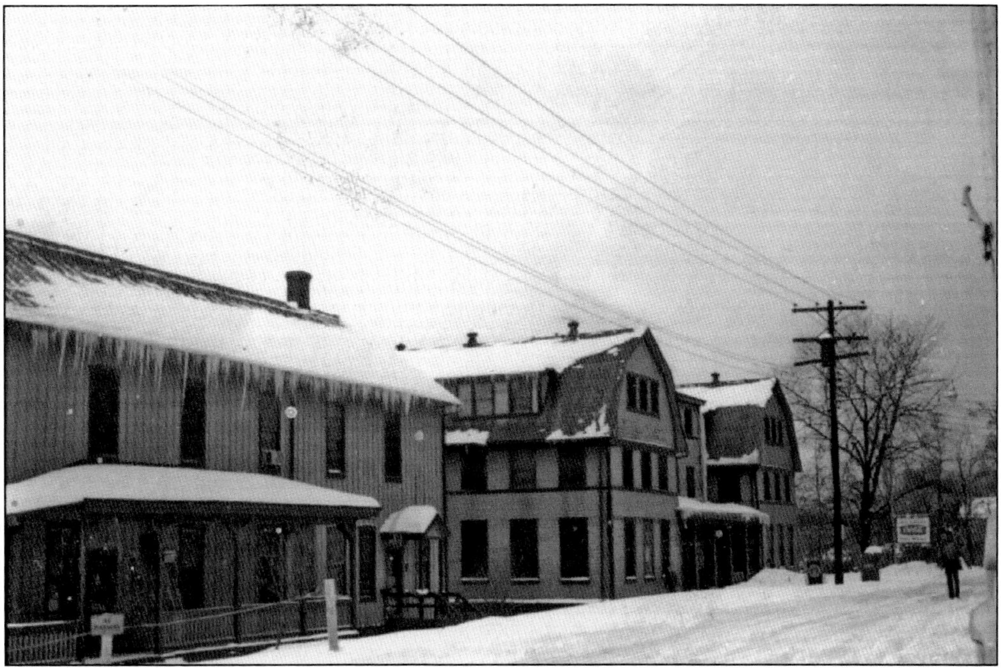

This 1961 winter photograph shows another view of the B&O hospital on the left. The barn-shaped building next to it is the YMCA. Just look at those icicles. (Courtesy Brunswick History Commission.)

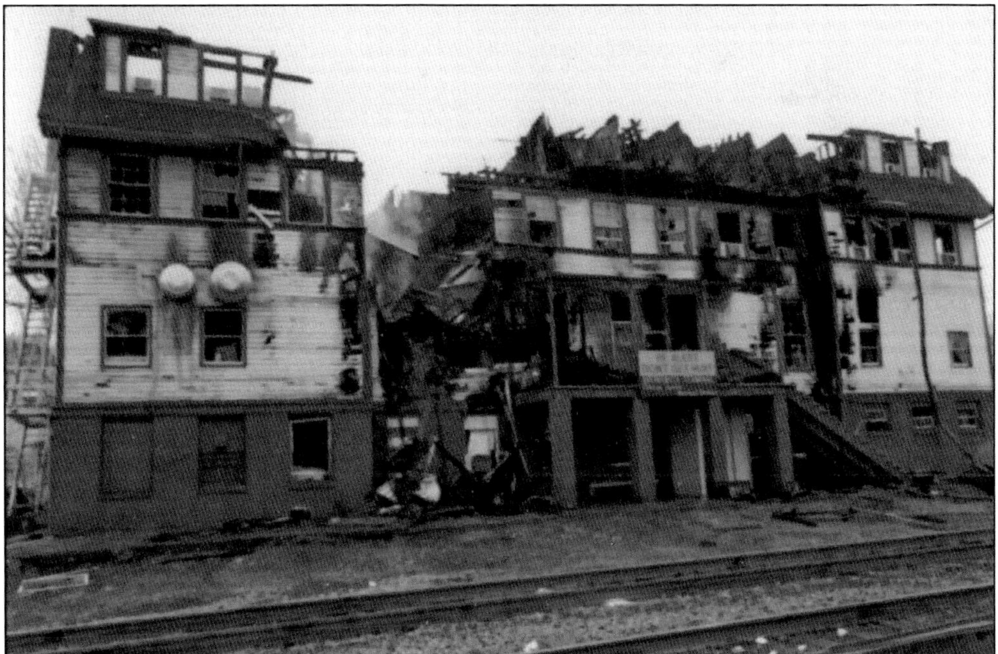

This image, taken trackside after the YMCA fire on November 9, 1980, shows the devastation wrought by the fire on this historic structure. (Courtesy Brunswick History Commission.)

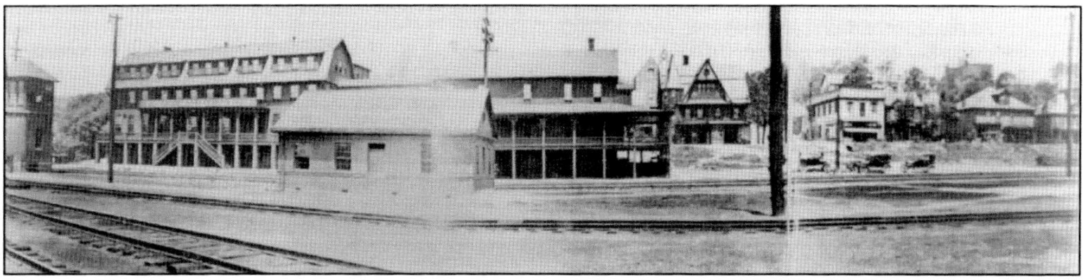

This wide-angle photograph shows various buildings in excellent perspective to each other. The structures pictured are, from left to right, the westbound rail tower (containing the Teletype operator and switch levers), the main YMCA building, the callers office (in front of the YMCA), the B&O hospital, Katie Barnard's boarding house (burned down in 1988), and a storefront. In the right-hand background is the Brunswick High School building. (Courtesy Brunswick History Commission.)

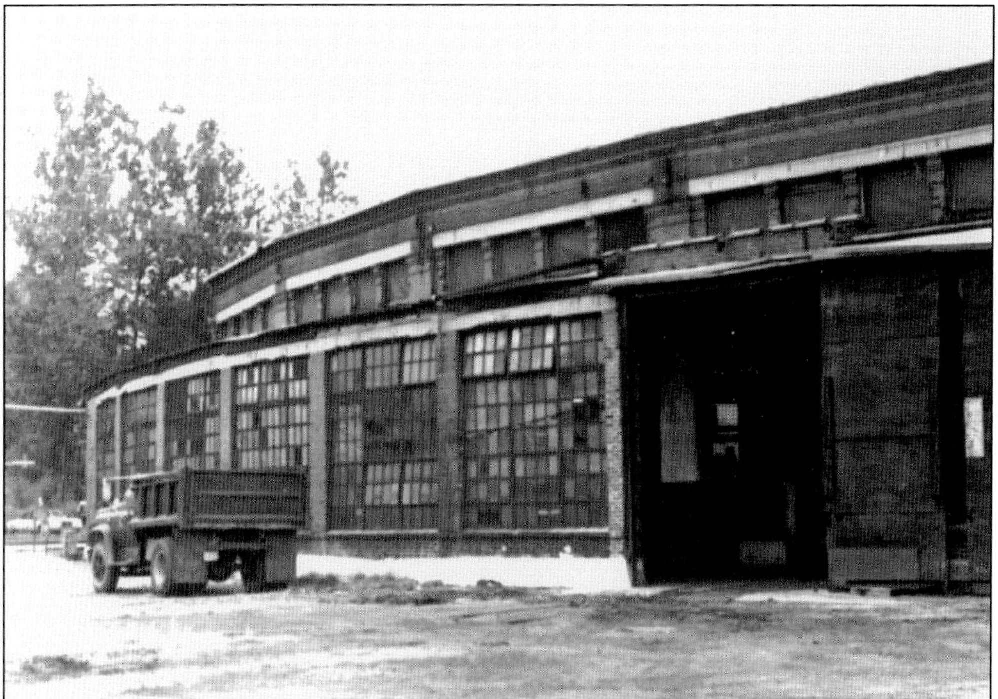

The first roundhouse in Brunswick was an iron structure built in June 1891. This brick roundhouse was constructed by the B&O Railroad in 1907, with an addition to complete the circular structure added in 1916. (Courtesy Brunswick History Commission.)

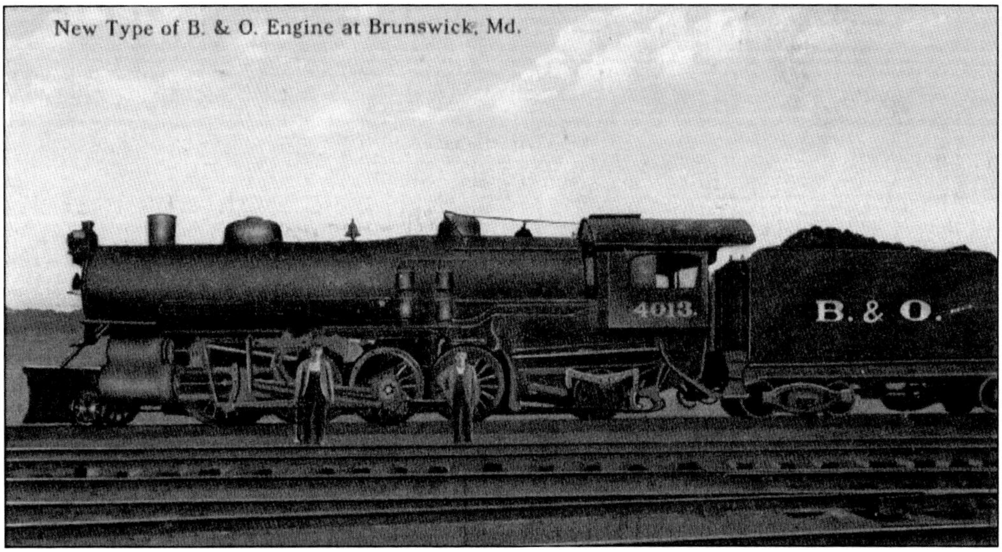

This old postcard advertised a new type of B&O engine on the tracks at Brunswick. This engine was known as a Class Q Mikado 2-8-2 freight engine from the first decade of the 20th century. The numbers 2-8-2 are from the Whyte System of wheel notation for steam locomotives and refer to the wheel arrangement. The first number refers to the leading wheels, the second to the coupled drive wheels, and the third to the number of supporting or trailing wheels. (Courtesy Brunswick History Commission.)

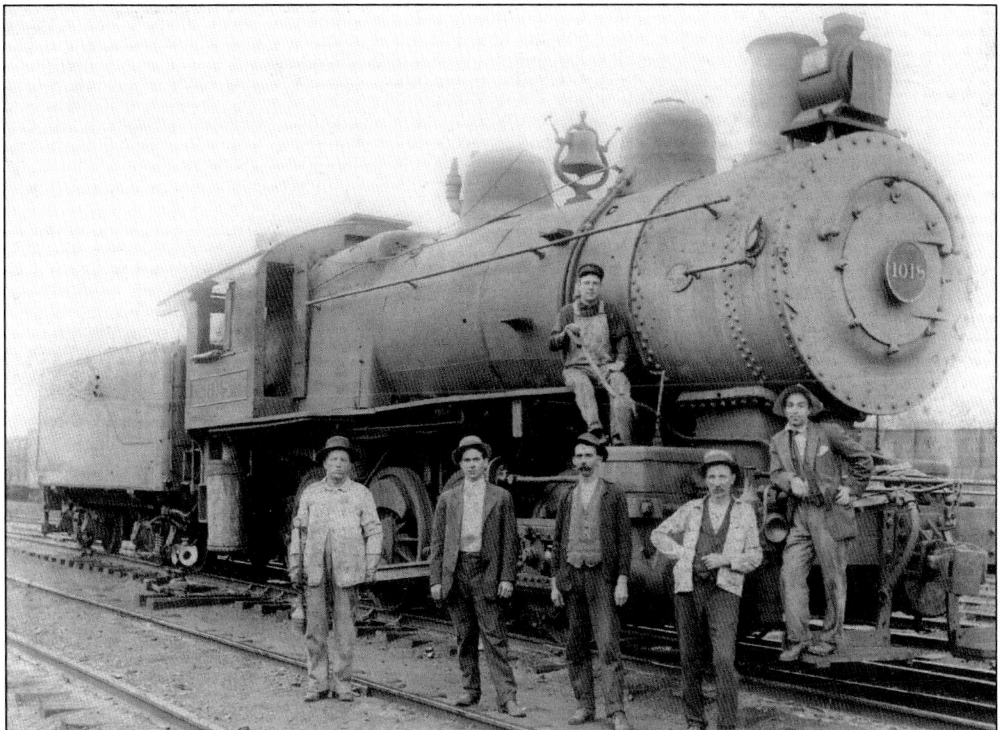

These men are posed by engine No. 1018, a Class L 8-wheel switcher, in Brunswick on July 29, 1912. (Courtesy Brunswick History Commission.)

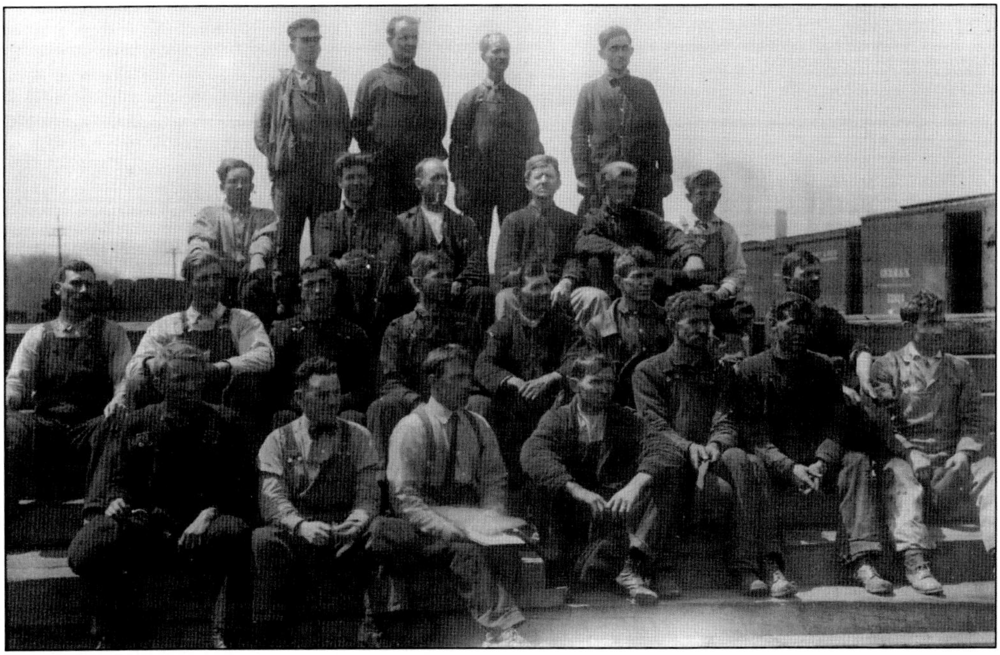

This 1914 group shot shows the B&O railcar yard employees. (Courtesy Brunswick History Commission.)

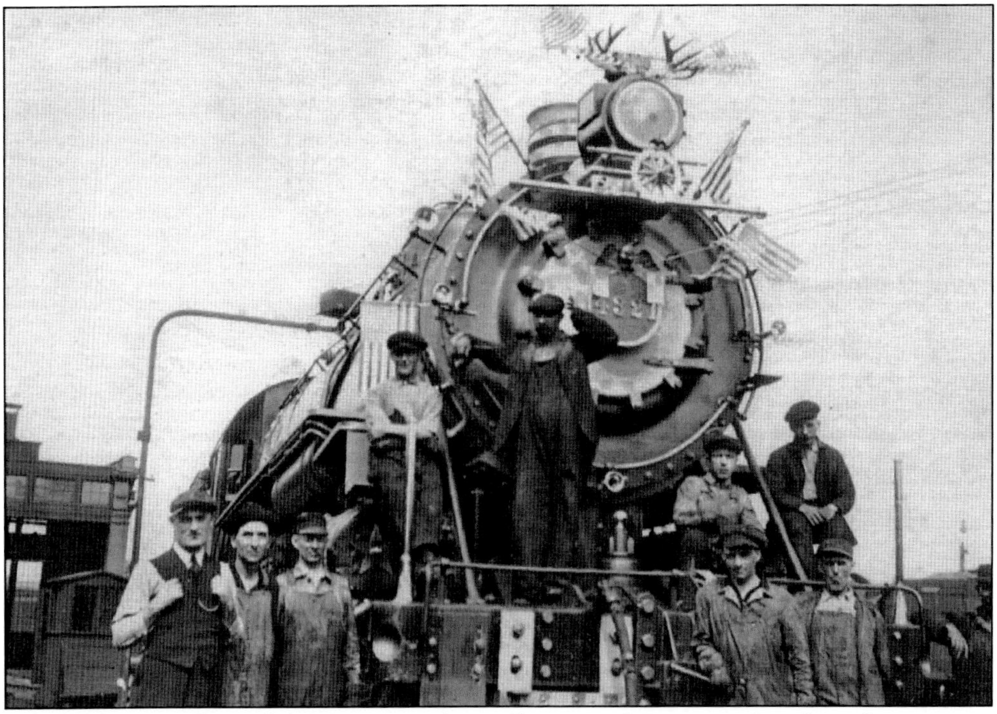

This 1920s image shows the train crew and roundhouse workers posing for a fun ride on engine No. 4321. Note the American flags and the headlight topped by the elk antlers. Men in the photograph are unidentified by location but include Charlie Lalloy, Clark Haller, and Harry A. Burns. (Courtesy Brunswick History Commission.)

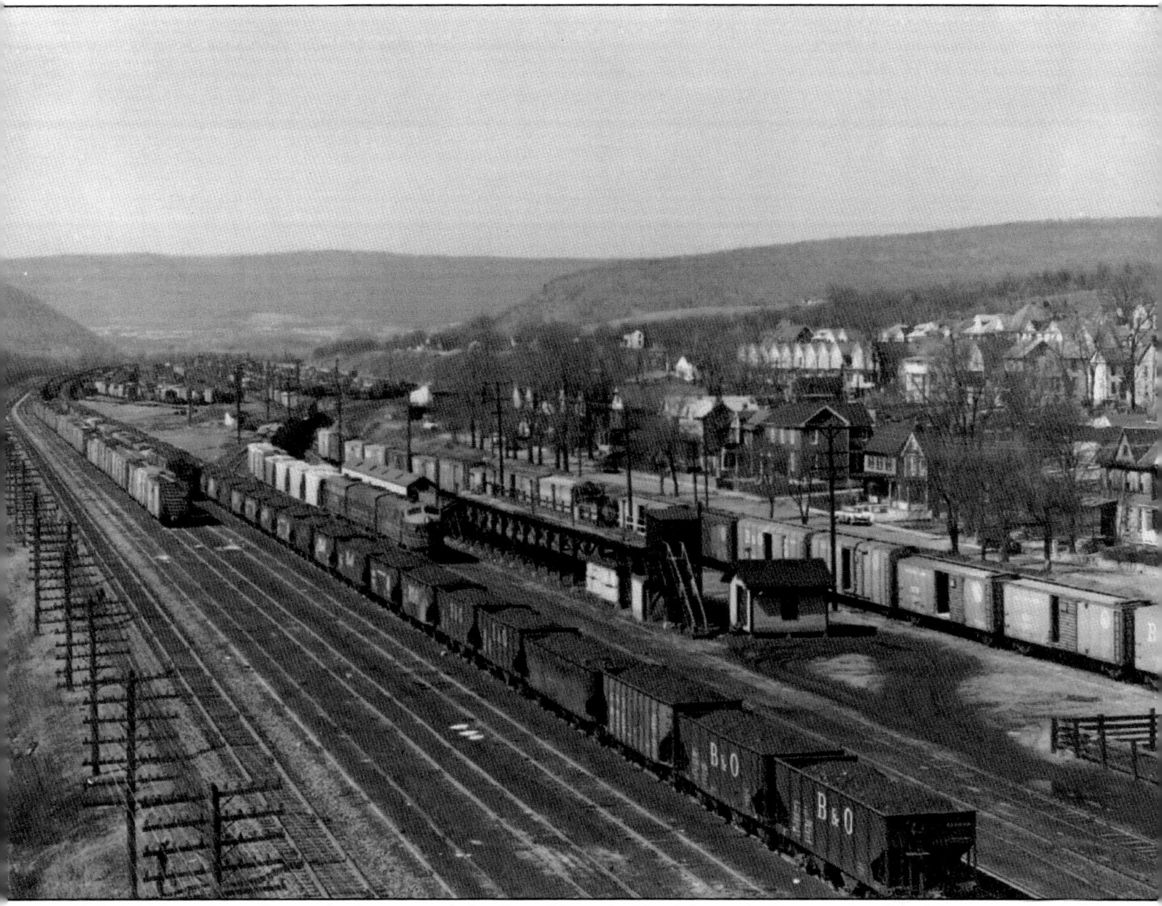

This *c.* 1950 image shows the Brunswick Railroad Freight Yard from the west, as well as houses in the west end of town. Note the railcars at the cattle-holding pen on the far right. The image also shows a freight train pulling out, the Fruit Growers Express office, and the platform for icing refrigerator cars, as well as the classification yard in the rear. (Courtesy Brunswick History Commission.)

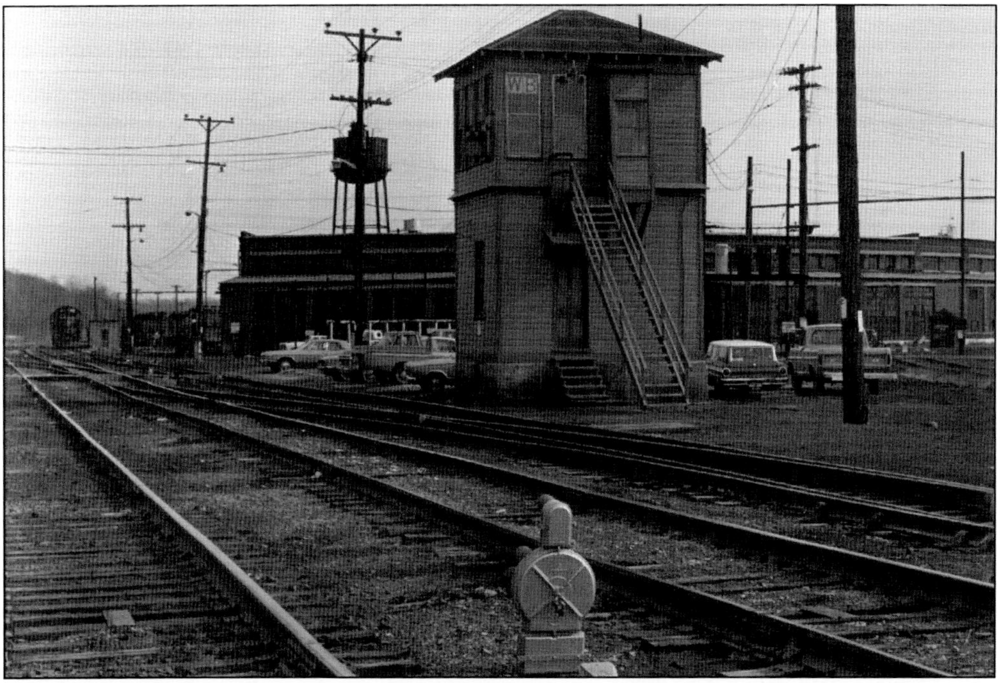

Here is a view of the tower on the westbound B&O tracks at Brunswick with the roundhouse in the background. (Courtesy Brunswick History Commission.)

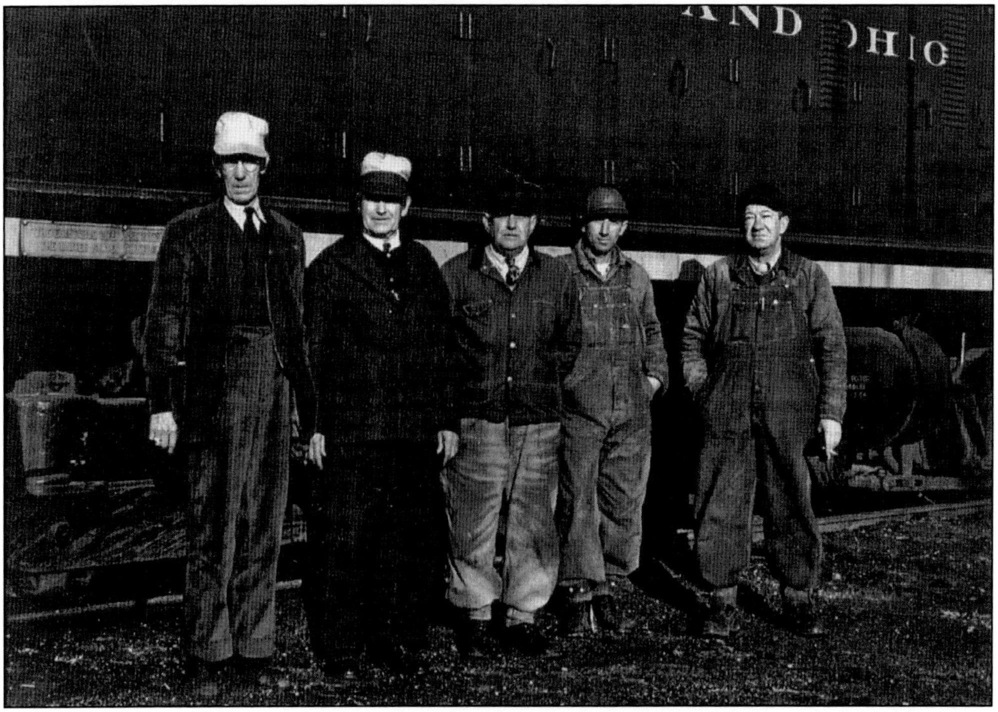

Here are some more B&O trainmen posing alongside the rails. The image shows, from left to right, Tom Keller, unidentified, Grayson Koogle, and two unidentified people. (Courtesy Brunswick History Commission.)

The B&O Railroad presented the town of Brunswick with this memorial bell. The bell is located in Railroad View Park on East Potomac Street on the site of the old YMCA. A few tables and benches are reminders that this was once a prime location for sitting and watching the trains. (Courtesy Brunswick History Commission.)

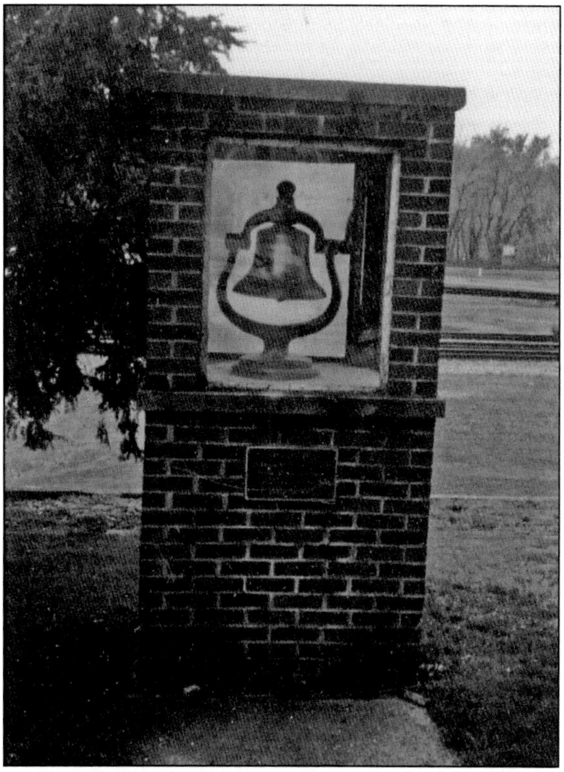

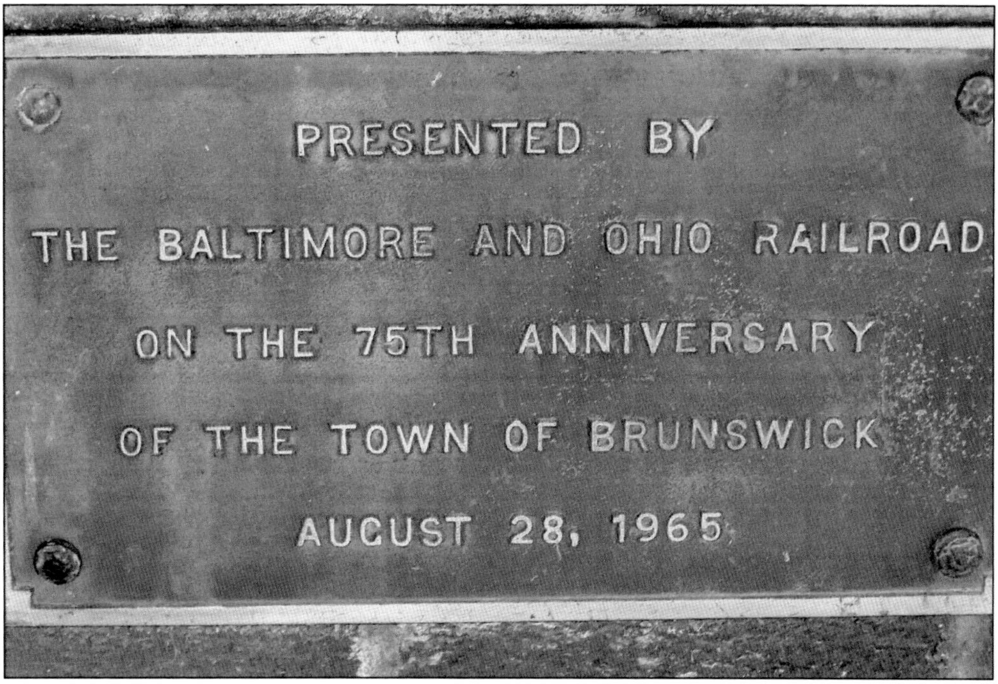

This is the plaque that is mounted on the bell at Railroad View Park. It was presented to the town on August 28, 1865, by the B&O Railroad in honor of the town's 75th anniversary. (Courtesy Mary H. Rubin.)

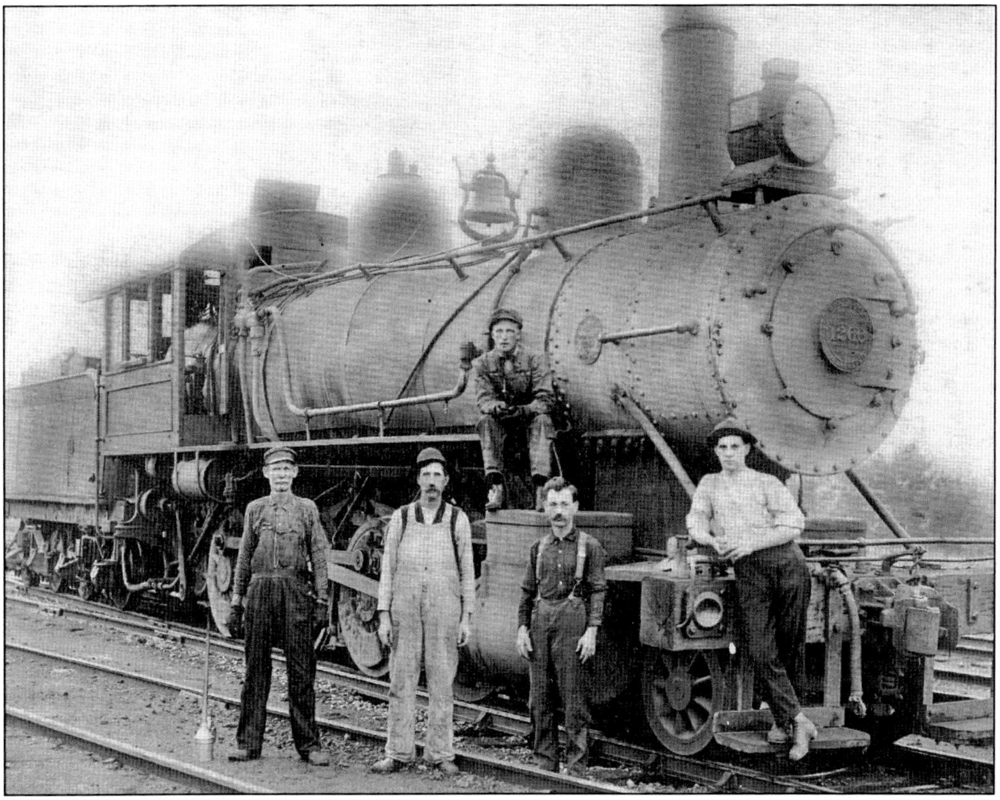

Here is another view of some Brunswick men with a B&O engine. Note the oilcan with the extra-long nozzle next to the man on the left. (Courtesy Brunswick History Commission.)

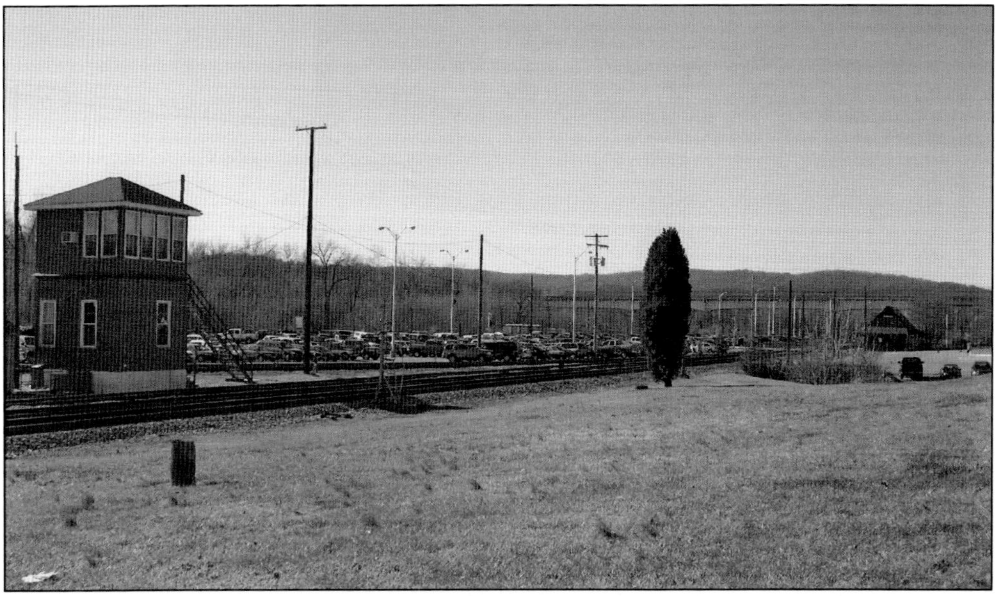

This view of the rail yards was taken from the vantage point of Railroad View Park on East Potomac Street. The Maryland Rail Commuter parking lots and the Brunswick train station can be seen in the background. (Courtesy Mary H. Rubin.)

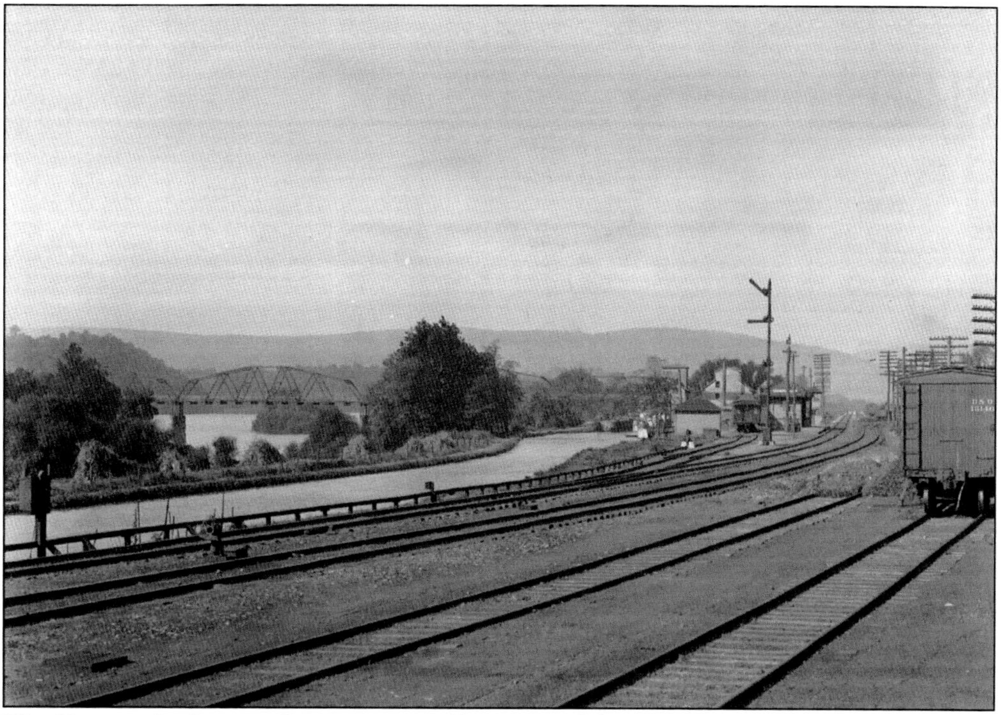

This Brunswick photograph gives an excellent view of the Potomac River on the far left, the canal running down the middle, and the rail tracks to the right. (Courtesy C&O Canal National Historical Park Headquarters.)

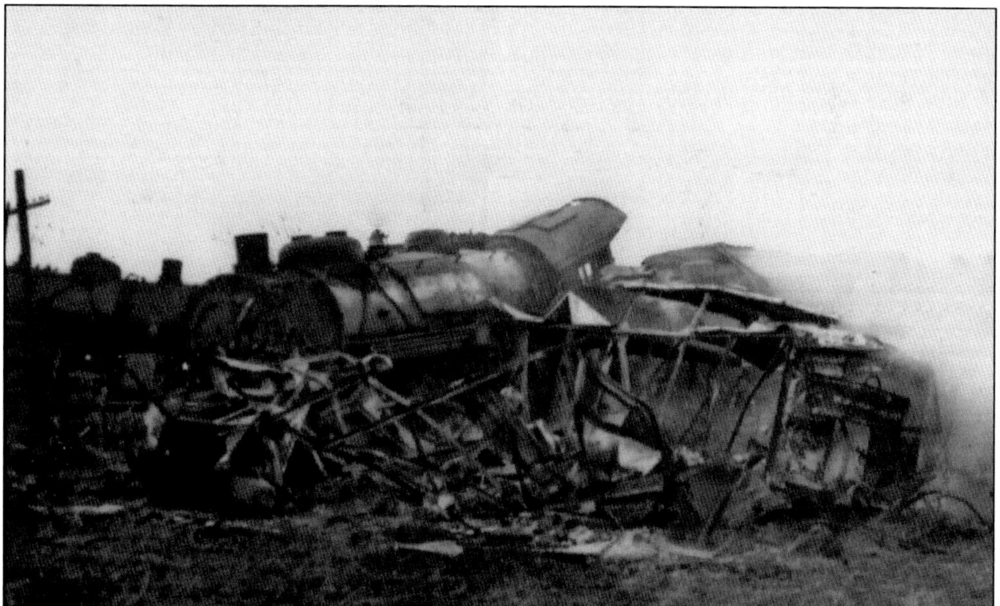

This image shows a tragic train wreck in nearby Point of Rocks in 1936. Accidents were a part of railroading life, reminding us that rail travel was not without its dangers. (Courtesy Brunswick History Commission.)

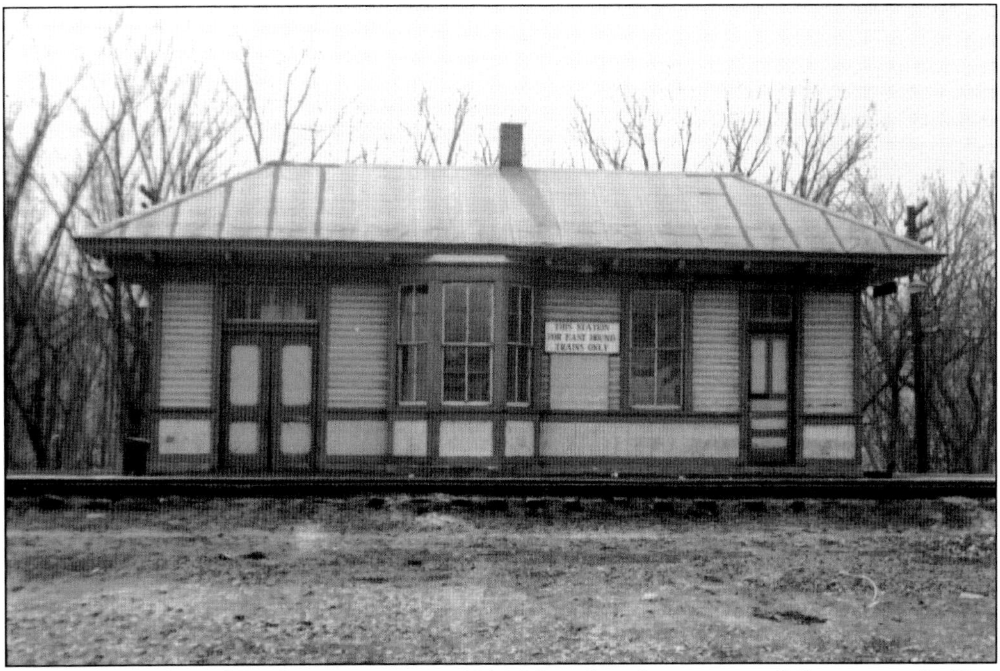

Here is the eastbound B&O train station c. 1904. Note that the sign says, "This station for East Bound trains only." (Courtesy Brunswick History Commission.)

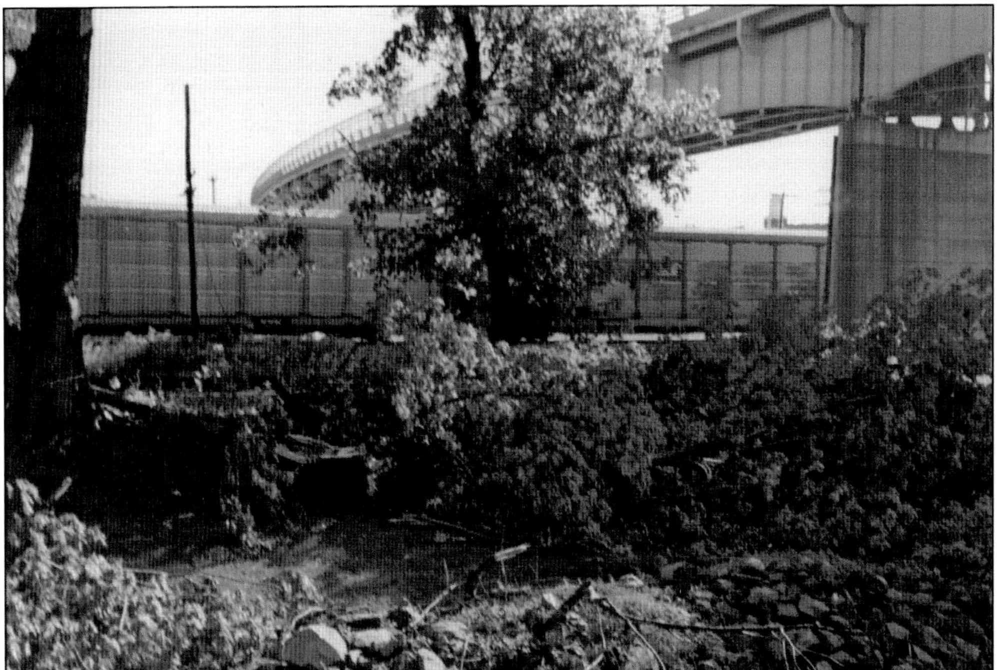

Here is another photograph taken near the new Potomac River bridge in Brunswick. This one shows storm damage after the July 19, 1996, tornado that moved through the area. Note the train moving under the bridge in the background. (Courtesy C&O Canal National Historical Park Headquarters.)

Five

People, Places, and Events

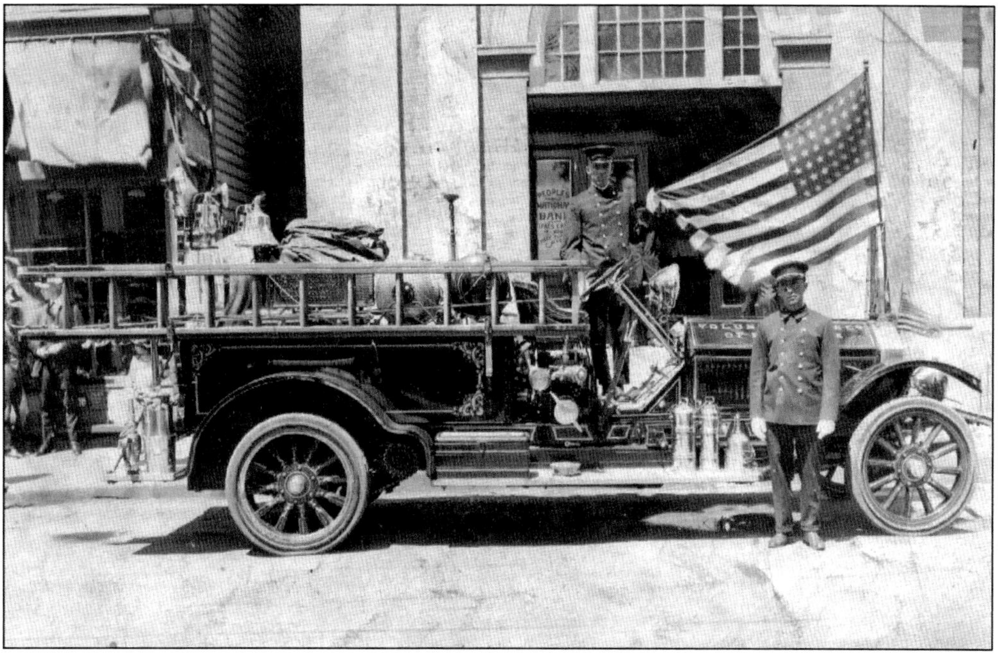

This photograph was taken in 1923 in front of the People's National Bank and shows Brunswick's first motorized fire engine, an American LaFrance. The men in the photograph are William C. Nuse (chief) and Cooper Draker. The engine had a 750-gallon-per-minute pump. Note the hand-rung bell mounted near the back and the solid rubber tires. (Courtesy Brunswick History Commission.)

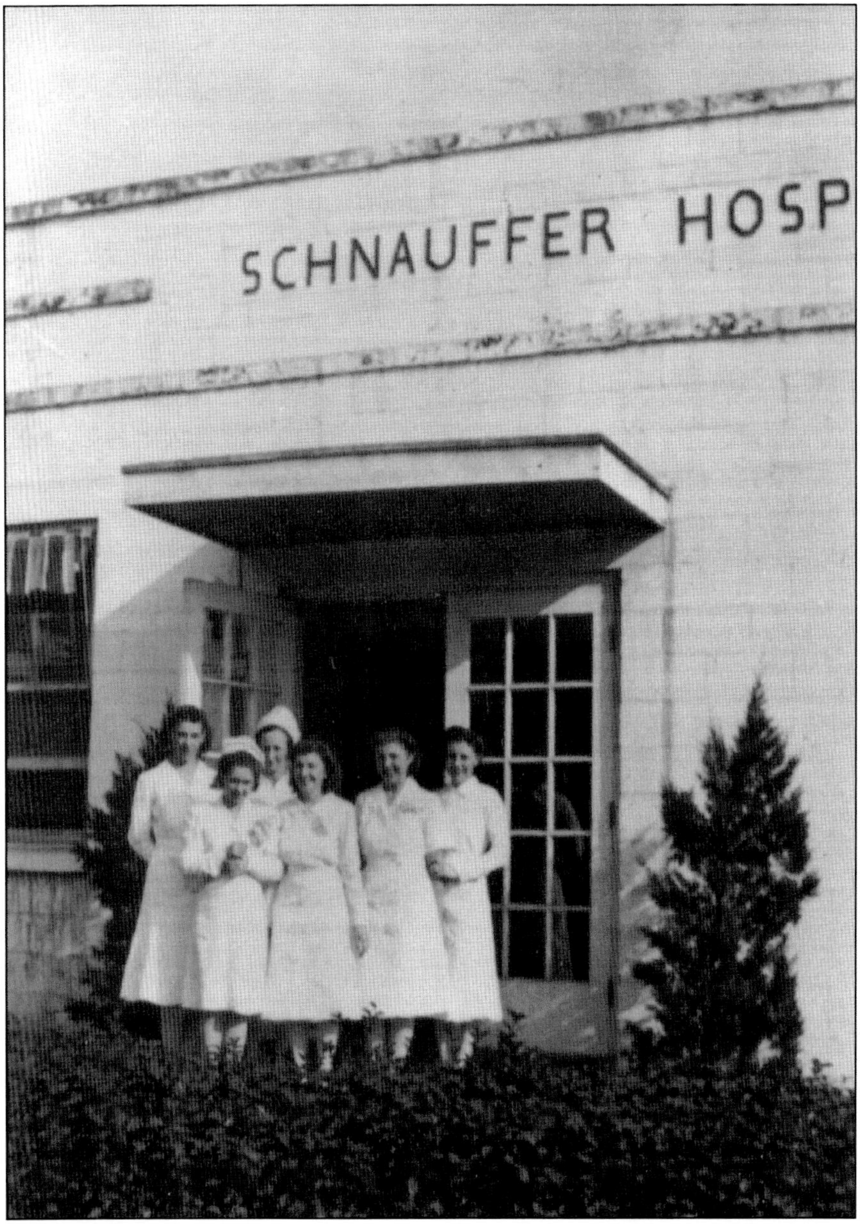

This group of nurses is posed outside the Schnauffer Hospital. The hospital was founded in 1932 by Dr. William Schnauffer Jr. Almost every kind of operation was performed, with Dr. Leo Gafney coming in by train from Washington, D.C., as needed for consultation or assistance with surgery. The hospital was considered well outfitted for its day, with an electrocardiogram, X-ray capabilities, oxygen tents, and more. The surrounding communities of Lovettsville, Sandy Hook, Weverton, Yarrowsburg, and Brownsville were all served by the hospital. After the hospital closed in July 1946, Brunswick's first health clinic was opened on the lower level of the empty town synagogue in 1947. Pictured are, from left to right, Connie Isaac Jenkins, L.P.N.; June Shewbridge Jones, R.N. (the first registered nurse at the hospital); Rebecca Snyder Blessing, R.N.; Ethel Wenner Trice, N.A.; Mae Fink, lab technician; and Louise M. Kimes, N.A. (Courtesy Brunswick History Commission.)

This photograph shows George Ernest "Amy" Ambrose with his Indian Chief motorcycle on North Maple Street. Amy became Brunswick's policeman in 1926 and was named the chief of police by 1937. During those years, he was the only operator of the police motorcycle and was known as the town's favorite policeman. (Courtesy Brunswick History Commission.)

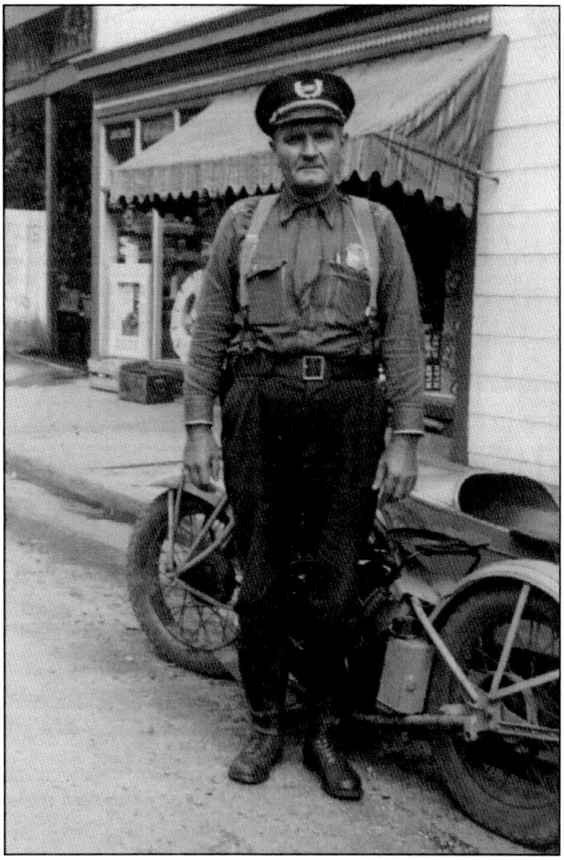

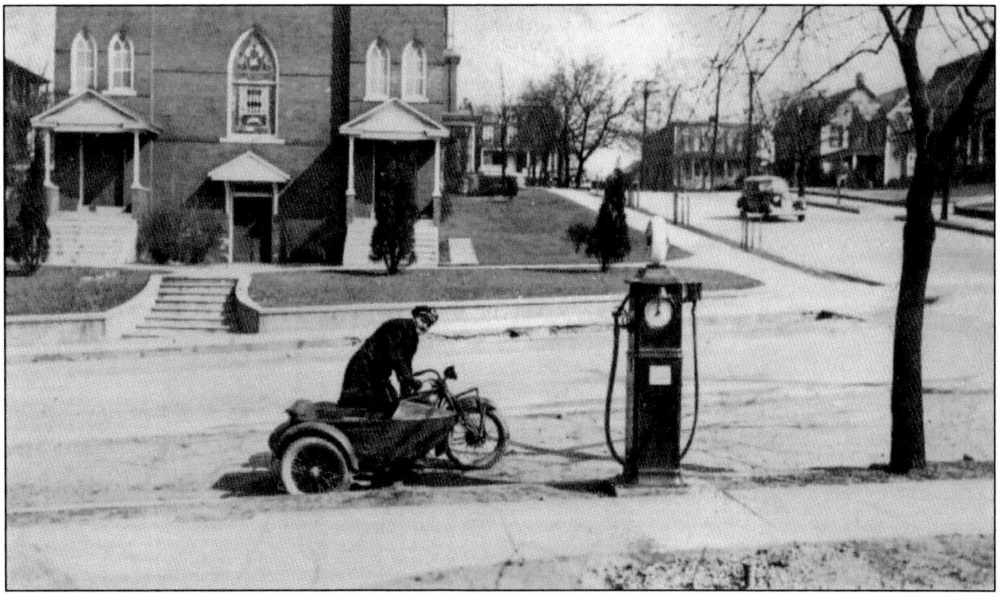

Here is another shot of Policeman Ambrose around 1930 with his bike by a gas pump in front of city hall. Bethany Evangelical Lutheran Church is in the background. Note the sidecar on the motorcycle. (Courtesy Brunswick History Commission.)

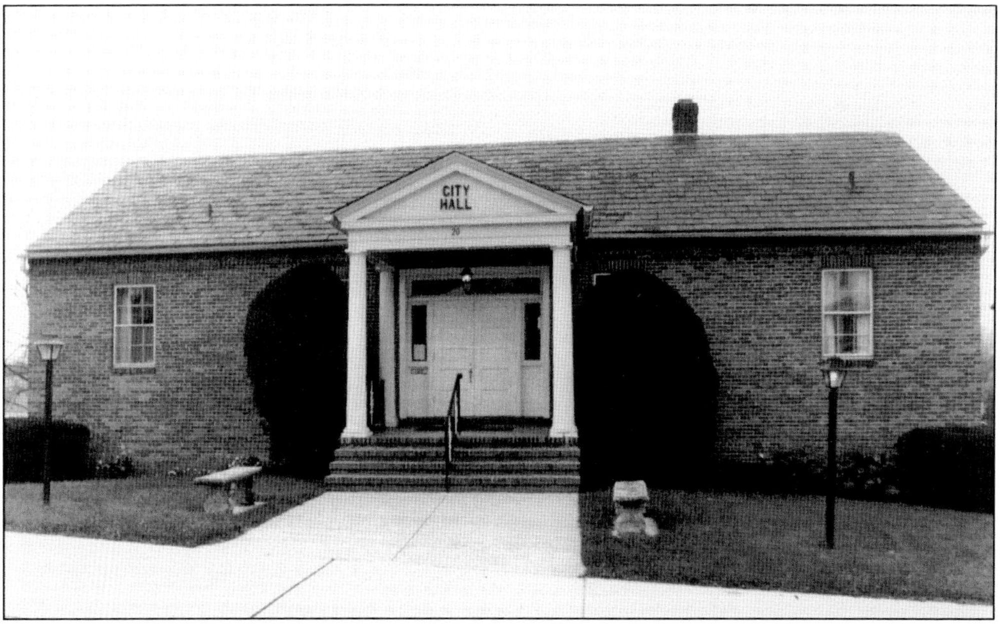

City hall has been located in several spots over the years. This photograph shows Brunswick City Hall when it was located at 20 A Street. The cement benches shown in this image had deteriorated to such an extent that they were removed in 1994. The building was completely taken over by the police department when city hall relocated to 1 West Potomac Street. (Courtesy Brunswick History Commission.)

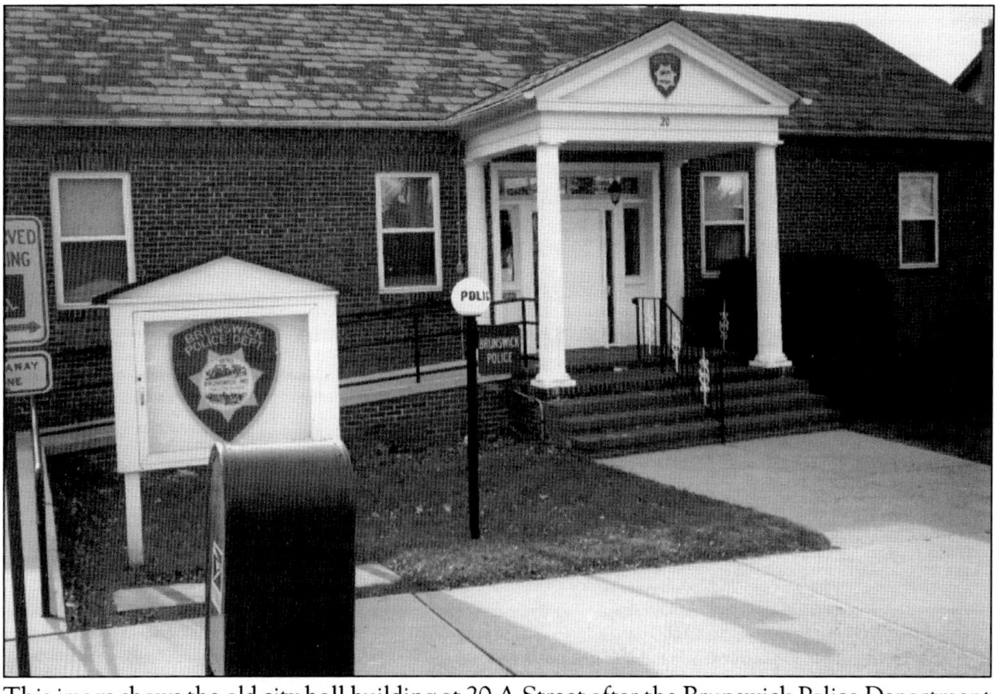

This image shows the old city hall building at 20 A Street after the Brunswick Police Department took it over. For many years, the police "lock up" was located in the basement, and the town meeting hall was upstairs. (Courtesy Brunswick History Commission.)

Here is the LaFrance fire engine when it arrived in town in 1923. Note the old Firemen's Hall building it is parked in front of on Delaware Avenue between Potomac and Brunswick Streets. (Courtesy Brunswick History Commission.)

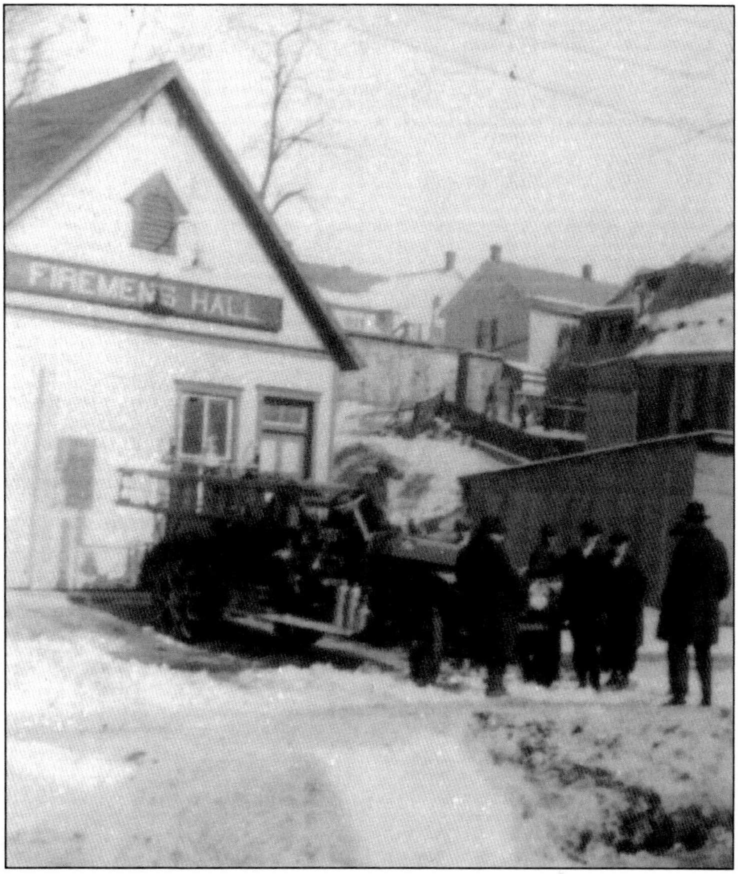

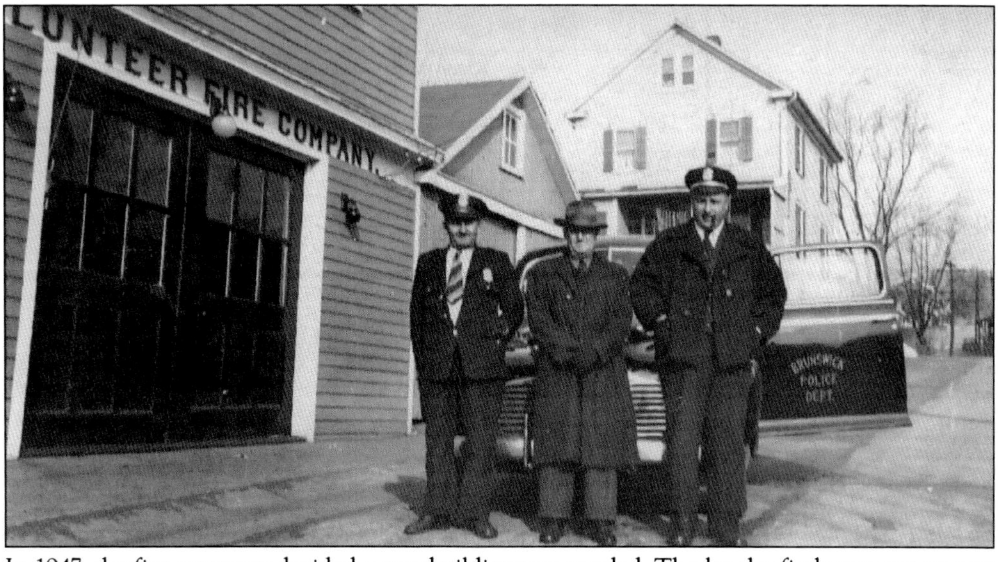

In 1947, the fire company decided a new building was needed. The lot the firehouse was on was purchased for $3,800, and the new building was completed in 1951. The first floor contained the trucks, while the second floor contained a ballroom and stage where many bands played over the years for town dances. (Courtesy Brunswick History Commission.)

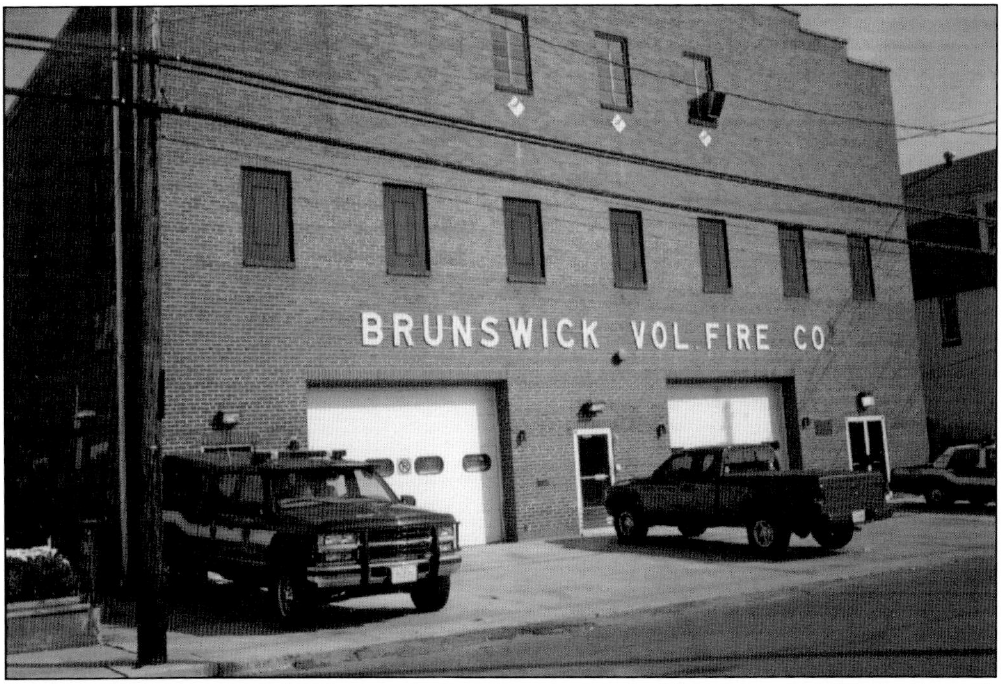

Here is a view of Brunswick's current volunteer fire company building taken in 2000. By the mid-1990s, the fire company included three engine trucks, a ladder truck, a tanker, a mini-pumper/brush truck combination, and a brush truck. (Courtesy Brunswick History Commission.)

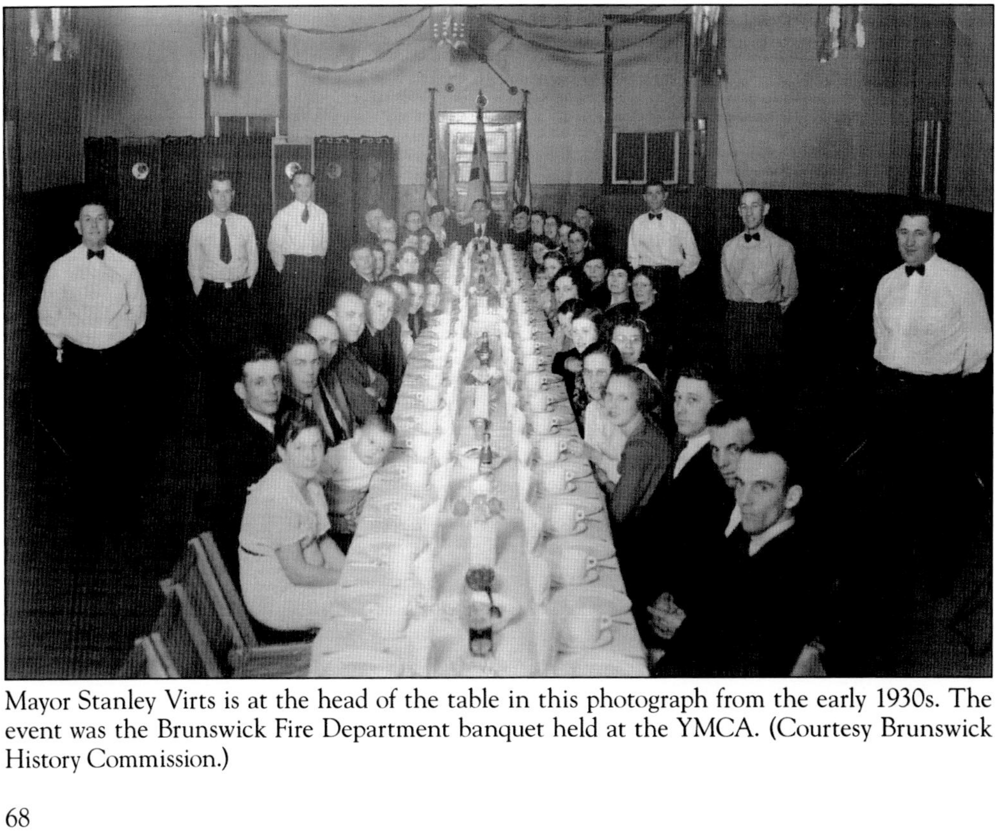

Mayor Stanley Virts is at the head of the table in this photograph from the early 1930s. The event was the Brunswick Fire Department banquet held at the YMCA. (Courtesy Brunswick History Commission.)

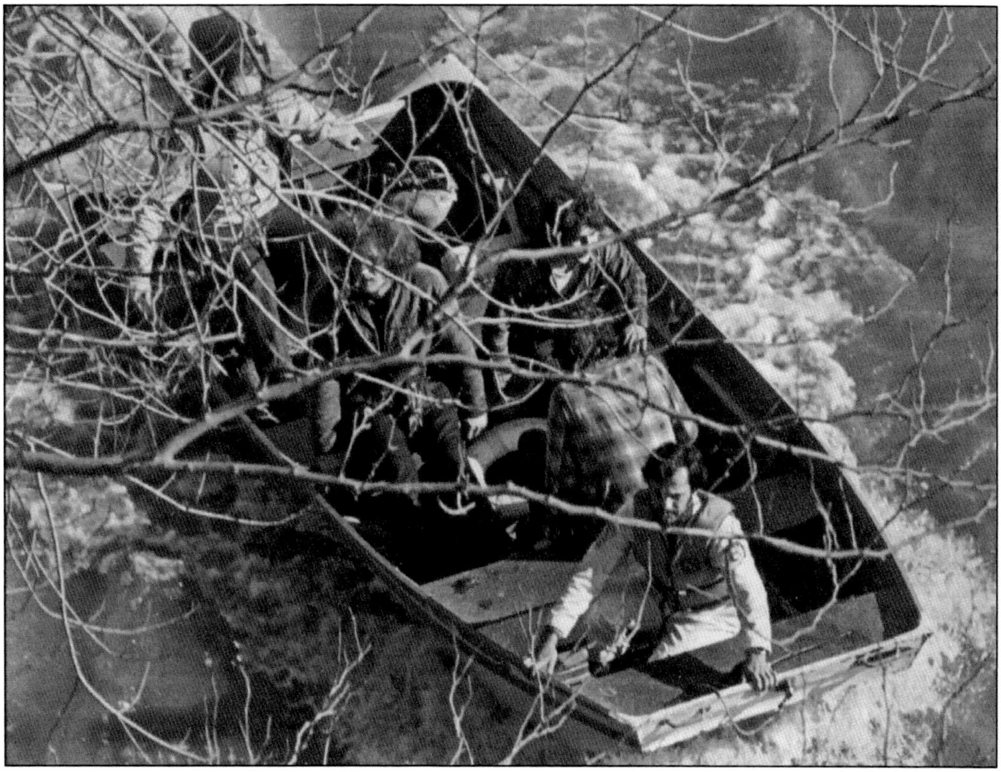

Brunswick's emergency services began in 1960 and have grown over the years to a professional, highly trained rescue company. Because of the town's location on the bank of the Potomac River, training in water emergencies and rescue operations is important. This *c.* 1970 photograph shows a river rescue operation. (Courtesy Brunswick History Commission.)

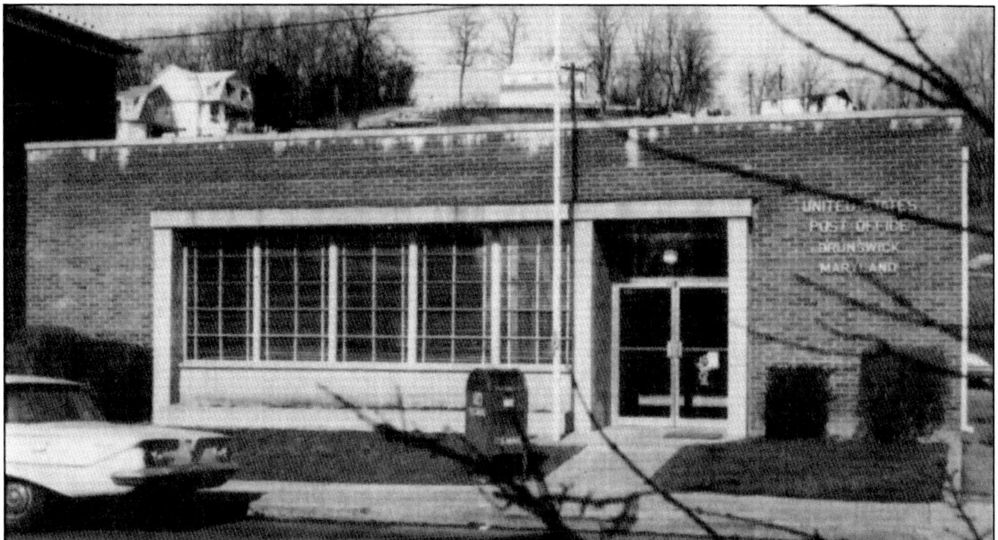

The post office in Brunswick has been housed in various buildings around town since its inception as the Barry Post Office in 1832. Here we see the current building, dedicated October 11, 1958, at 315 Brunswick Street. (Courtesy Brunswick History Commission.)

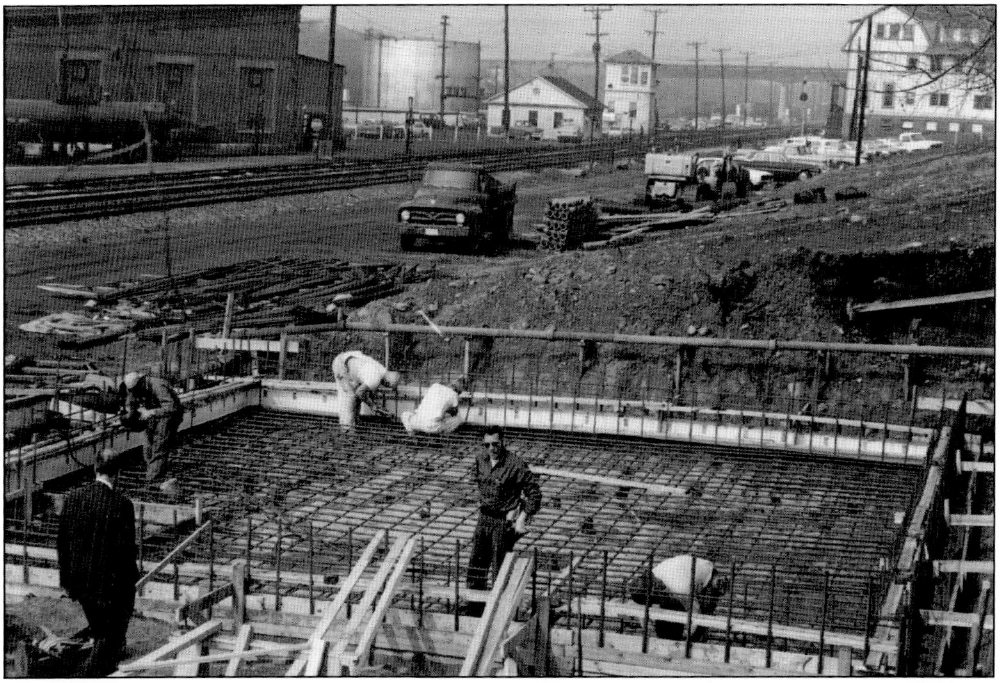

In 1989, construction began on a new water treatment plant. During the early years, private wells, cisterns, and a town well served the water needs of Berlin. The town's first reservoir was completed on Souder Road in 1922. (Courtesy Brunswick History Commission.)

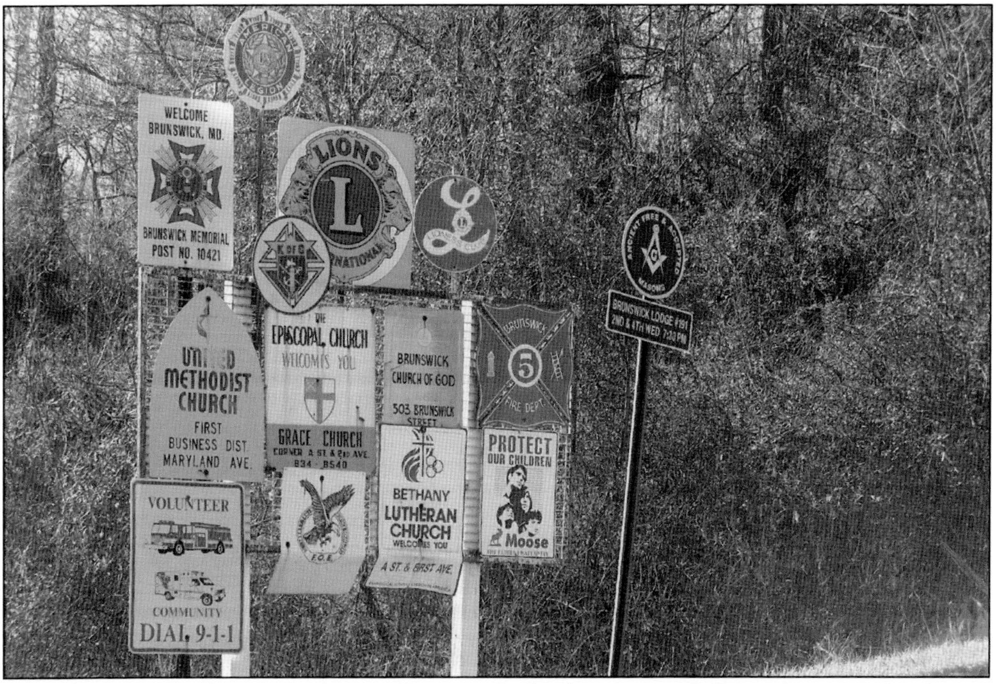

As with so many other communities, Brunswick also has a group of signposts outside of town noting its various churches and community groups. This group of signs is on Petersville Road on the right-hand side heading south toward downtown. (Courtesy Mary H. Rubin.)

The gentleman in this picture is Brunswick's first mayor, John L. Jordan Jr. He served the town from 1890 to 1892 and then again from 1898 to 1900. Jordan also served as county clerk from 1891 to 1897, as well as justice of the peace. (Courtesy Brunswick History Commission.)

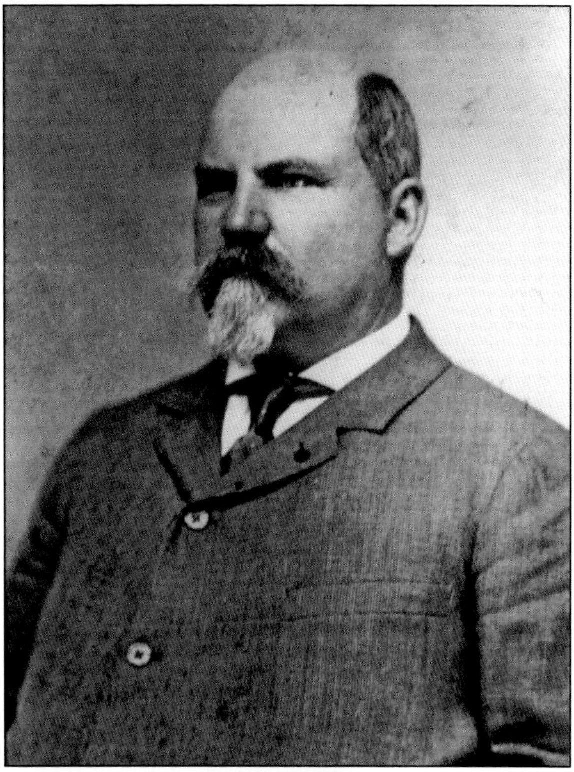

Below is a selection of books on the shelves at the Brunswick Library. The Brunswick Library Association was formed on March 1, 1962, and one room was leased at 317 Brunswick Street. With 3,500 books, the library opened its doors on April 23, 1963. The library later became part of the Frederick County Library System, and a dedicated library building was constructed at 915 North Maple Avenue and opened on April 9, 1989. (Courtesy Brunswick History Commission.)

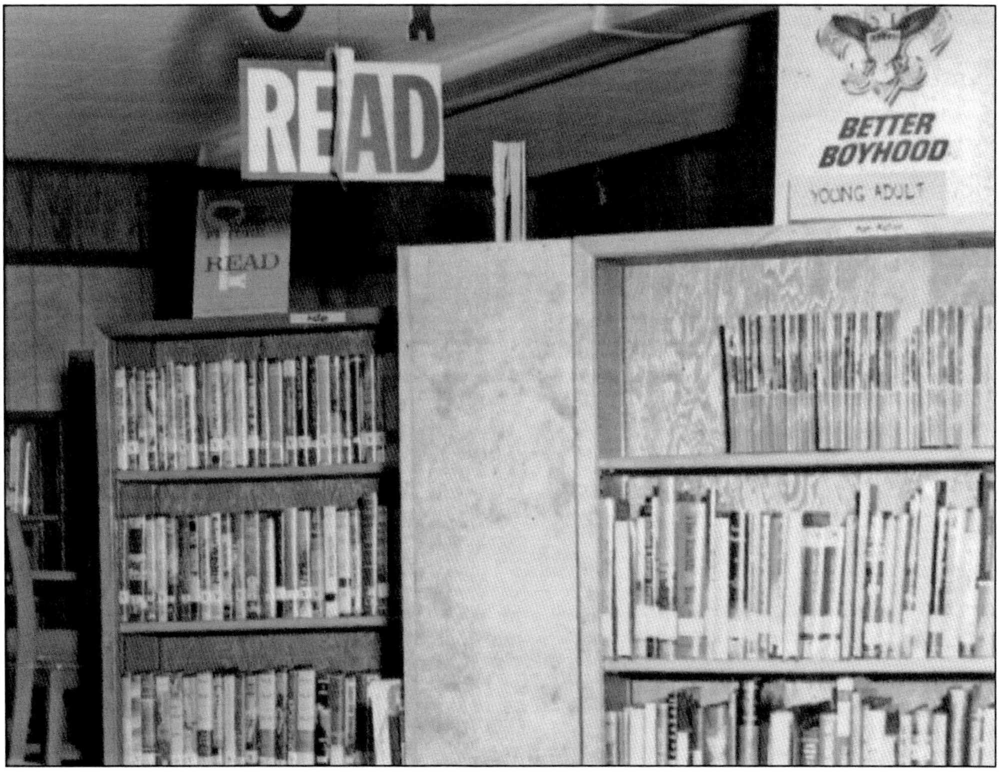

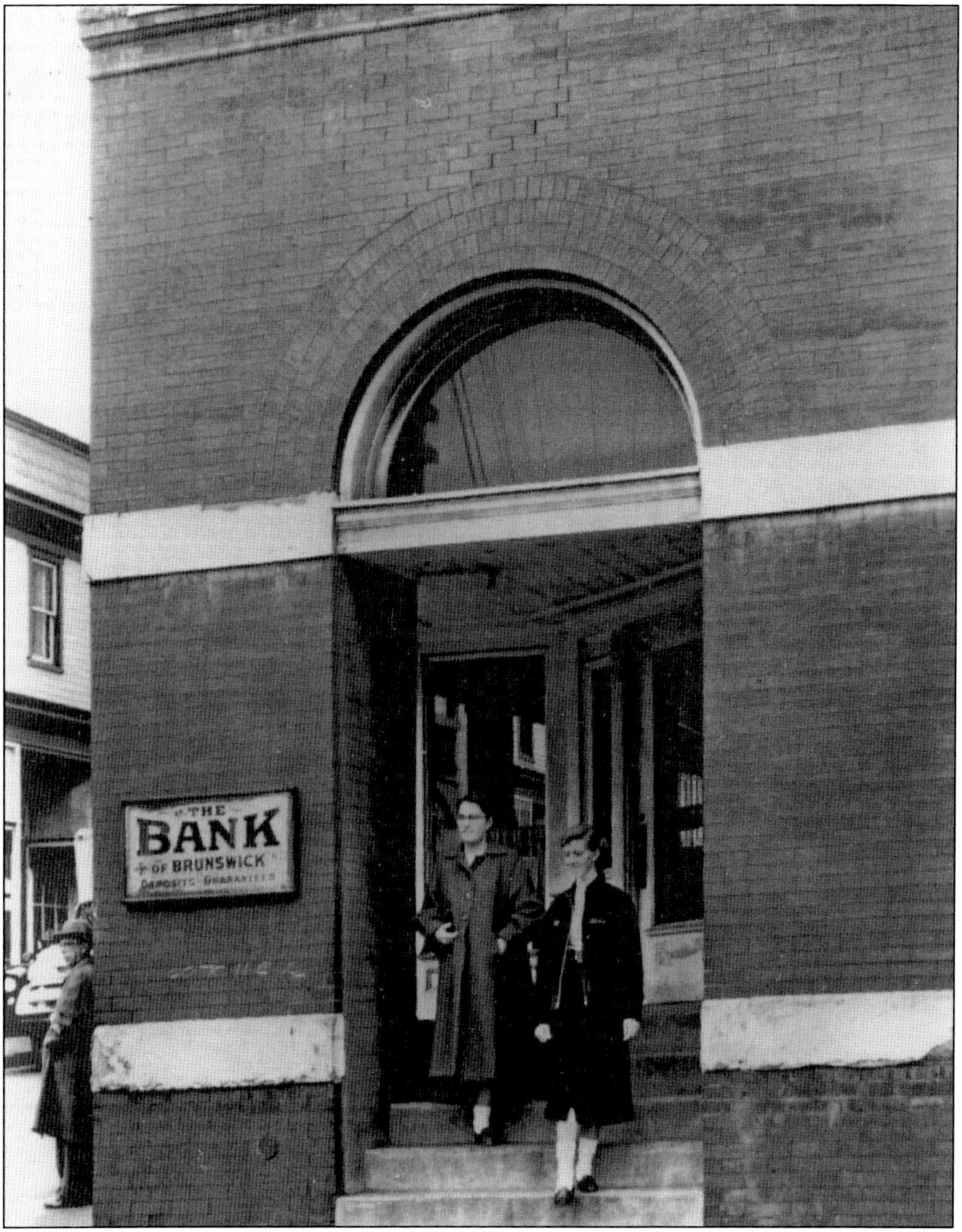

Here is a photograph of the Bank of Brunswick on the corner of North Maple Avenue and West Potomac Street. Incorporated by stockholders in 1915, the bank originally occupied space in the Red Men's Hall until this building was purchased in 1920. An interesting story in the bank's history dates back to the Depression years when, on March 6, 1933, Pres. Franklin D. Roosevelt called a seven-day "bank holiday" to allow Congress to implement emergency bank measures to halt the total collapse of the national economy. The stability of the Bank of Brunswick resulted in it being one of the banks allowed to re-open after the holiday. (Courtesy Brunswick History Commission.)

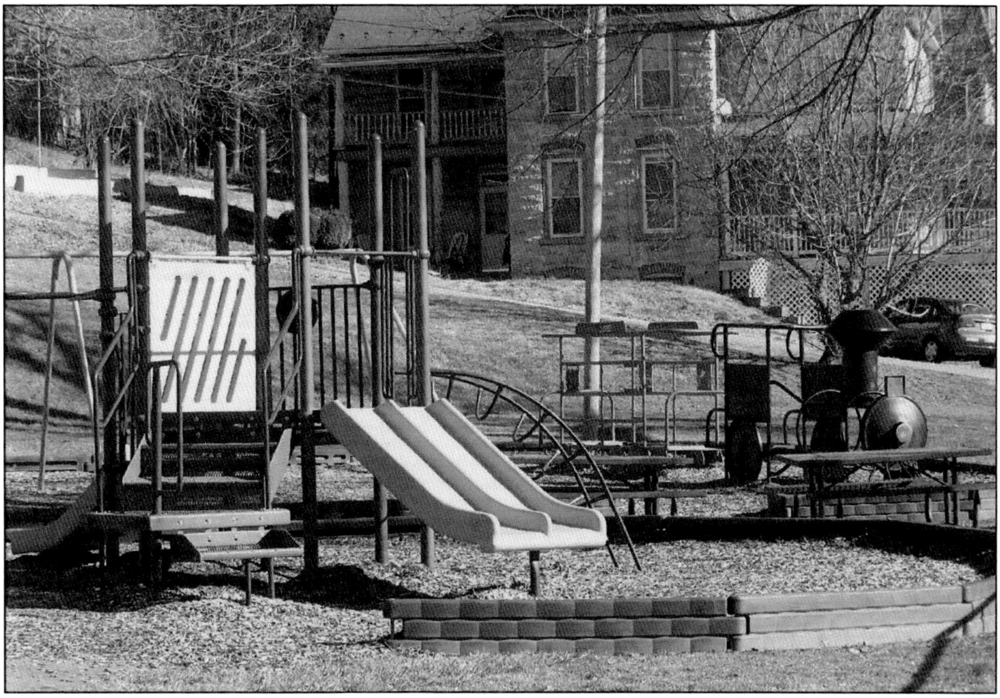

One of numerous parks throughout town, the Brunswick City Park is shown in these images. The park, located on the corner of East Potomac Street and Gum Spring Road, was deeded to the town on May 22, 1895, with the stipulation that it be used for a public park and no other purpose. Note that one of the climbing apparatus is in the form of a train locomotive, another nod to the city's heritage. (Courtesy Mary H. Rubin.)

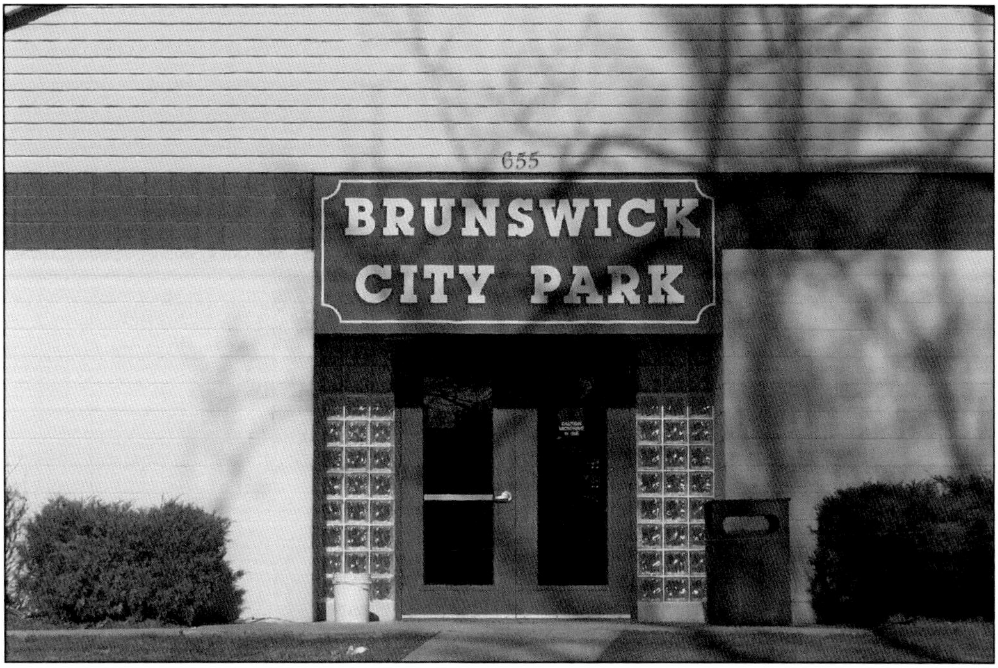

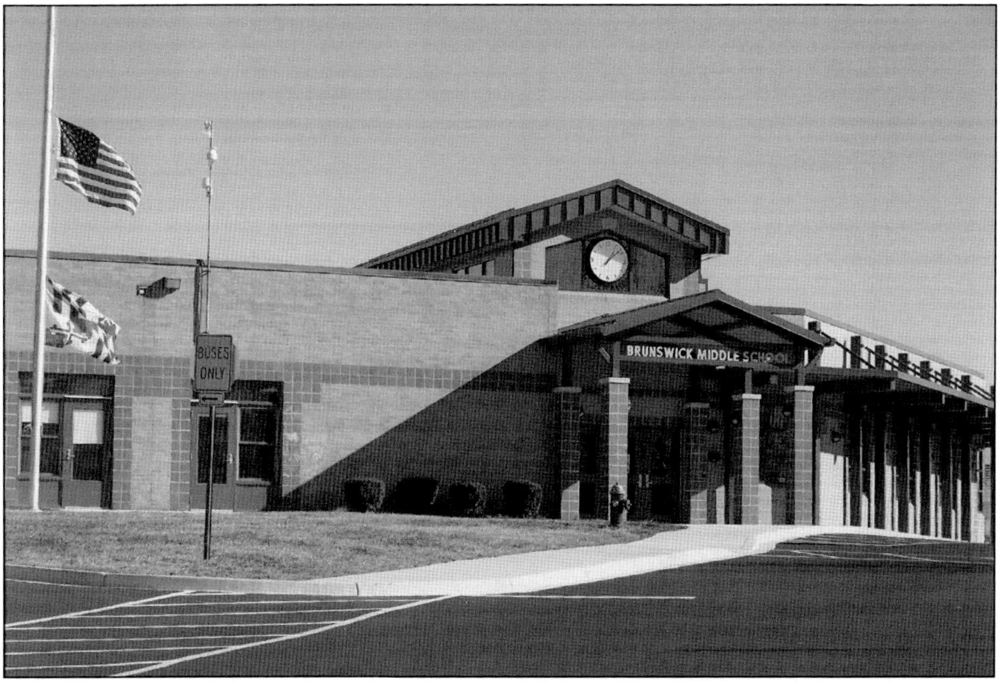

Here is an image of today's modern Brunswick Middle School. Note the American and Maryland state flags flying at half-mast—this image was taken during the 30-day national mourning period after the death of Pres. Gerald Ford in 2006. (Courtesy Mary H. Rubin.)

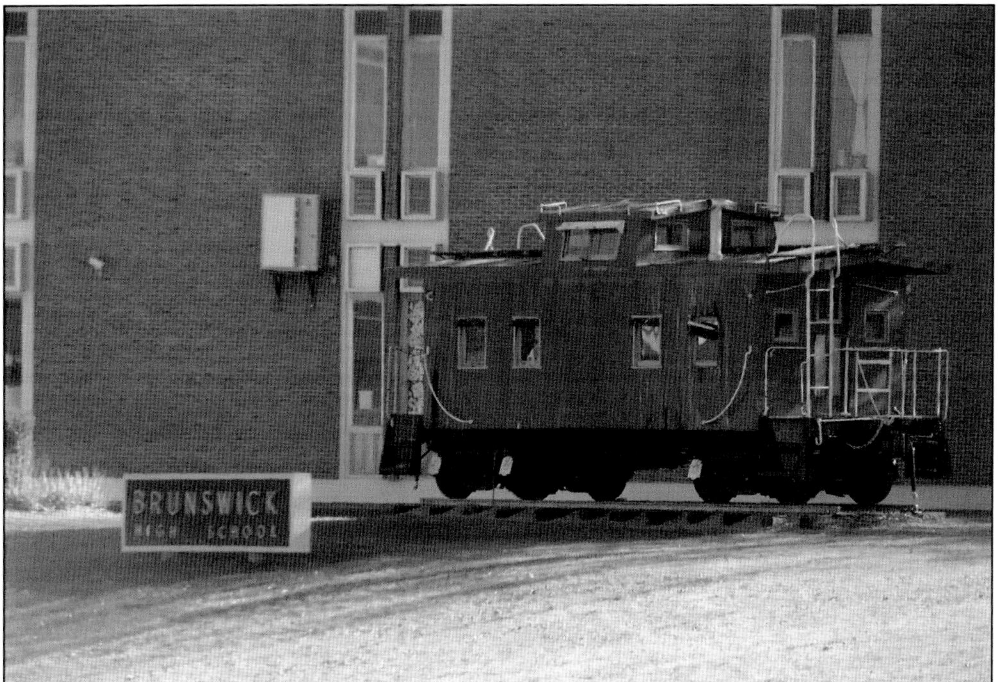

Brunswick's modern high school building still has a hint of the community's past with this old caboose parked on the grounds of the school. (Courtesy Mary H. Rubin.)

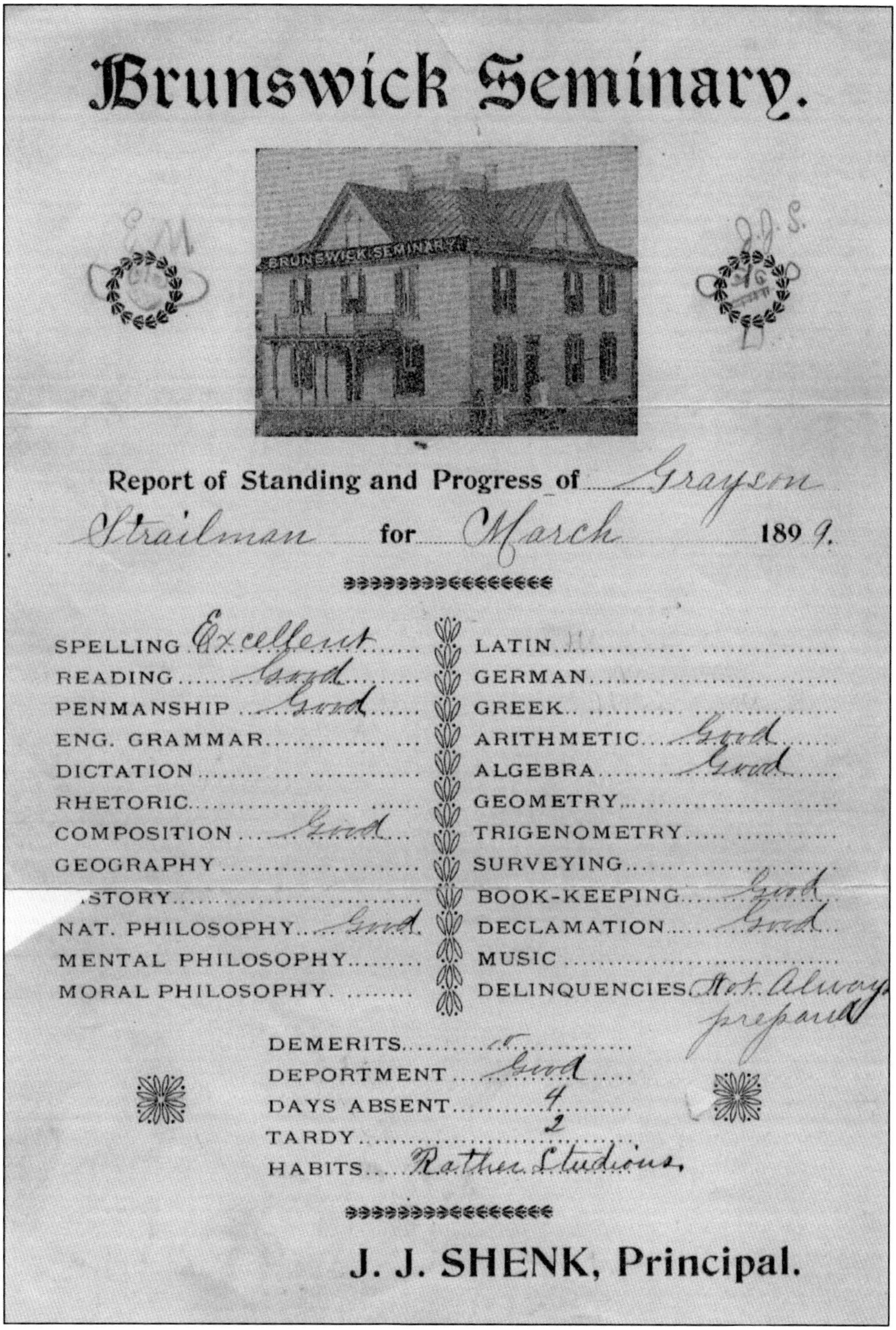

Brunswick Seminary.

Report of Standing and Progress of Grayson Strailman for March 1899.

SPELLING	Excellent	LATIN	
READING	Good	GERMAN	
PENMANSHIP	Good	GREEK	
ENG. GRAMMAR		ARITHMETIC	Good
DICTATION		ALGEBRA	Good
RHETORIC		GEOMETRY	
COMPOSITION	Good	TRIGENOMETRY	
GEOGRAPHY		SURVEYING	
[illegible]STORY		BOOK-KEEPING	Good
NAT. PHILOSOPHY	Good	DECLAMATION	Good
MENTAL PHILOSOPHY		MUSIC	
MORAL PHILOSOPHY		DELINQUENCIES	Not Always prepared

DEMERITS 0

DEPORTMENT Good

DAYS ABSENT 4

TARDY 2

HABITS Rather Studious.

J. J. SHENK, Principal.

This image shows a March 1899 report card from the Brunswick Seminary. Note the wide variety of items on which students might be graded. This report for Grayson Strailman indicates that the pupil was "rather studious." Also known as "Shenk's Seminary," the private school was founded by John J. Shenk and his wife in 1890. The school accepted both boys and girls and was described as a "progressive preparatory school for college and the active affairs of life" and offered "tuition and board at reasonable rates." (Courtesy Brunswick History Commission.)

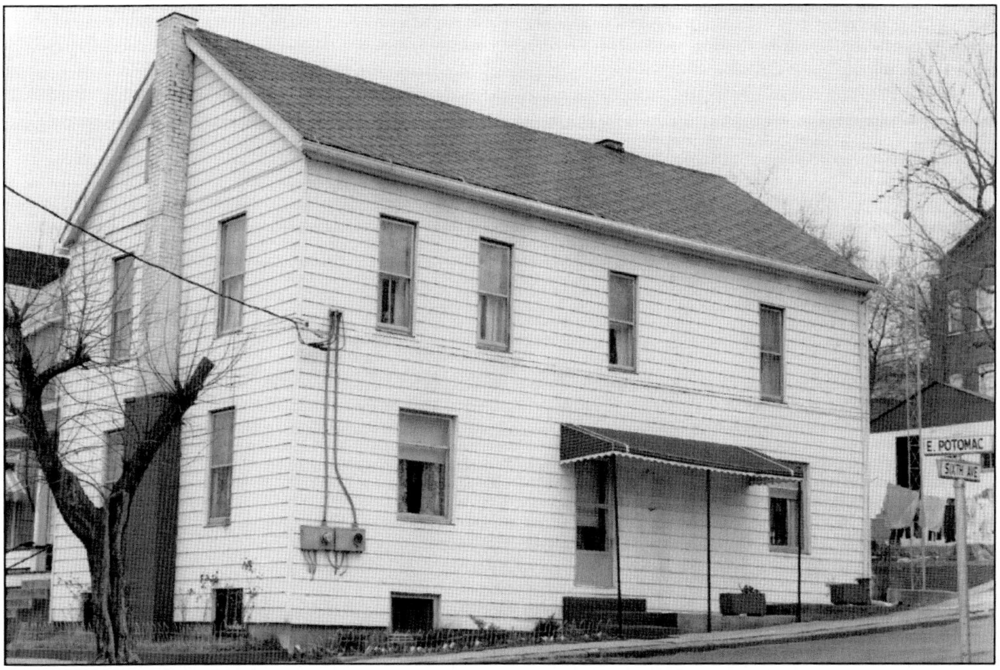

Brunswick's first high school was housed in one room of this building, the Westall House (which was also a residence at the time), on the corner of East Potomac Street and Sixth Avenue. The school opened in September 1900 with 31 pupils. The first principal, county native Thomas W. Troxell, made $150 per term. Prior to the opening of the high school in Brunswick, many students attended school in Frederick, traveling by train at 7:25 a.m. and returning home at 7:00 p.m. with homework still to be completed before bedtime. (Courtesy Brunswick History Commission.)

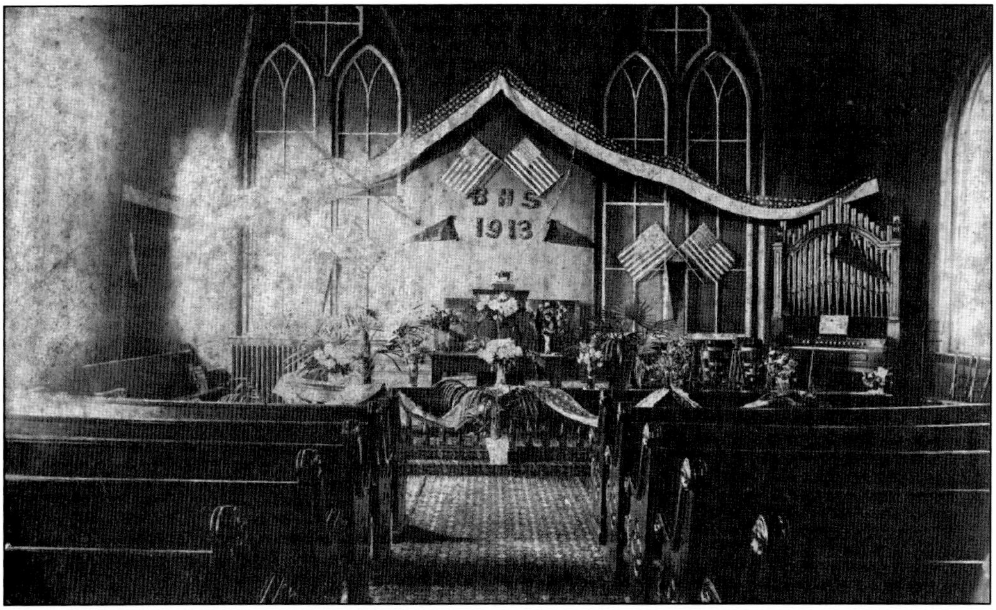

This 1913 photograph shows the United Methodist Church on Maryland Avenue all decked out with flags and bunting in honor of that year's Brunswick High School graduation ceremonies. (Courtesy Brunswick History Commission.)

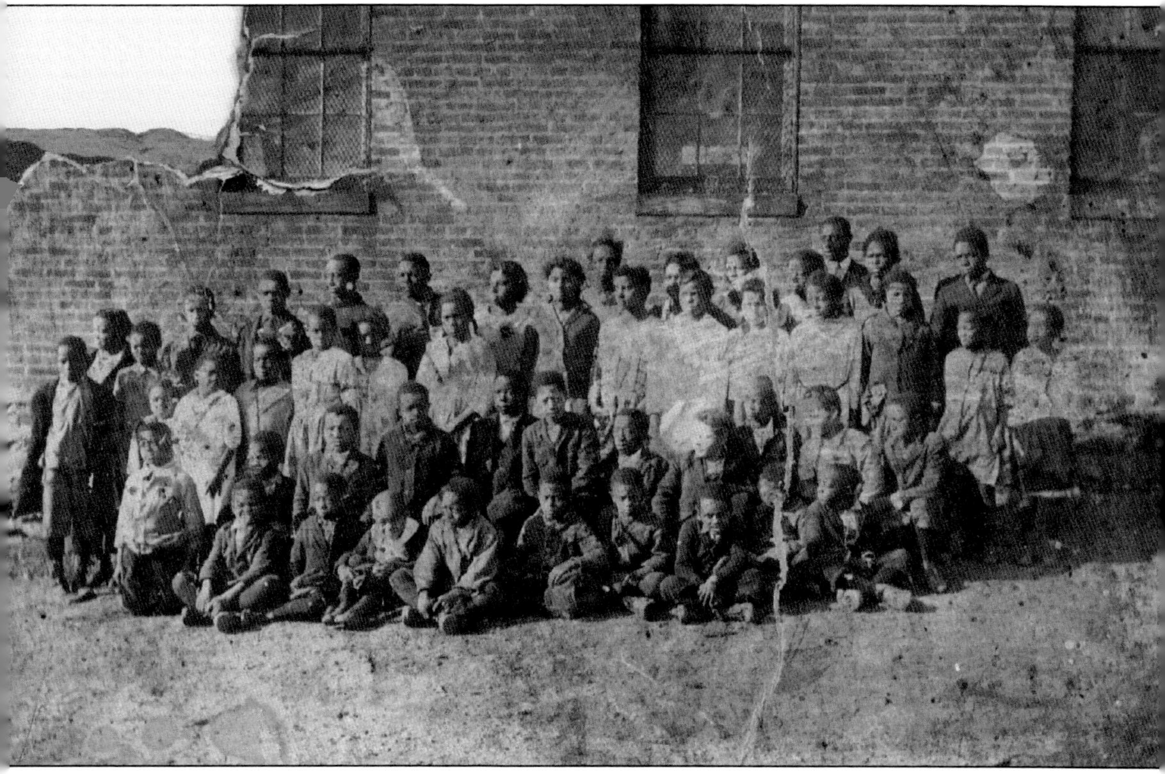

Prior to school integration in 1954, Brunswick's African American students attended their own segregated classes. At first, a corncrib on the Wenner farm was used as a schoolroom. In 1901, a house was rented at 37 West I Street where 41 students were enrolled. This photograph shows a later, one-room brick schoolhouse at 40 West J Street. An early teacher, Robert McDaniel, came by train from Harpers Ferry, West Virginia, each day to teach grades one through seven. If students wished to continue their studies after grade school, they needed to travel to Frederick to attend Lincoln High School. Some of these students used the B&O trains for their daily travel back and forth to school. (Courtesy Brunswick History Commission.)

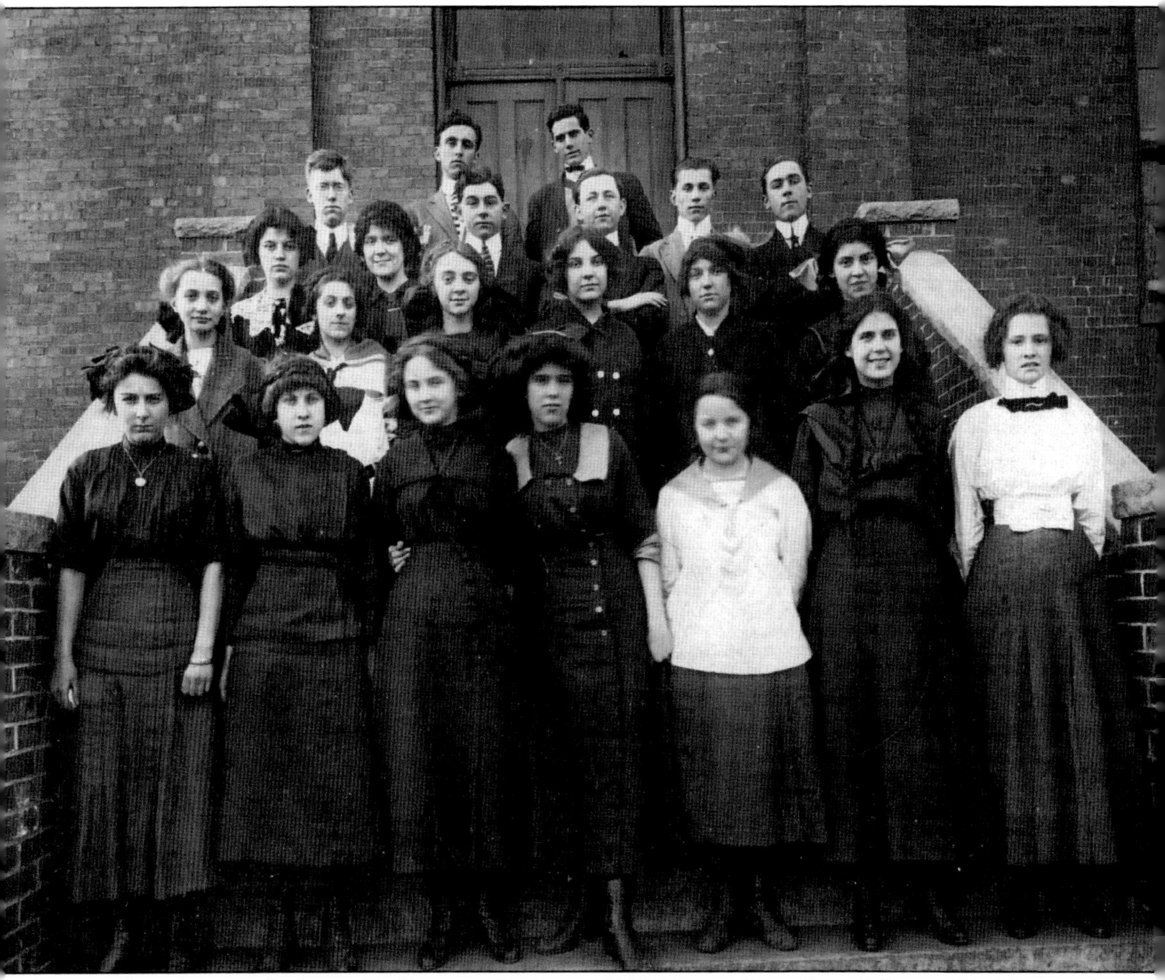

This photograph shows the Brunswick class of 1915. Pictured are, from left to right, (first row) unidentified, O. McDonald Miller, E. Sigafoose Stewart, Helen Hammond, Beatrice Smith Hartman, Nellie Mehrling, and Hazel W. Good; (second row) Mary Kaetzel Brocken, Edith Wenner Vanpelt, three unidentified, and Georgia Hood; (third row) unidentified, Lavinia Hood, and four unidentified; (fourth row) unidentified, Hillary Mills, and unidentified. (Courtesy Brunswick History Commission.)

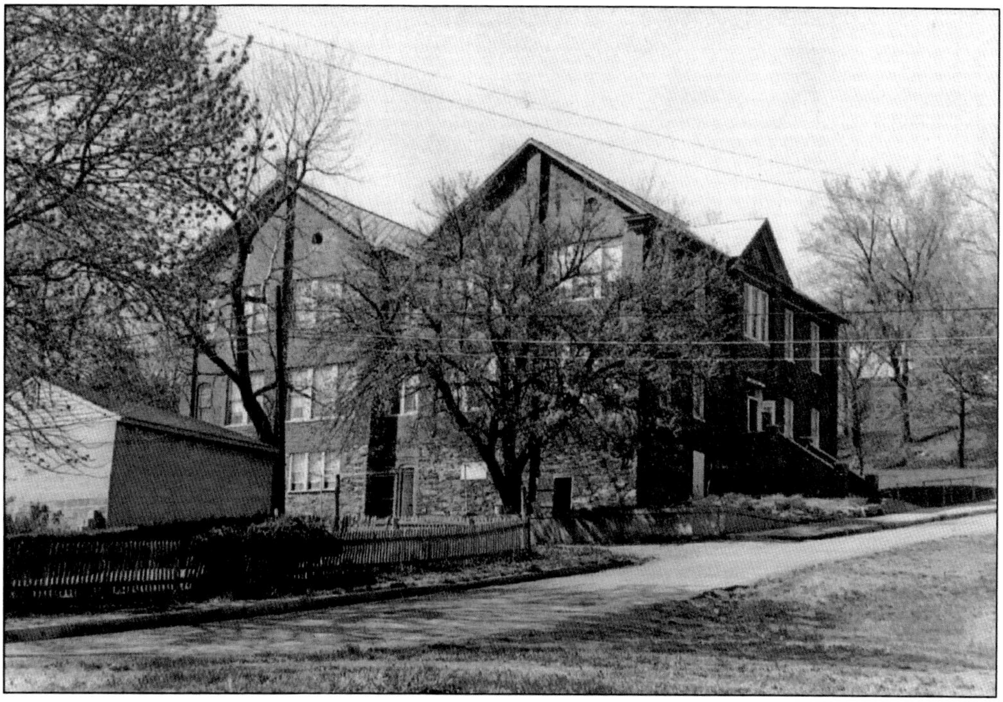

This image shows the East Brunswick School at Sixth Avenue and A Street around 1905. The B&O Railroad donated the land for the school in 1892. Another school, West Brunswick School, on Brunswick Street was also in existence. Children living east of Maple Avenue went to East Brunswick while those living west of Maple went to West Brunswick. A modern elementary school was built in 1952 on Central Avenue. (Courtesy Brunswick History Commission.)

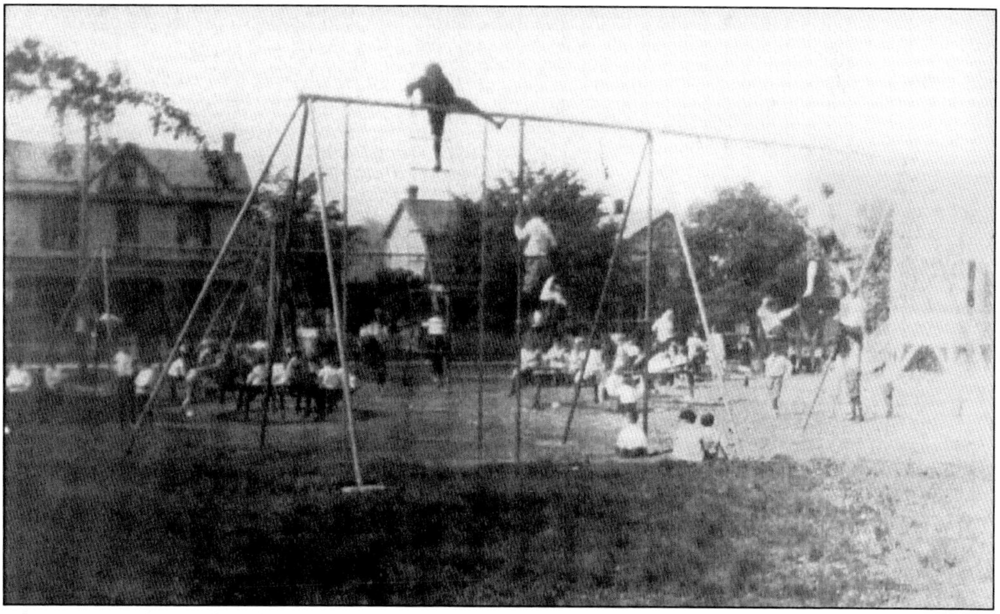

This picture shows the playground at West Brunswick School. The playground is located where the post office now stands. Note the ladder that allowed the boy in the photograph to climb to the top of the swings. (Courtesy Brunswick History Commission.)

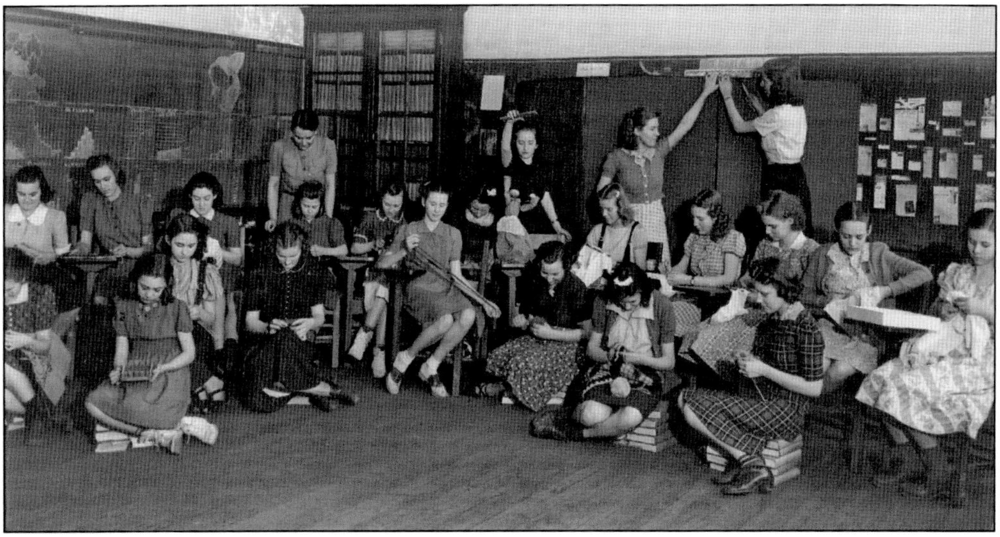

This 1940 photograph from the *Garnet and Gold* yearbook shows the Handwork Club at Brunswick High School. Sitting on those stacks of books to pose for the picture had to be pretty uncomfortable for those unfortunate enough not to be seated at one of the desks. (Courtesy Brunswick History Commission.)

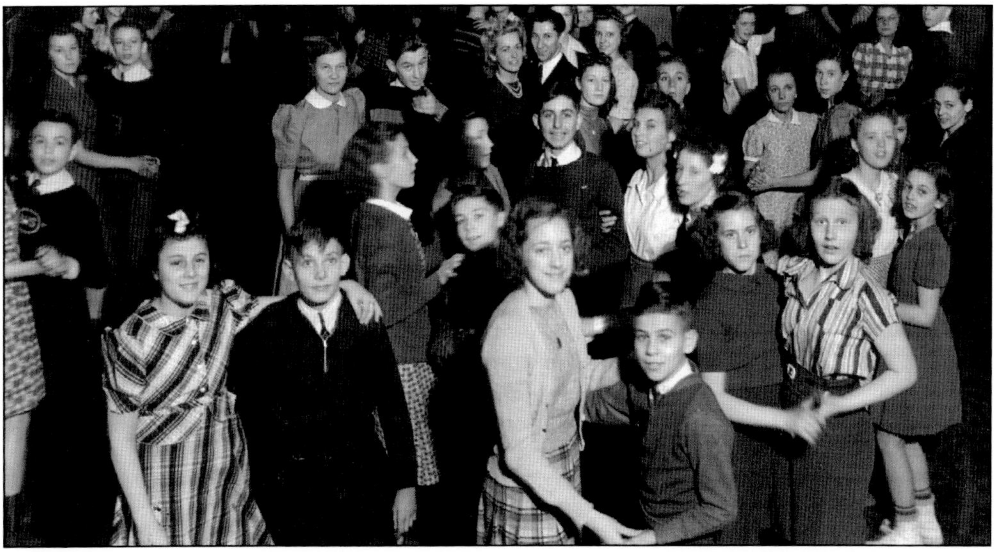

This image of the Dance Club was taken for the high school's 1940 *Garnet and Gold* yearbook. This was clearly a popular activity based on the size of the crowd in the picture. (Courtesy Brunswick History Commission.)

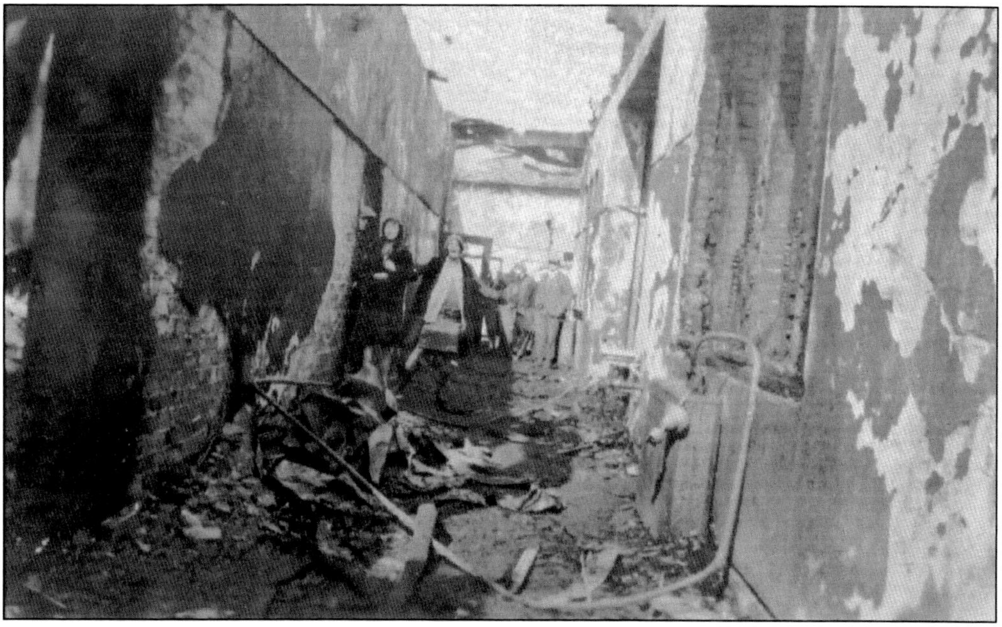

Brunswick High School was devastated by a fire in February 1928. This photograph shows the structure in the aftermath of the blaze. After the fire, students attended classes in various places around town until renovation and expansion of a new school was completed in September 1928. (Courtesy Brunswick History Commission.)

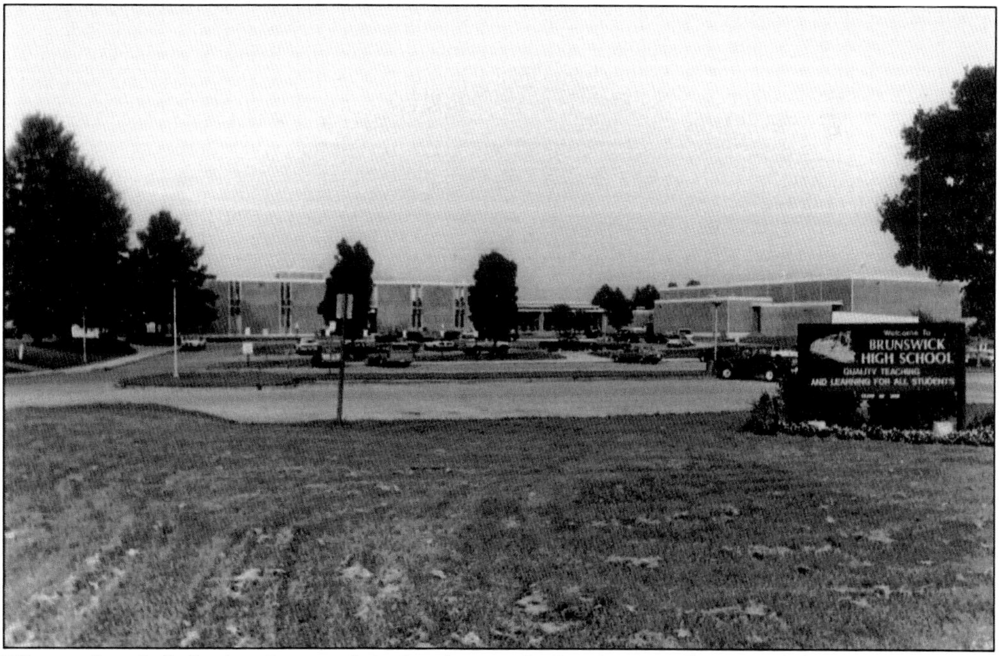

The newly refurbished and expanded school created after the 1928 fire served the community well until it met the wrecking ball in June 1965. A new high school welcomed students in the fall of 1965 at a new location on Cummings Drive. (Courtesy Brunswick History Commission.)

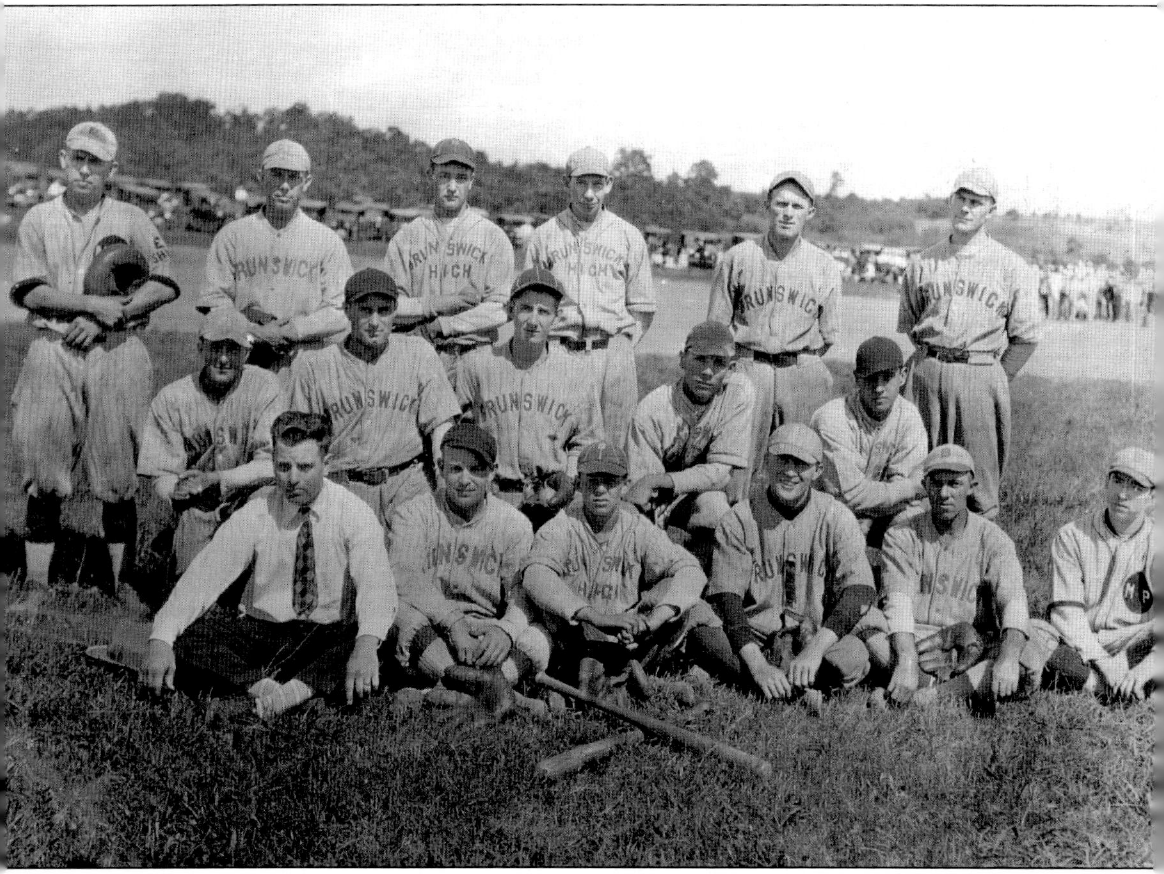

This undated photograph shows the Brunswick baseball team. Pictured from left to right are (first row) Paul Koogle, unidentified, Edgar Burch, unidentified, Lawrence Nelson, and John "Jack" Brady; (second row) unidentified, Paul Orrison, unidentified, Willis Connor, and Charles Magolis; (third row) Charles "Chum" Mills and five unidentified. (Courtesy Brunswick History Commission.)

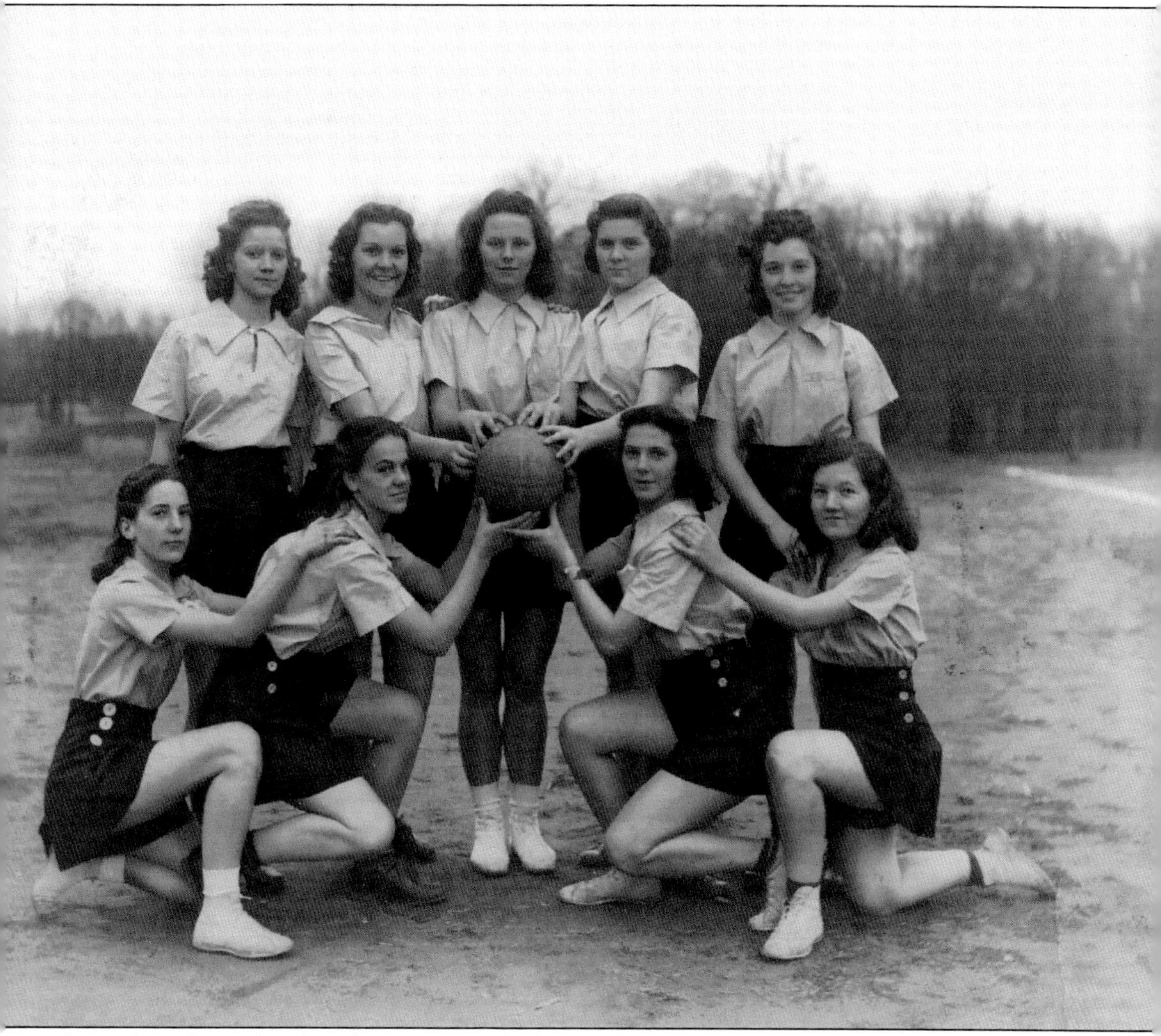

Sports have long played a role in Brunswick's history for both girls and boys. This picture shows the Brunswick High School girl's basketball team from 1940. Pictured are, from left to right, (first row) Mary Pearl Koogle, Jessie Brown, Agnes Burch, and Ruth Ellen Sherrad; (second row) Mary Ellen Roby, Ella Mae Virts, Jane Grams, Aileen Michael, and Adelaide Webber. (Courtesy Brunswick History Commission.)

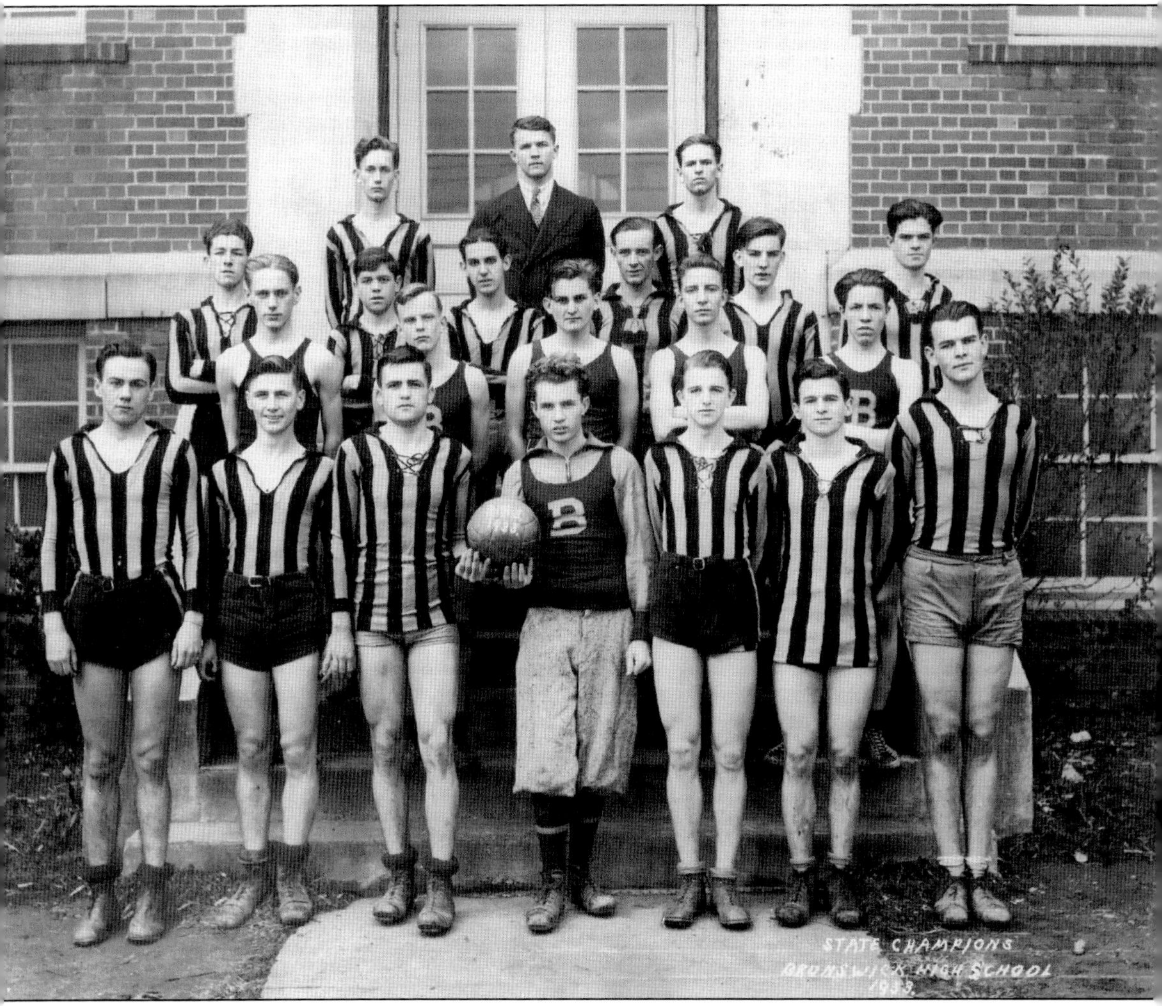

This photograph shows the Brunswick High School state soccer champions in 1933. Pictured are, from left to right, (first row) Hammer Orndorff, Harry Woods, Bud Walker, Nelson Strathern, Gordon Bingham, Bill McLaughlin, and Bill Jenkins; (second row) Ray Crabil, John Hammond, Edward Looker, James Bingham, and Matthew Donaldson; (third row) Gerald Barnard, Carl McQuillen, Earl Nokes, Marty Garrot, Deray Lowry, and Anthony Cramer; (fourth row) Ray Reynolds, Ho Smith, and Donald Williams. (Courtesy Brunswick History Commission.)

Staging various productions was common in communities large and small across the country in the early 1900s. This image is a program cover from an operetta of *Snow White* staged by the students of the Brunswick schools for the school-year closing exercises in 1910. (Courtesy Brunswick History Commission.)

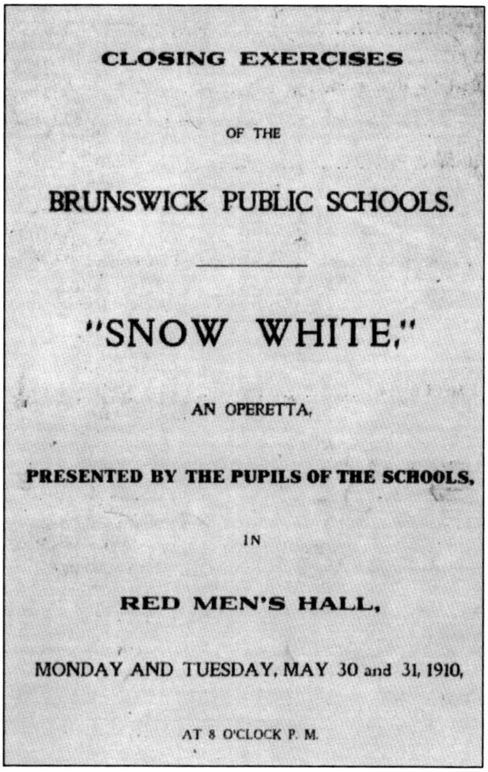

CLOSING EXERCISES

OF THE

BRUNSWICK PUBLIC SCHOOLS.

"SNOW WHITE,"

AN OPERETTA,

PRESENTED BY THE PUPILS OF THE SCHOOLS,

IN

RED MEN'S HALL,

MONDAY AND TUESDAY, MAY 30 and 31, 1910,

AT 8 O'CLOCK P. M.

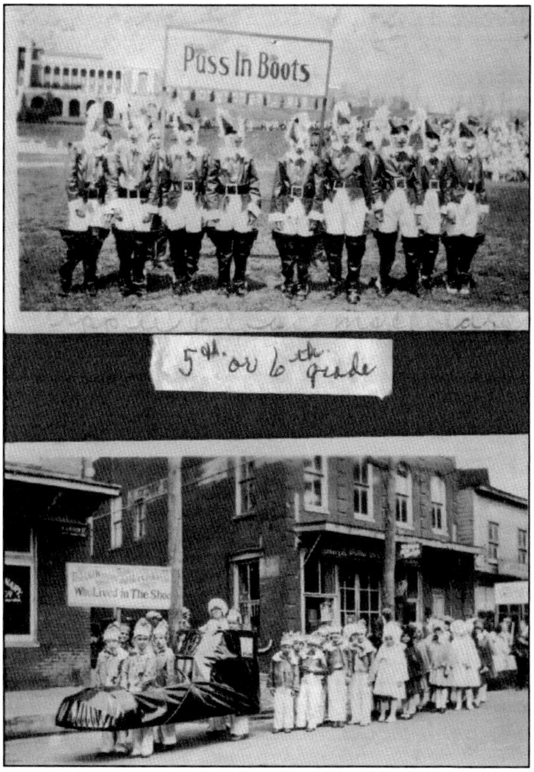

Even the younger students were involved in community productions. Here are some images of Brunswick students participating in the Apple Blossom Parade in Winchester, Virginia, in 1927. Students dressed to represent characters from the children's stories *Puss in Boots* and *The Old Lady Who Lived in a Shoe*. The Shenandoah Apple Blossom Festival was a staple activity for Brunswick schoolchildren, particularly during the years 1924–1930. (Courtesy Brunswick History Commission.)

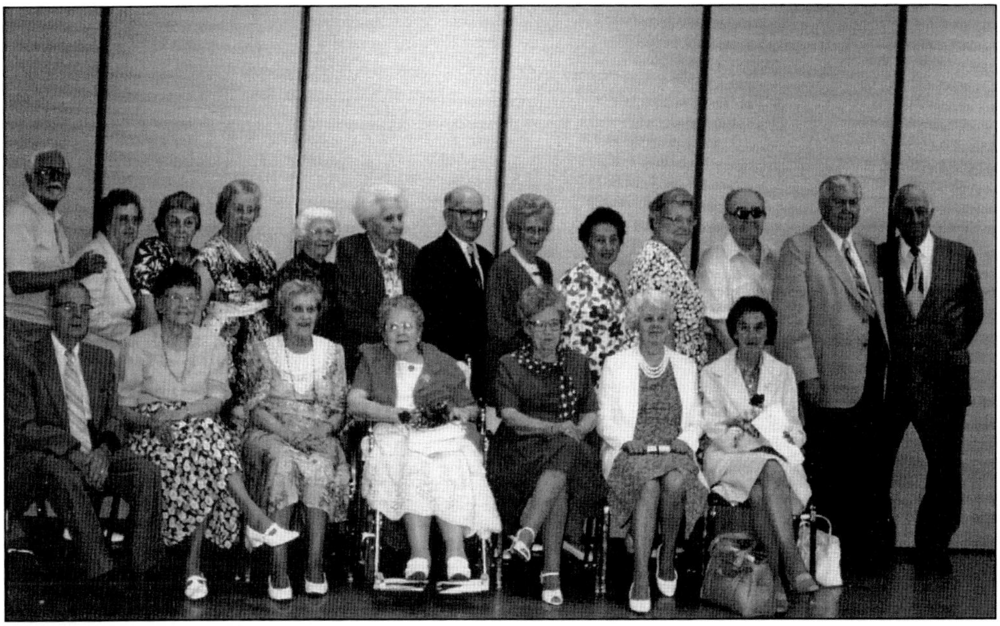

Do you recognize any of these people? This is the Brunswick High School class of 1931 at their 61st reunion, held at the YMCA on Souder Road in 1992. (Courtesy Brunswick History Commission.)

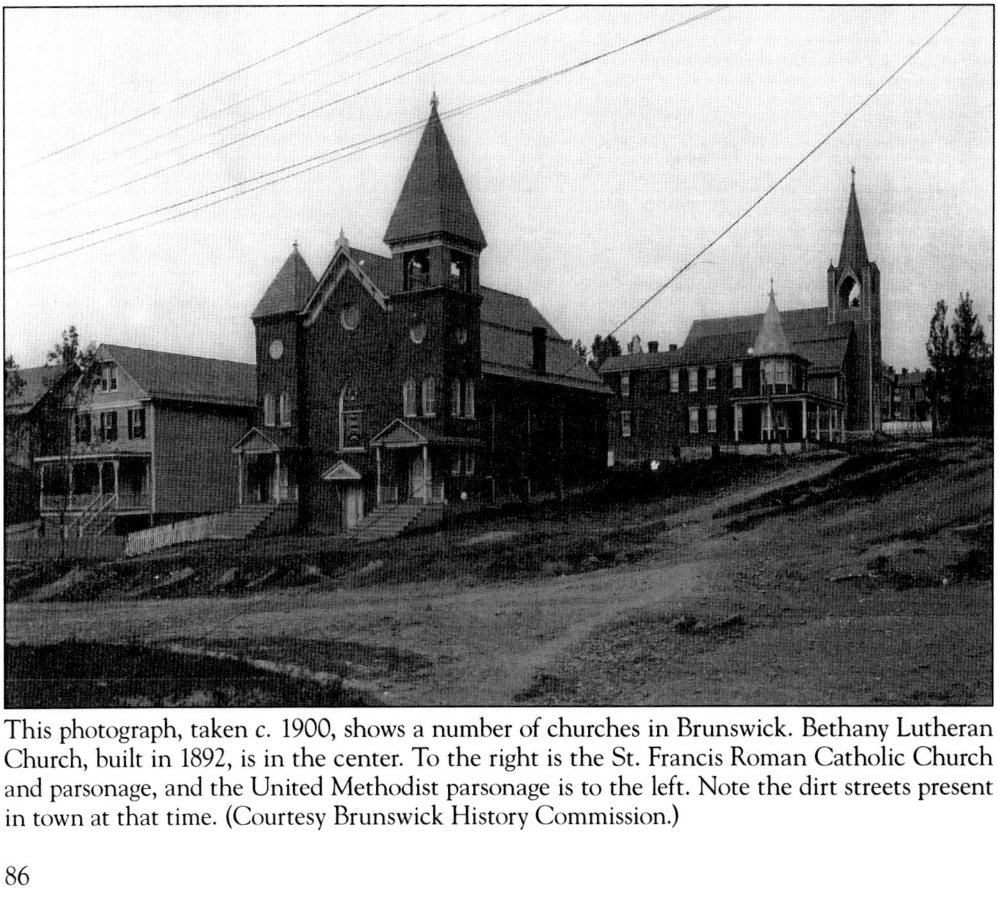

This photograph, taken *c.* 1900, shows a number of churches in Brunswick. Bethany Lutheran Church, built in 1892, is in the center. To the right is the St. Francis Roman Catholic Church and parsonage, and the United Methodist parsonage is to the left. Note the dirt streets present in town at that time. (Courtesy Brunswick History Commission.)

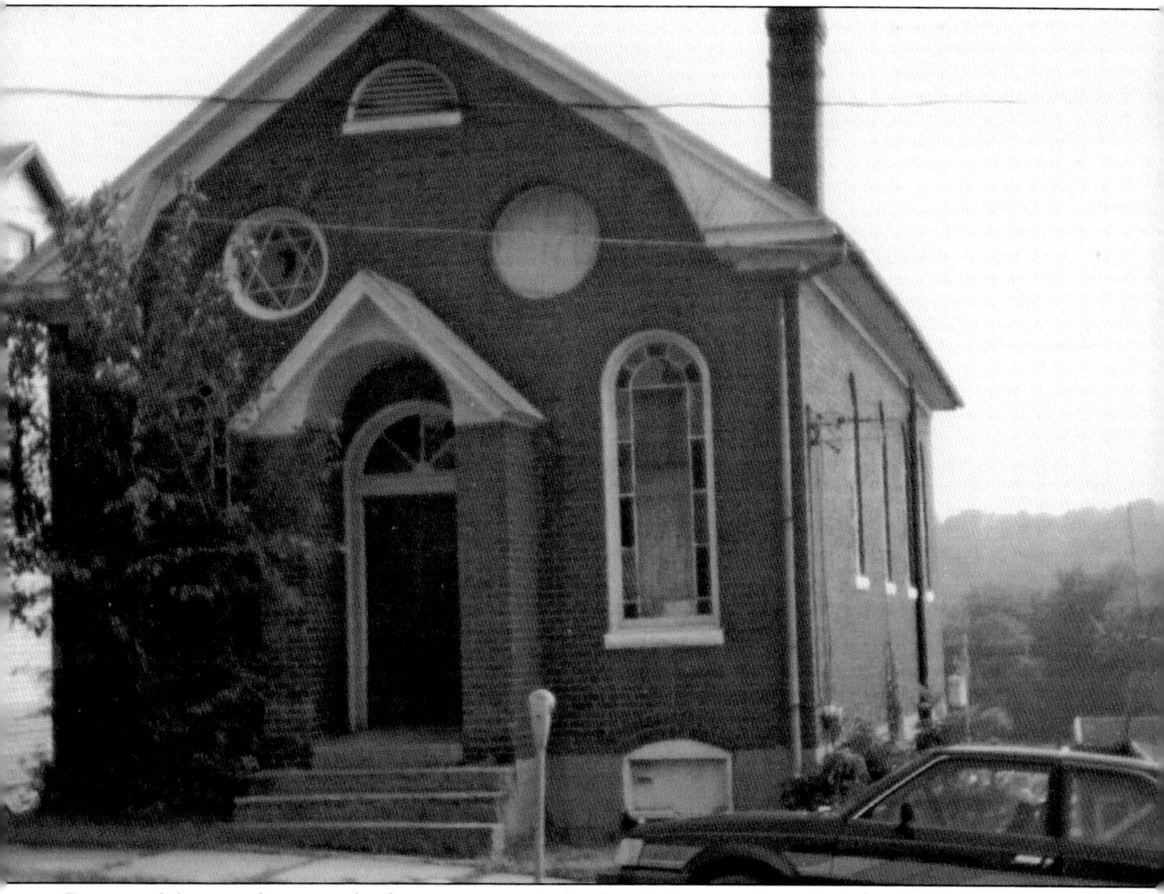

Brunswick became home to the first synagogue in Frederick County when Beth Israel Congregation built its synagogue on A Street in 1917. The Jewish community in Brunswick was never large and often joined with Jewish communities from Hagerstown, Frederick, Baltimore, and Charles Town, West Virginia, for regular services or special celebrations. The building remained synagogue property until 1959, when it was sold by H. N. Werntz, the last surviving trustee of the congregation. The building served various purposes over the years, including being the International Red Cross headquarters and a doctor's office. Werntz also conducted all the kosher slaughtering of meat and fowl for the Jewish families of Brunswick. (Courtesy Brunswick History Commission.)

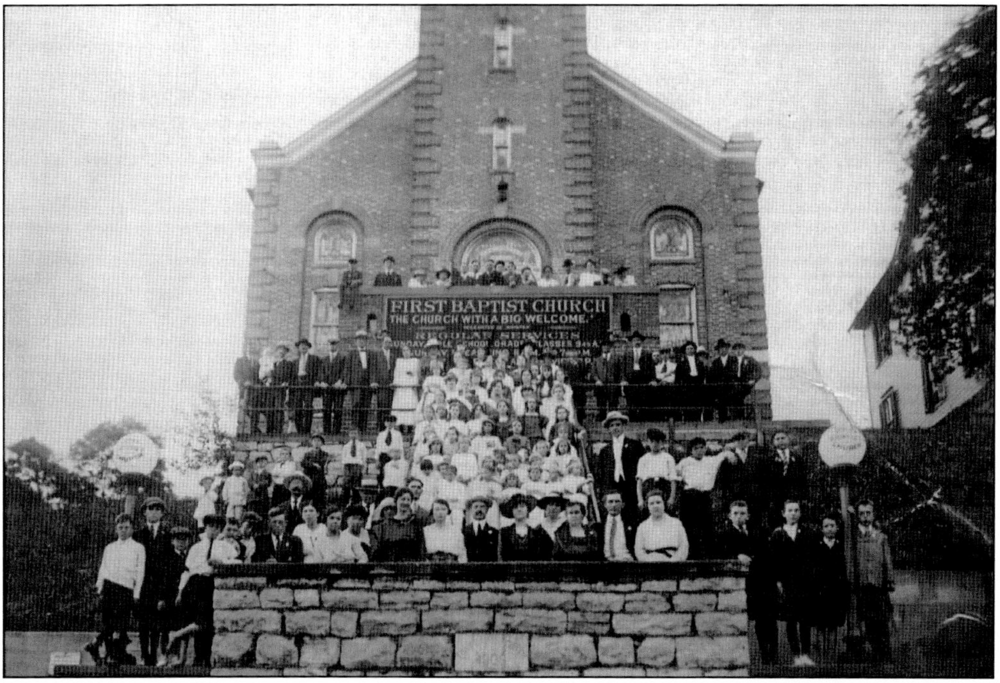

The First Baptist Church was organized on January 21, 1906. The cornerstone for the church was laid on July 28, 1908, and services were first held on January 1, 1909. This photograph shows the congregation gathered in front of the church on the first Sunday it was open. (Courtesy Brunswick History Commission.)

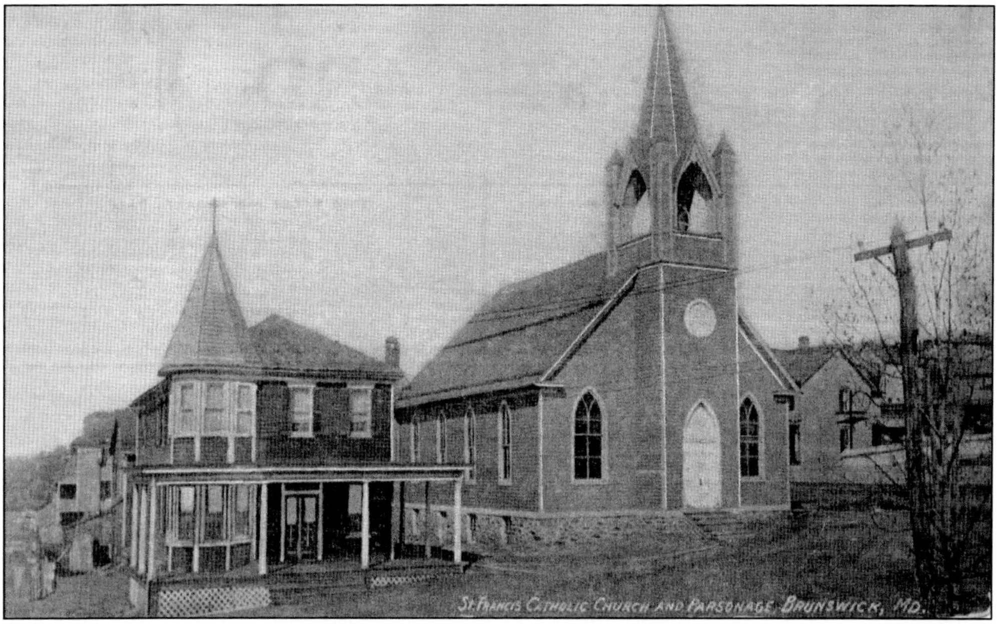

Here is the St. Francis Catholic Church and parsonage built in 1901 on First Avenue. Construction also included a school and convent. Four sisters from the Baltimore archdiocese came to teach at the school. The sisters continued to teach there until the late 1920s. The school continued to operate under lay teachers until it closed in 1938. (Courtesy Brunswick History Commission.)

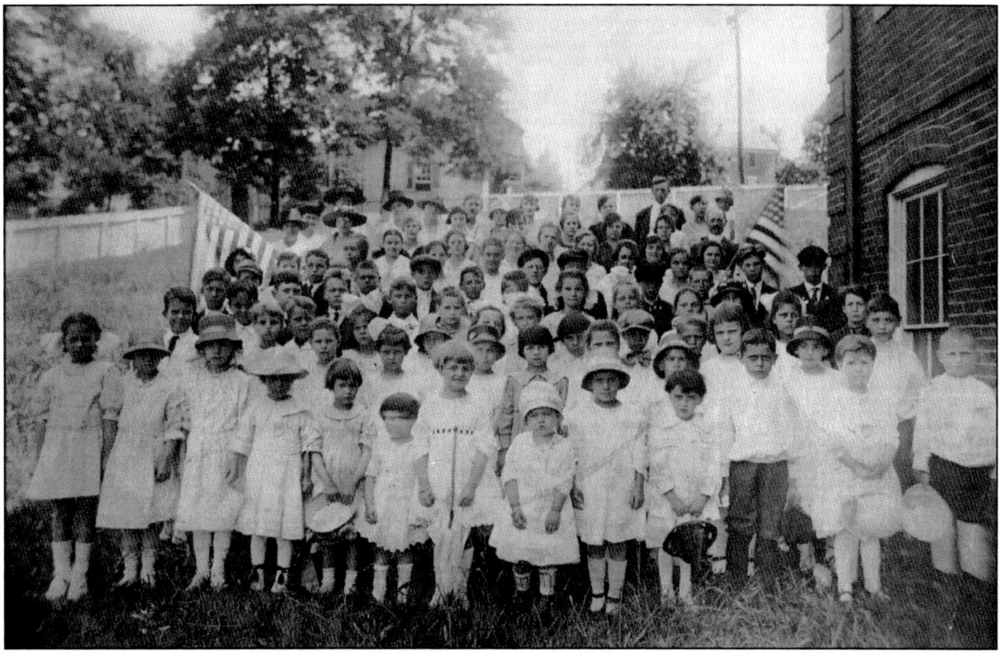

This photograph shows Lavetta Kelly's 1919 Sunday school class at the Baptist church. The First Baptist Church was organized on January 21, 1906, with Rev. Benjamin D. Porter as the first pastor. (Courtesy Brunswick History Commission.)

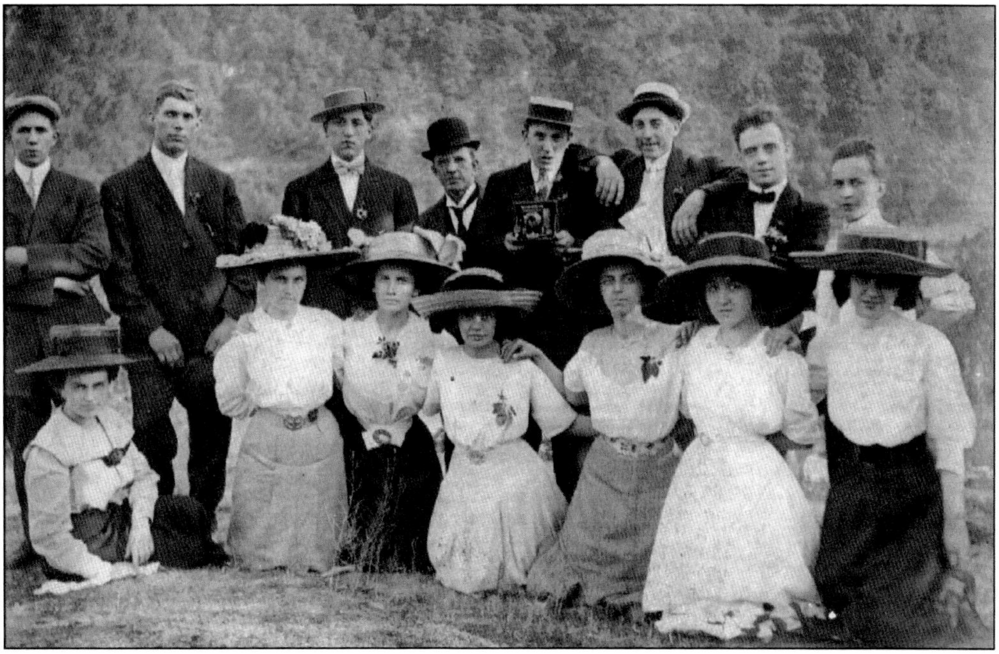

This image is from the Brunswick Methodist Church Sunday school picnic at Harpers Ferry, West Virginia, in 1912. The B&O Railroad ran trains sponsoring these picnics. The men in the photograph, standing from left to right, are Charlie Smith, Harry Mace, L. B. Darr, Reverend Sanner, C. Brother Barger, Frank Cover, Joseph Roberts, and Reverend Sanner's son. The women in the photograph are unidentified. (Courtesy Brunswick History Commission.)

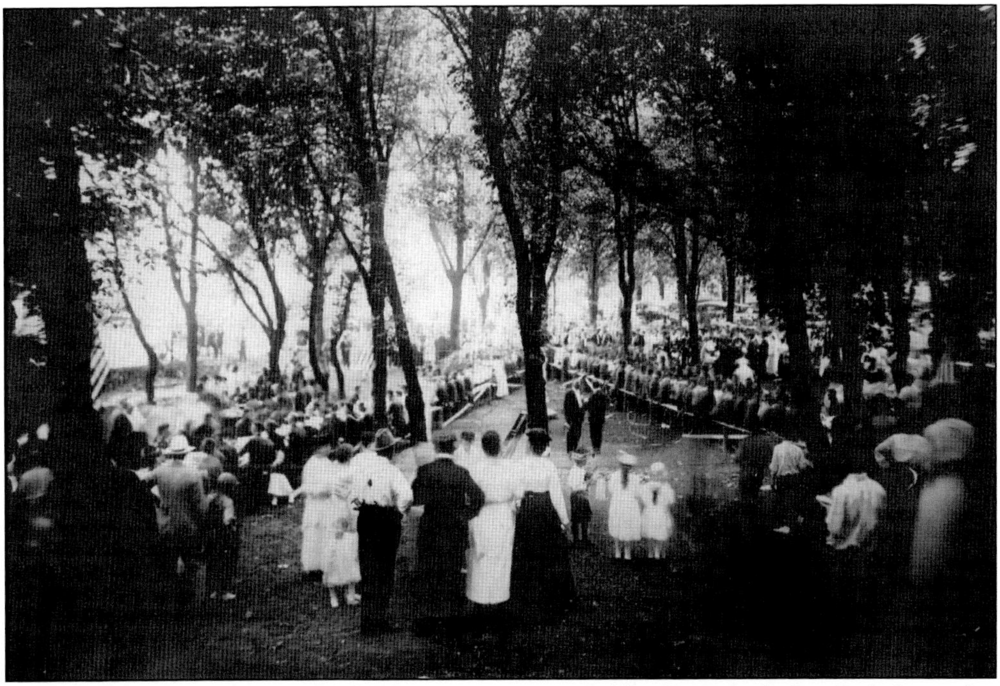

This event to welcome home World War I veterans was held in Brunswick City Park, located at East Potomac Street and Gum Spring Road. Note the huge turnout for the event. The park, one of several in town, has been used for many events through the years, including dances, family reunions, and public meetings. (Courtesy Brunswick History Commission.)

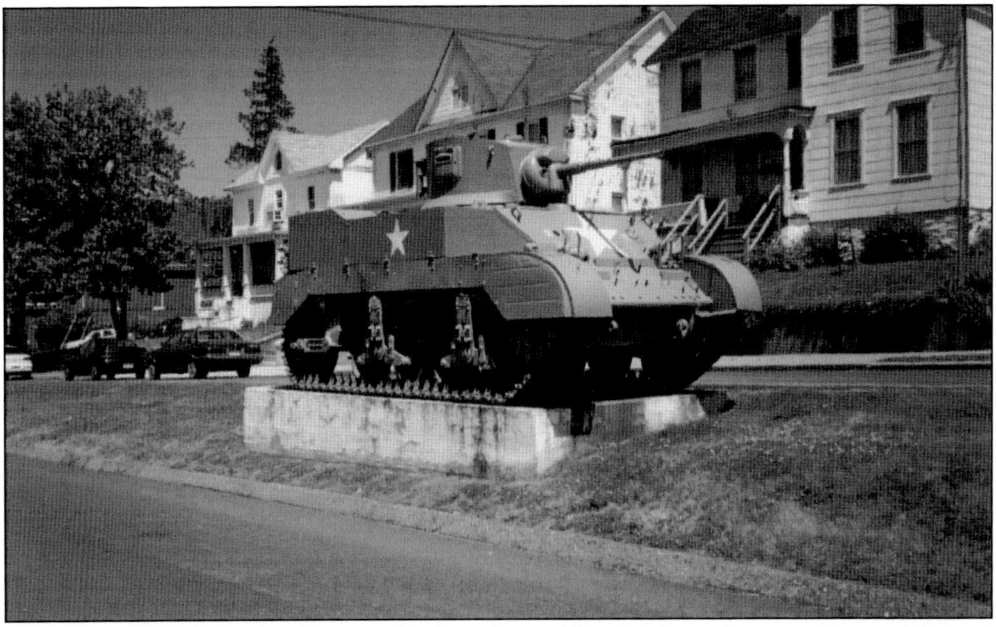

This army tank is located in Memorial Park in the middle of A Street between First and Second Avenues. A World War I cannon was originally located here, but it was scrapped during World War II. This World War II tank was dedicated on August 31, 1946. (Courtesy Brunswick History Commission.)

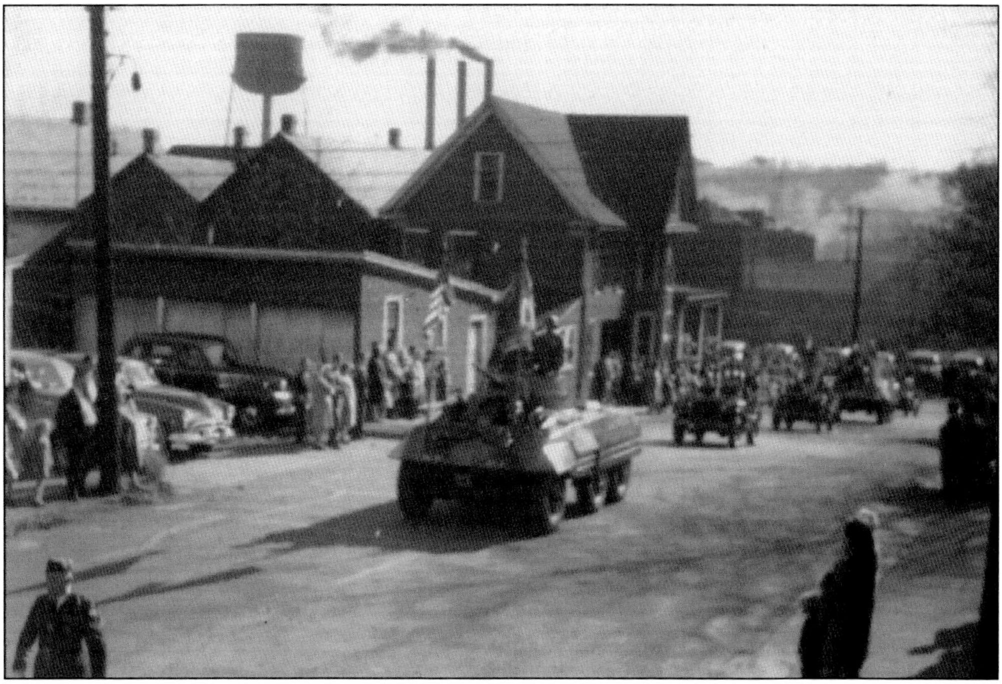

Taken in the 1930s, this photograph shows one of many Armistice Day (now Veteran's Day) parades held in Brunswick over the years. Shown here turning up Third Avenue from East Potomac Street, the parade ended at Memorial Park on A Street for a formal ceremony honoring veterans. There was a grandstand, speeches, band music, and a firing squad. (Courtesy Brunswick History Commission.)

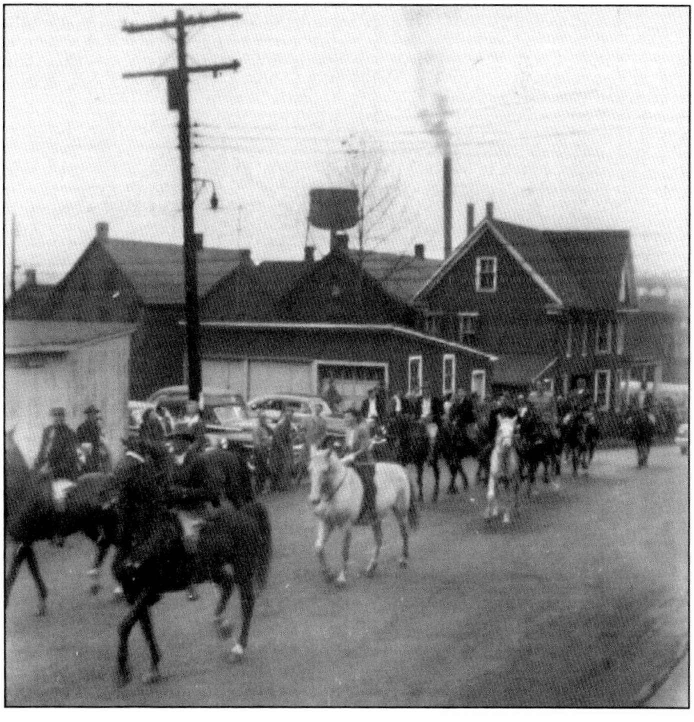

Here is another image from a 1930s Armistice Day Parade showing the Silver Bit Riding Club of Petersville Farmers Woods. At the time of this parade, Memorial Park on A Street still had a World War I–era 155-millimeter cannon. The cannon was later replaced with a World War II tank. (Courtesy Brunswick History Commission.)

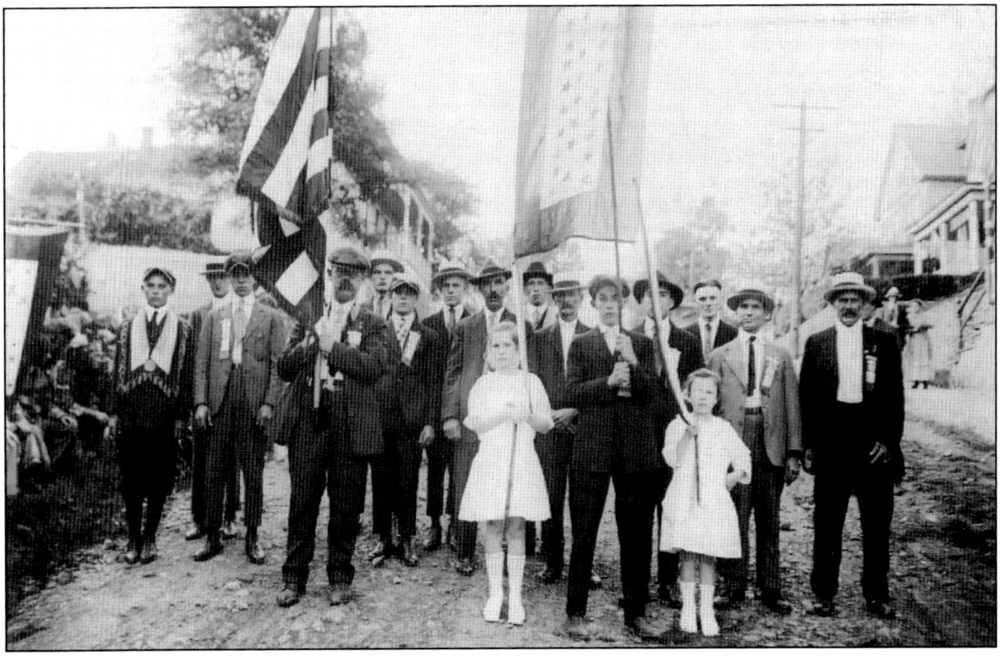

Taken on Virginia Avenue, this image shows the Junior Order of American Mechanics' armistice celebration. The man with the moustache standing behind the girl on the left is Ephraim Schrader. (Courtesy Brunswick History Commission.)

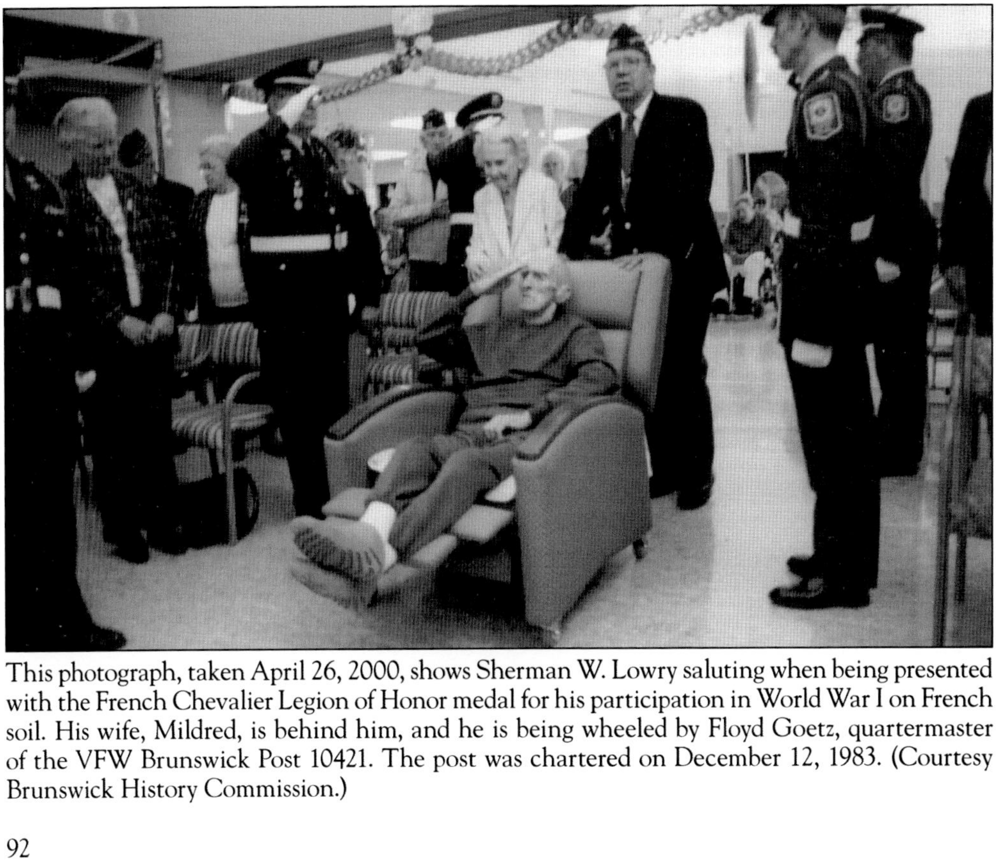

This photograph, taken April 26, 2000, shows Sherman W. Lowry saluting when being presented with the French Chevalier Legion of Honor medal for his participation in World War I on French soil. His wife, Mildred, is behind him, and he is being wheeled by Floyd Goetz, quartermaster of the VFW Brunswick Post 10421. The post was chartered on December 12, 1983. (Courtesy Brunswick History Commission.)

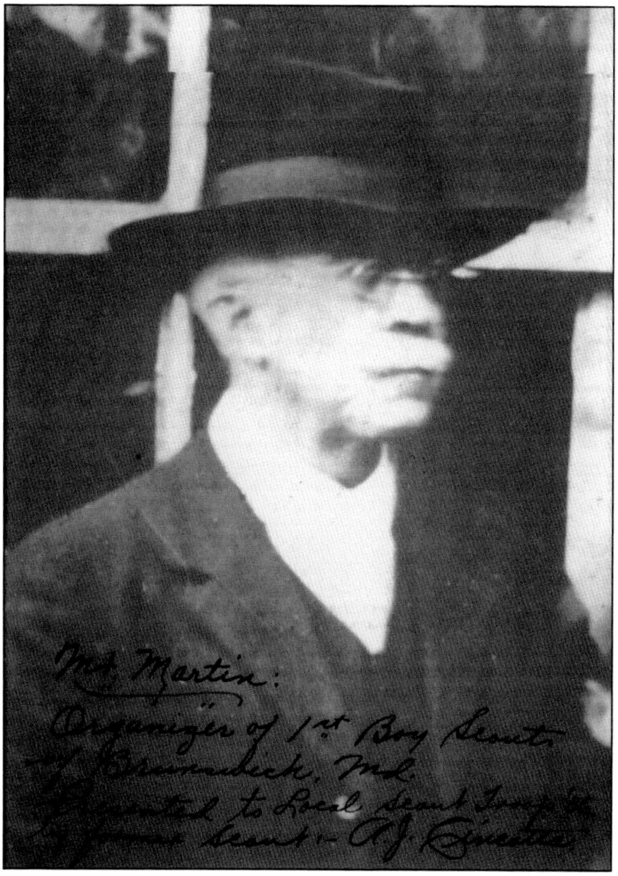

This image shows Rev. Luther Martin, organizer of the first Boy Scouts of America in Brunswick. Author of the poem "I Am Going Back to Brunswick," he served as pastor of the Brunswick Presbyterian Church on A Street from about 1907 until the church disbanded in 1918. (Courtesy Brunswick History Commission.)

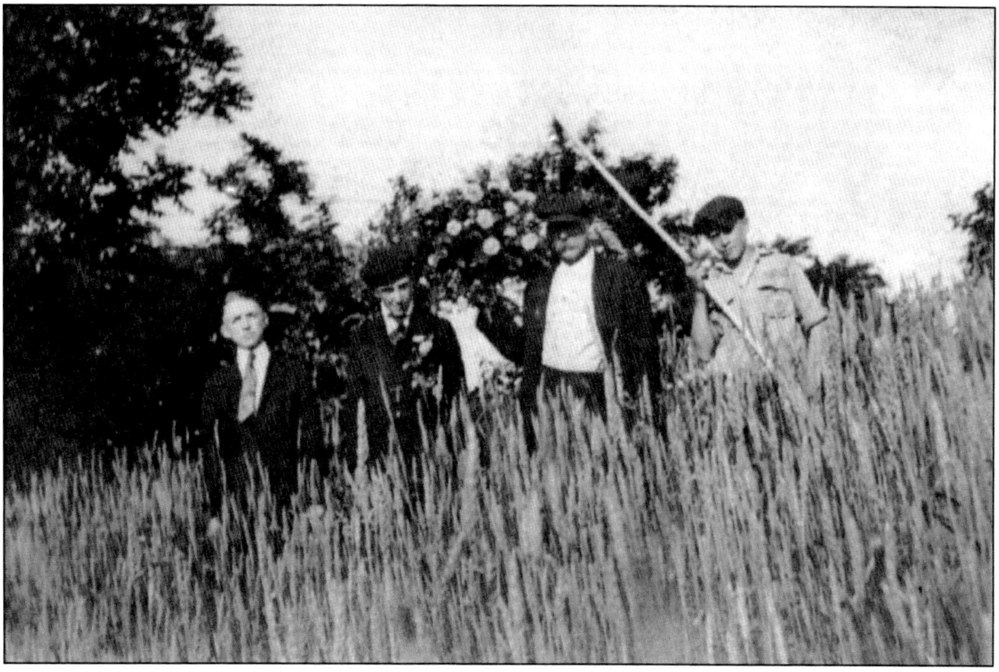

Scouting began in Brunswick around 1915, and the town was home to Boy Scout Troop No. 2. This photograph, taken in 1920, shows some of the Scouts on a hike to the Virginia Springs, a source of Brunswick's water supply. Pictured are, from left to right, William Deener, Raymond Funk, scoutmaster George A. Hood, and Lewis Rice. Brunswick also offered Girl Scouts for girls beginning in 1921. (Courtesy Brunswick History Commission.)

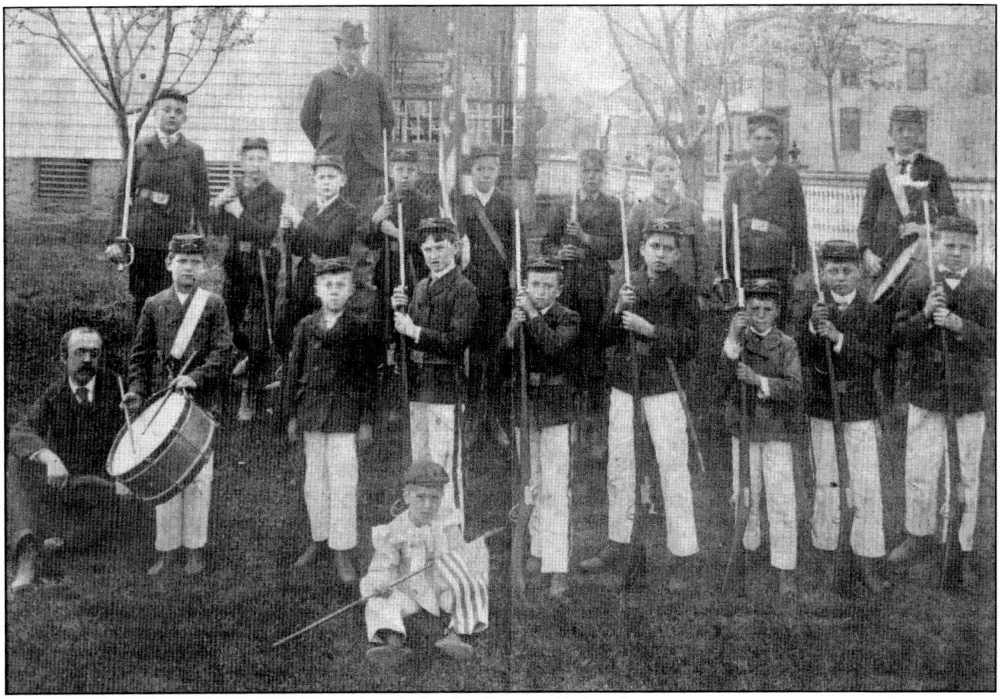

This 1909 image, taken at the home of Judge Jordan on West Potomac Street, shows the Brunswick Boy's Club. Founded by Rev. Luther Martin of the Brunswick Presbyterian Church, the group's cry was "O. G. F. Boom!" and each member had an insignia pin inscribed with the initials OGF (standing for Old Glory Forever) and the American flag. Today's Brunswick Boy Scout Troop No. 277 can trace its beginnings back to this boy's club. A Shell filling station was later constructed on this site. (Courtesy Brunswick History Commission.)

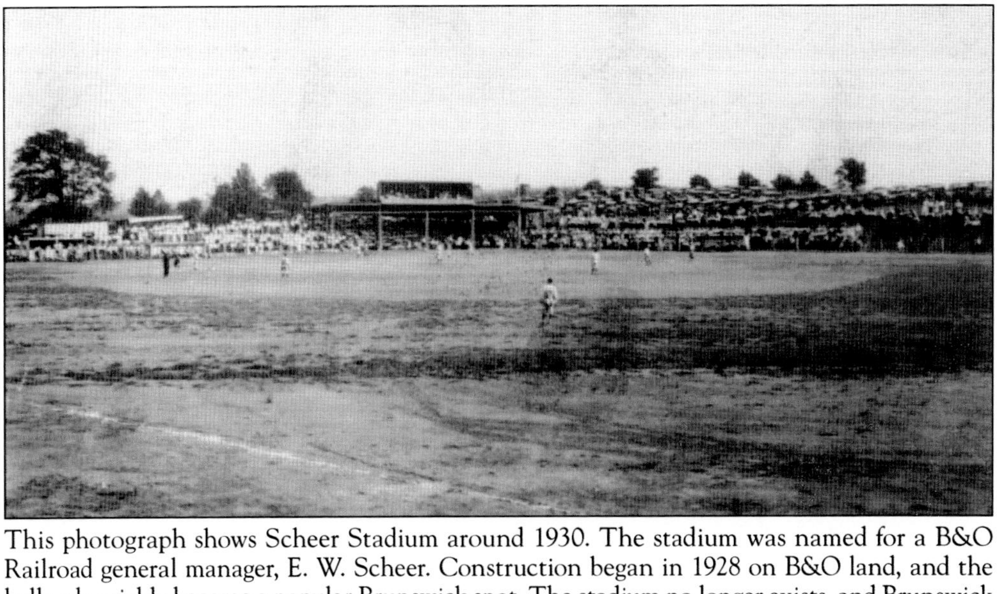

This photograph shows Scheer Stadium around 1930. The stadium was named for a B&O Railroad general manager, E. W. Scheer. Construction began in 1928 on B&O land, and the ballpark quickly became a popular Brunswick spot. The stadium no longer exists, and Brunswick High School and athletic fields now occupy the area that was once crowded with baseball fans. (Courtesy Brunswick History Commission.)

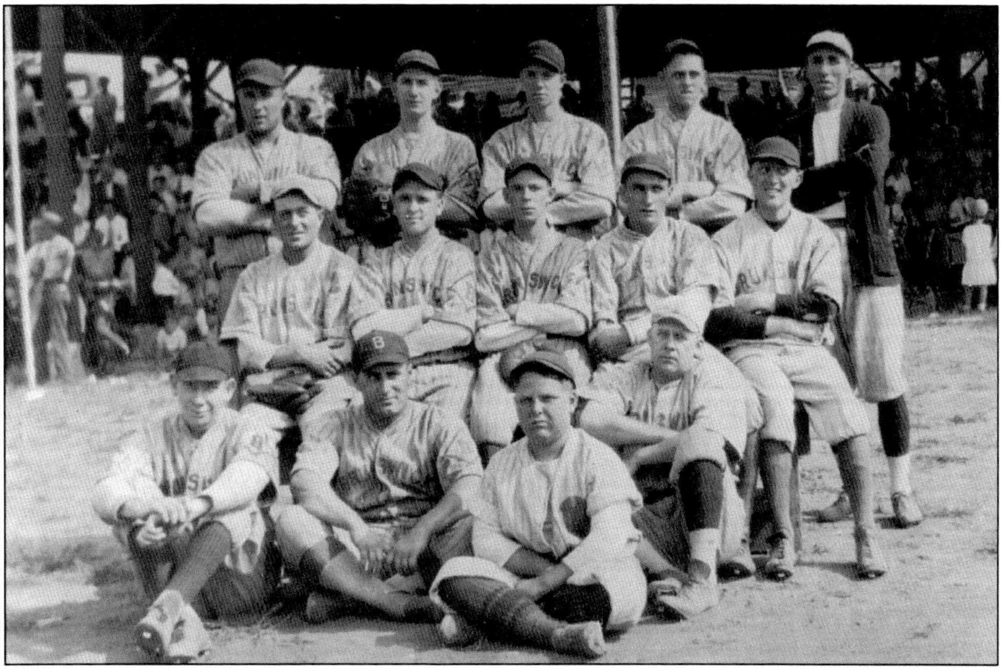

This photograph shows the Brunswick team of the Frederick County League from 1938 to 1940. Pictured are, from left to right, (first row) Ronald Mohler, Paul Orrison, Corky Virst (batboy), and John "Piper" Mills; (second row) Frank "Bony" Hartman, Preston "Press" Phillips, Edgar Burch, unidentified, and Lawrence Nelson; (third row) Lee Merriman, John Fleetwood, Ernest Burch, Marvin Youkins, and Harvey Butler. (Courtesy Brunswick History Commission.)

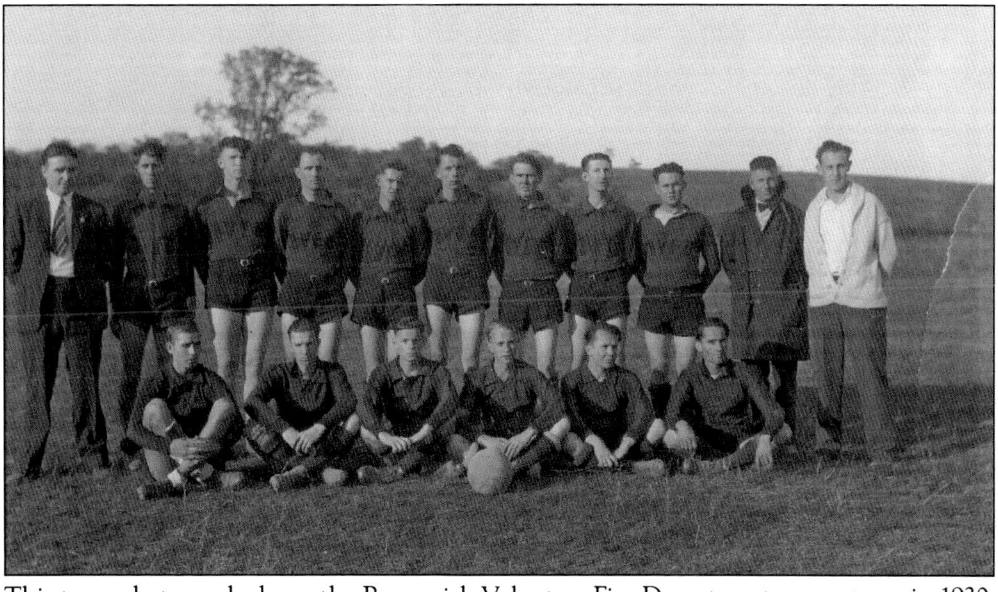

This team photograph shows the Brunswick Volunteer Fire Department soccer team in 1930. From left to right are (seated) B. Nokes, Earnest Burch, Ed Burch, H. W. Ellen, H. Mole, and V. Decker; (standing) R. Funk (manager), ? Day, O. Smith, T. Tucker, C. Grams, W. Conor, R. Grams, J. Fleetwood, G. Smith, F. Shafer (ticket collector), and C. Porter (referee). (Courtesy Brunswick History Commission.)

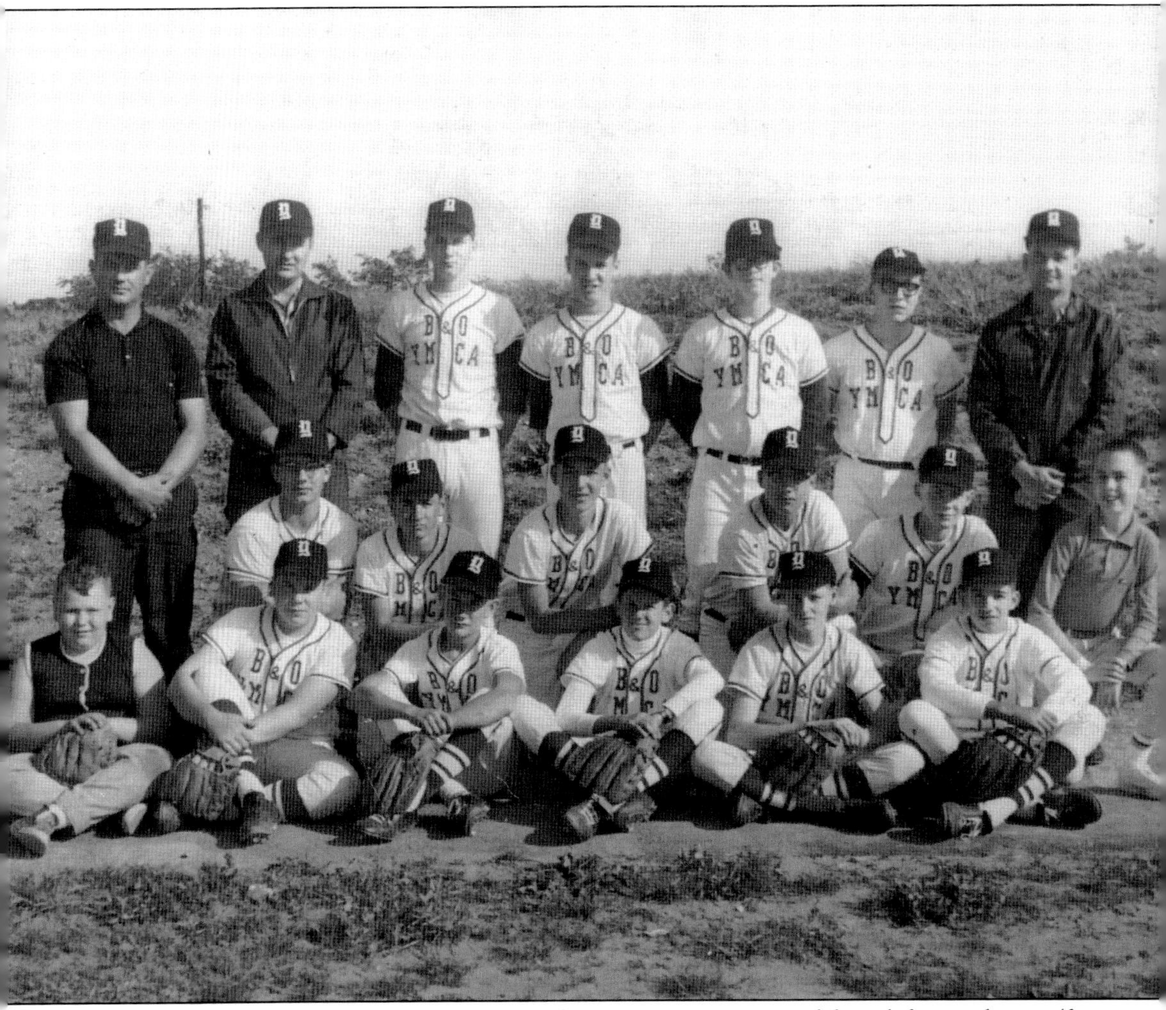

This 1968 image shows the Brunswick Little League team. Pictured from left to right are (first row) "Blooch" Daugherty, Rick Campbell, Wayne Daugherty, Eddie Haller, Larry Woods, and Dick Haller; (second row) Michael Deener, Terry Marshall, Craig Crowl, "Mitch" Deener, Larry "Buzzie" Proudfoot, and Bill Cauley (scorekeeper); (third row) Herman "Nookie" Deener (coach), James Haller, Paul Gaither, Paul Orrison, Bill Roundsley, Roland Eagle, and Larry Proudfoot (assistant coach). (Courtesy Brunswick History Commission.)

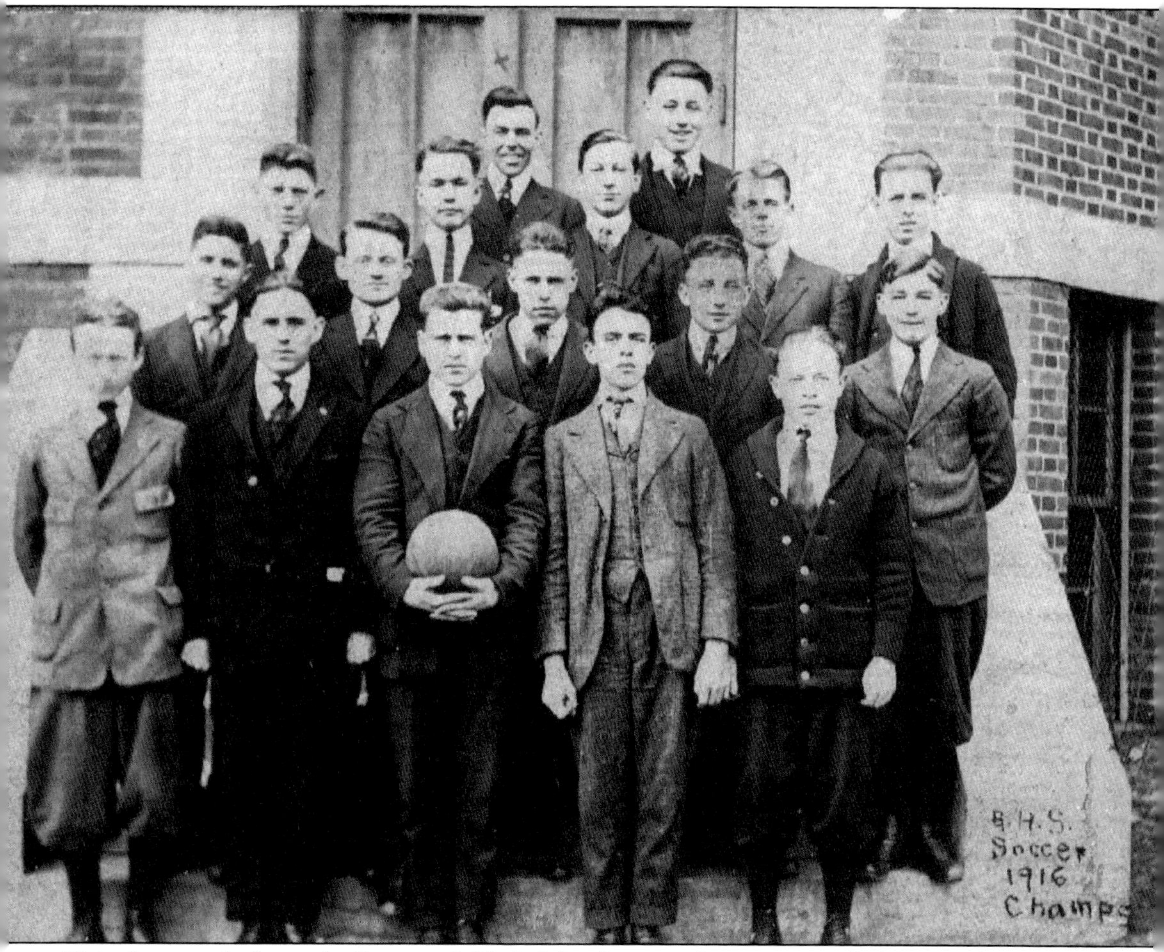

This photograph shows the Brunswick High School soccer champions in 1916. Pictured are, in no known order, Howard Chambers, William Harrington, Paul Koogle, Bricose Karn, Reginald Shewbridge, Richmond Wenner, Floyd Compton, Wes Schnauffer, George Karn, John Rittle, Russell Mills, Leonard Davis, Mark Adams, Elsworth McBride, Andrew Bissett, R. X. Day (coach), and Lee Feete. (Courtesy Brunswick History Commission.)

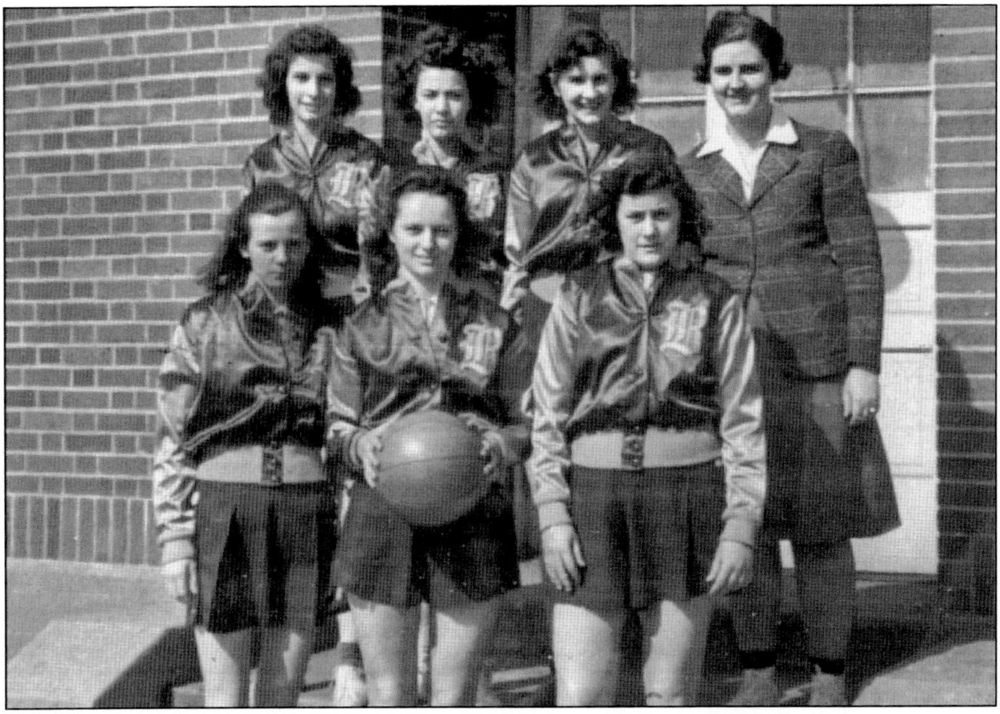

This March 31, 1942, image shows one of the girls' basketball teams. Pictured are, from left to right, (first row) Ruth Norris, ? Powers, and Doris Price; (second row) ? Merriman, Crenell Mulkey, June Foster Mohler, and Betty "Mac" McCaffrey. (Courtesy Brunswick History Commission.)

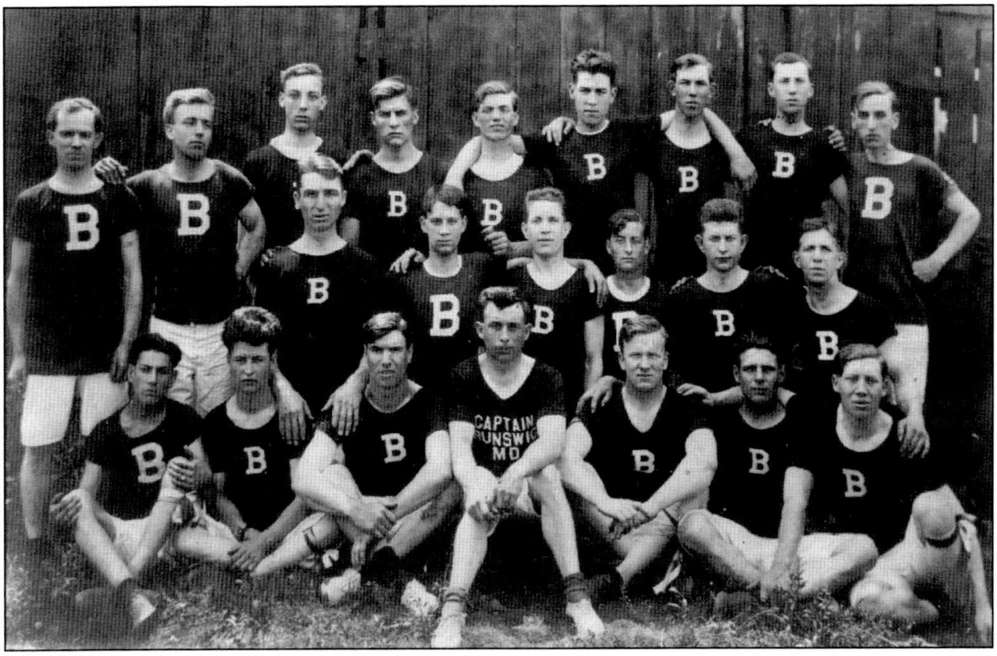

This undated photograph shows another of Brunswick's sports teams. No members are identified by name, nor is the sport indicated, though the captain is seated in the middle of the first row. (Courtesy Brunswick History Commission.)

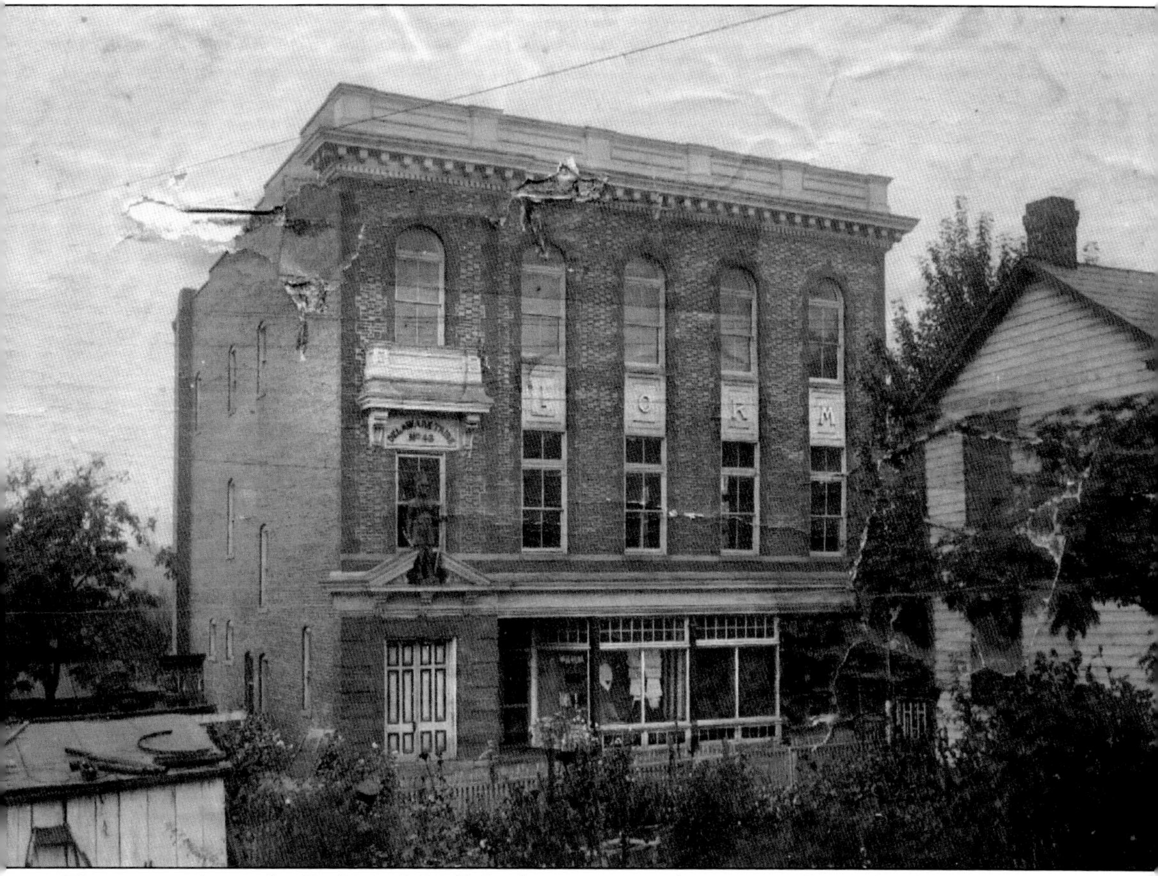

This image shows the Red Men's Hall, built in 1904 on the corner of Maryland Avenue and Potomac Street. Delaware Tribe No. 43 of the Improved Order of Red Men (IORM) was formed in Brunswick on July 5, 1867, and was Brunswick's oldest fraternal organization. Once having as many as 306 members in 1906, the tribe suffered from declining membership and disbanded in 1945. Today the Brunswick Railroad Museum and C&O Canal Visitor's Center are located in the building. (Courtesy Brunswick History Commission.)

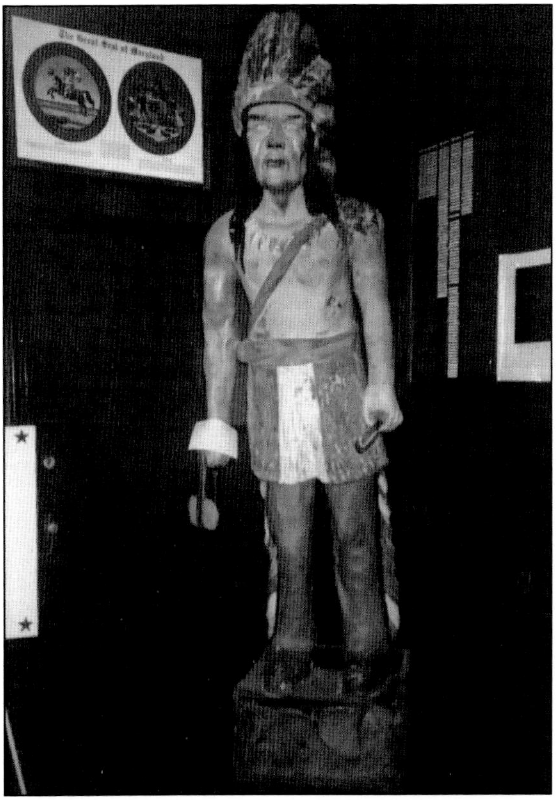

This image shows the "Red Man statue" once mounted above the entrance to Red Men's Hall. The statue is now located on the second floor of the Brunswick Railroad Museum. The second floor of Red Men's Hall was once a popular location for social events such as dances and public meetings. During the 1920s, the post office was located on the first floor, as well as Freeman's Bakery. (Courtesy Brunswick History Commission.)

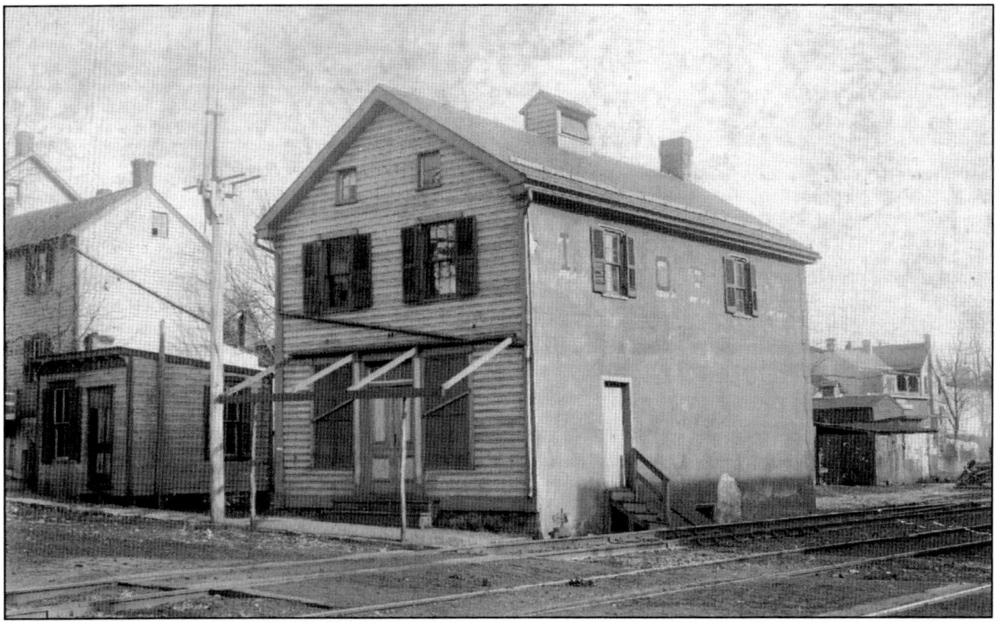

This 1873 photograph shows the first Red Men's Hall on the corner of Virginia Avenue and Walnut Street. Other groups, such as Masonic Lodge 191 and the Knights of Pythias, also used the building for meetings. Note how close to the building the rail tracks were laid. (Courtesy Brunswick History Commission.)

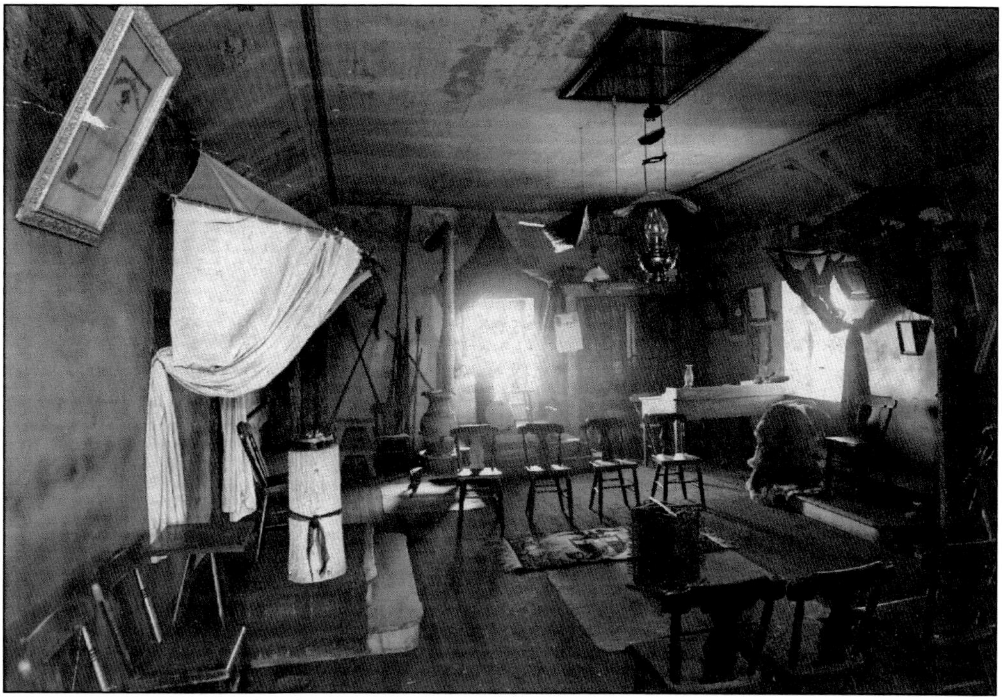

Here is an interior view of Red Men's Hall in 1873. Note the large framed charter hanging on the wall. The organization had strict rules and imposed fines on members for infractions such as spitting on the floor of the "wigwam" or fishing on Sunday. (Courtesy Brunswick History Commission.)

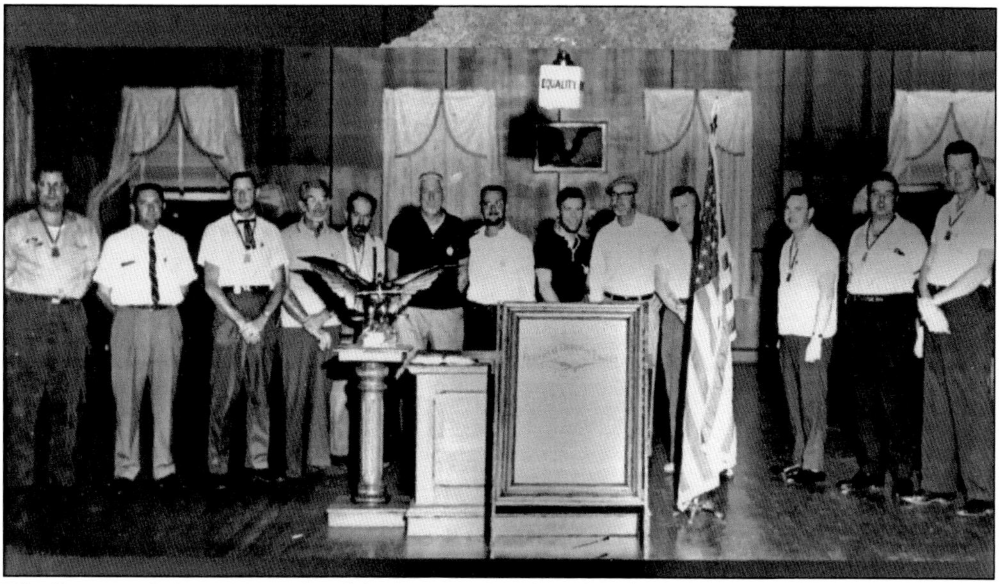

The Brunswick Aerie No. 1136 of the Fraternal Order of Eagles (FOE) was organized on June 30, 1905, under W. O. Suter of Hagerstown Aerie No. 694 and Jacob Clatterback of Cumberland Aerie No. 245. This image shows the FOE officers during the town's Diamond Jubilee Days. Pictured are, from left to right, unidentified, Mac Barger, Ernie Wineholt, Ortence Smoot, John Darr, Meredith Axline, unidentified, Harold Penwell, Rabbitt Hawes, Howard Wheeler, Kenny Giffin, Norman Greenfield, and Thomas Maloney. (Courtesy Brunswick History Commission.)

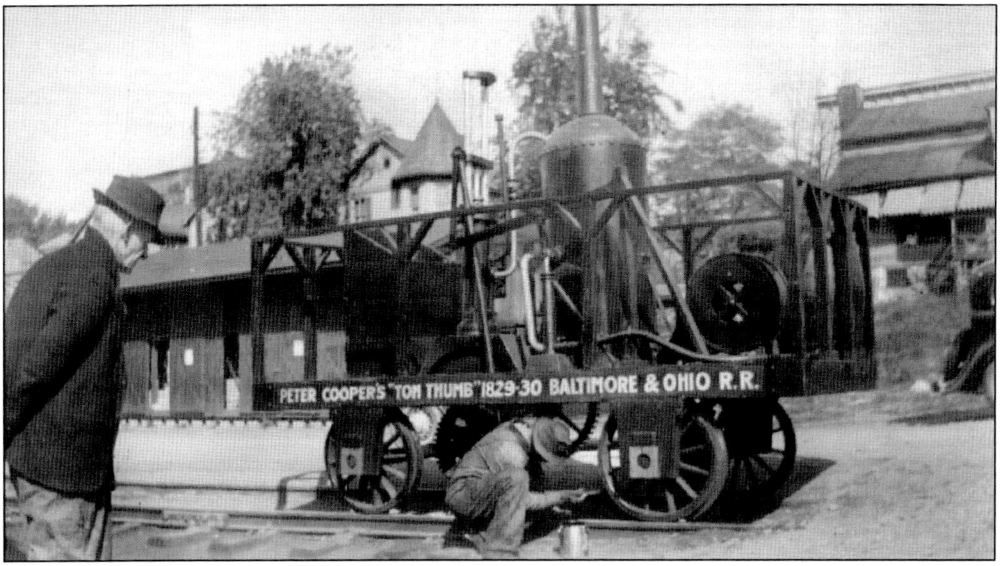

Brunswick enjoyed its Golden Jubilee in 1940, celebrating 50 years since the town became incorporated under the name Brunswick. This photograph shows Peter Cooper's 1829 "Tom Thumb" train from the B&O Railroad. The "Tom Thumb" engine pulled the nation's first passenger train between Baltimore and Ellicott Mills, Maryland, on May 24, 1830. The "Tom Thumb" visited Brunswick in honor of the jubilee. (Courtesy Brunswick History Commission.)

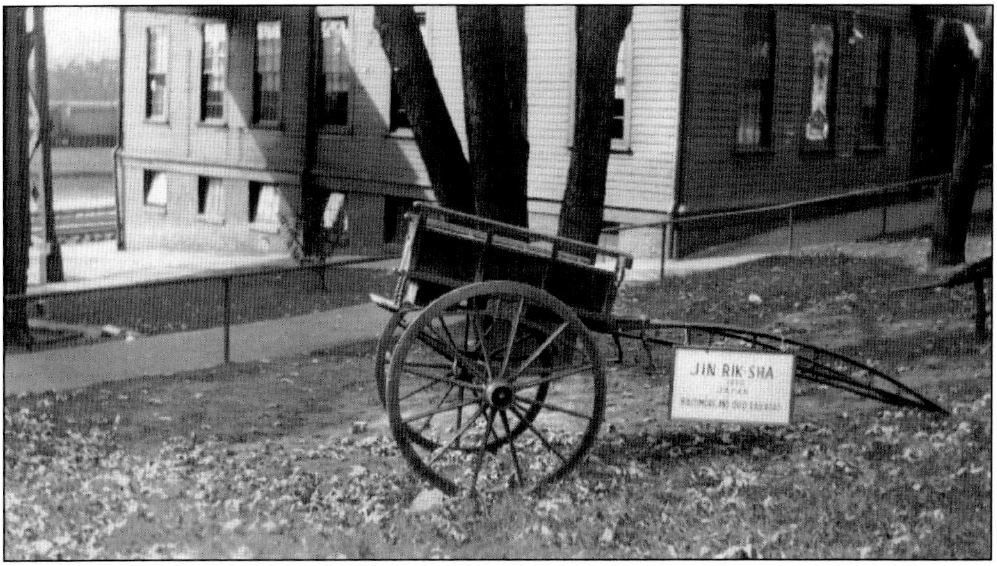

Other modes of transportation besides trains were also on display in Brunswick during the 1940 jubilee. This photograph shows a Jin Rik Sha, built in 1860, on display outside the B&O YMCA building. (Courtesy Brunswick History Commission.)

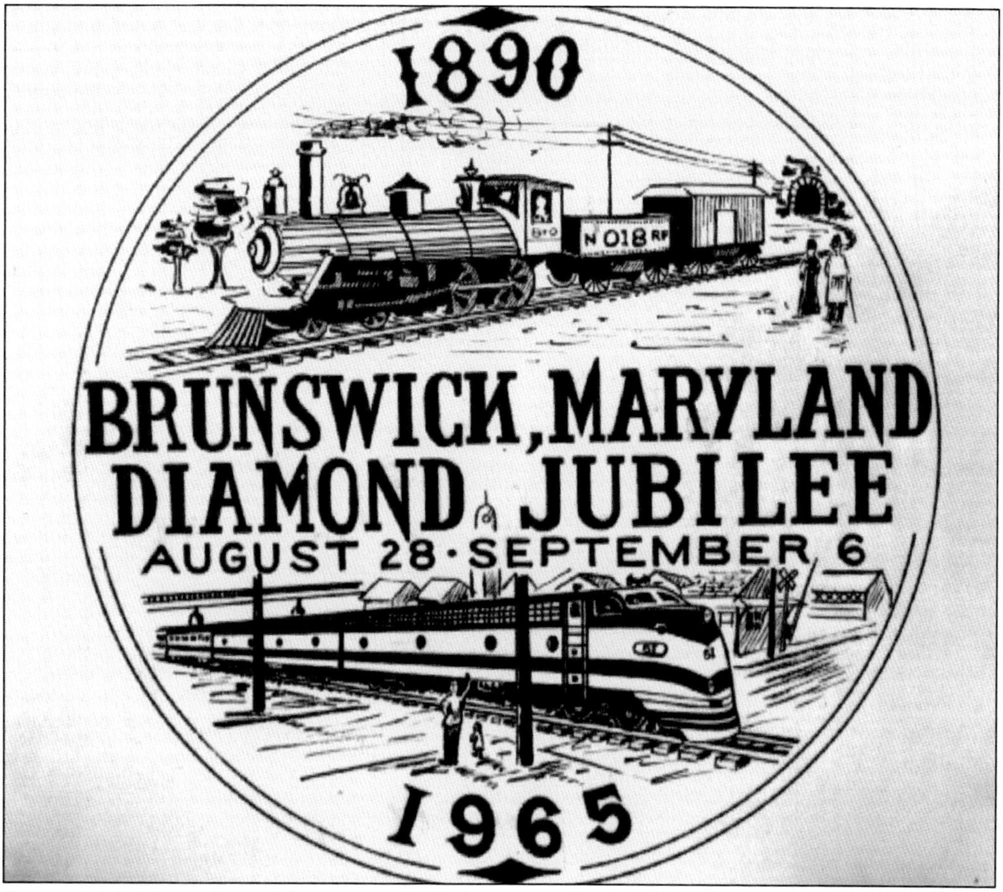

Brunswick held another celebration in 1965, this time a Diamond Jubilee commemorating 75 years since the town's incorporation on April 8, 1890. With the depiction of an old steam engine on the top and a modern diesel train on the bottom, this decal from the event shows the importance of the railroad for the town. (Courtesy Brunswick History Commission.)

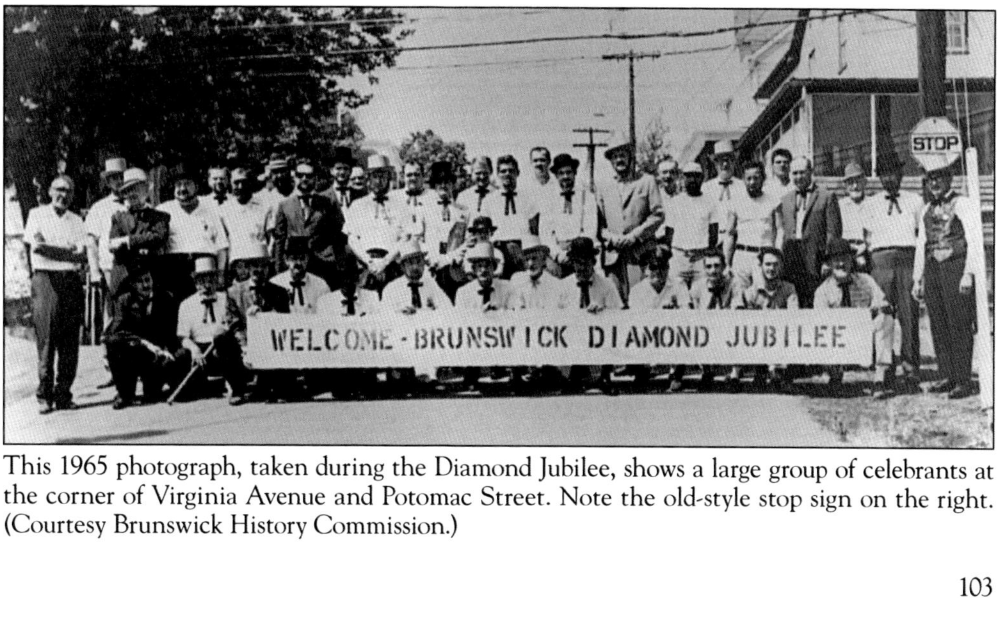

This 1965 photograph, taken during the Diamond Jubilee, shows a large group of celebrants at the corner of Virginia Avenue and Potomac Street. Note the old-style stop sign on the right. (Courtesy Brunswick History Commission.)

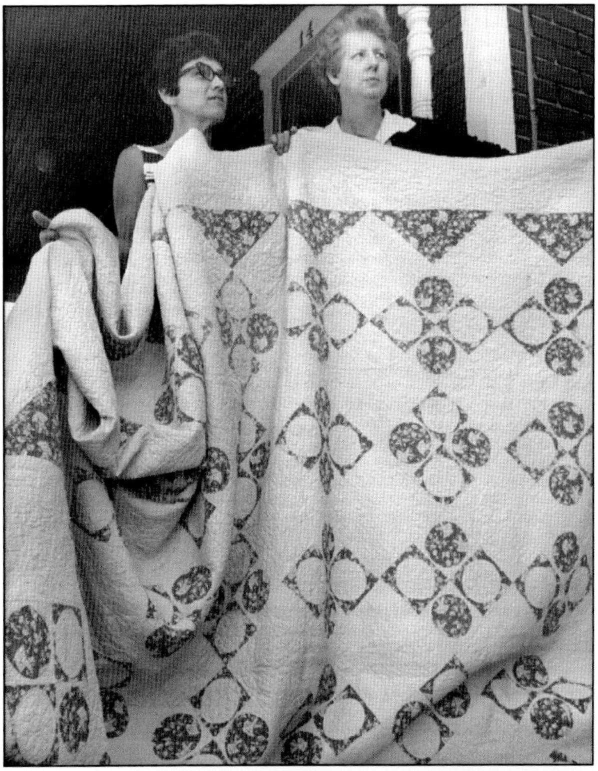

Mary Margrabe (left), publicity director, helps Gretchen M. Rollison (right) with a quilt made between 1830 and 1850. The photograph was taken at the Potomac River Festival on August 6, 1971, the third year of the festival. (Courtesy Brunswick History Commission.)

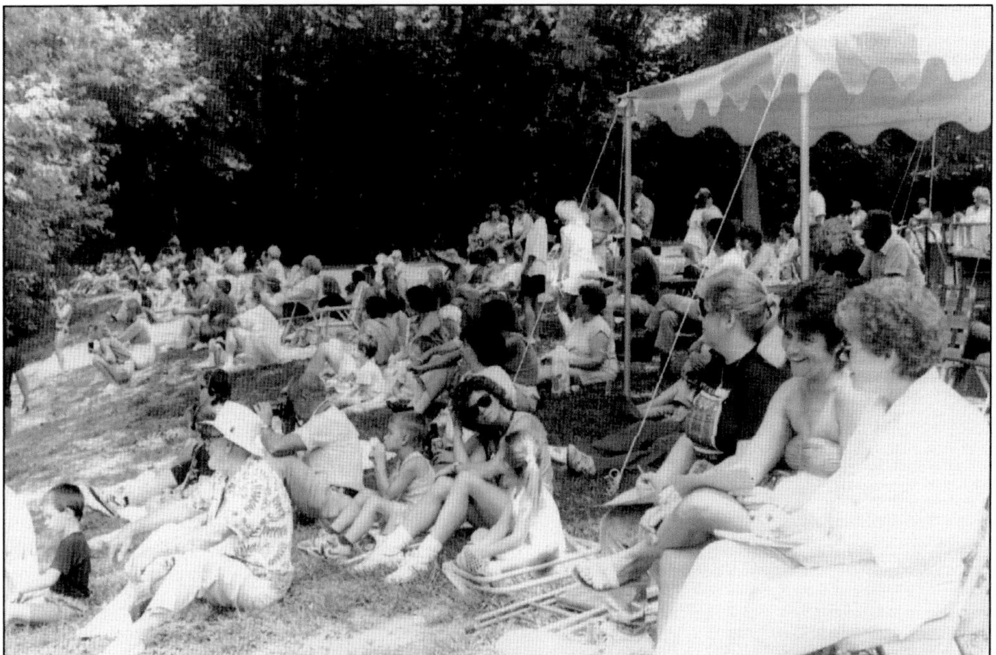

Here we see a crowd gathered on the banks of the river to watch a wacky boat race. Participants build all sorts of strange craft to race along the Potomac River. (Courtesy Brunswick History Commission.)

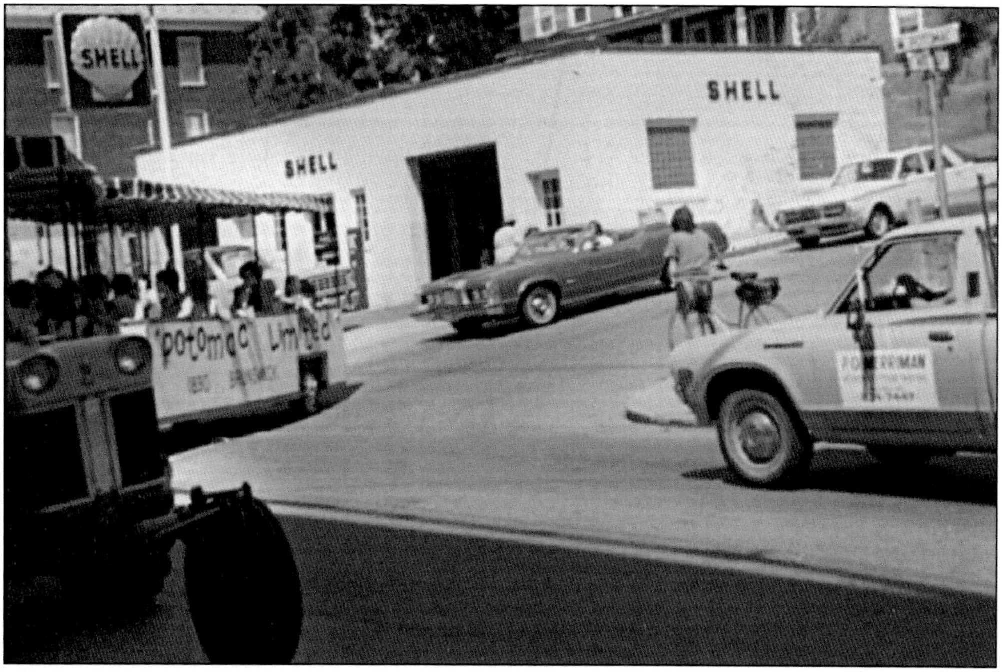

This Railroad Days photograph was taken in 1974. Note the tractor pulling a tram decorated as the *Potomac Limited* train. The tram is rounding the corner onto West Potomac Street. (Courtesy Brunswick History Commission.)

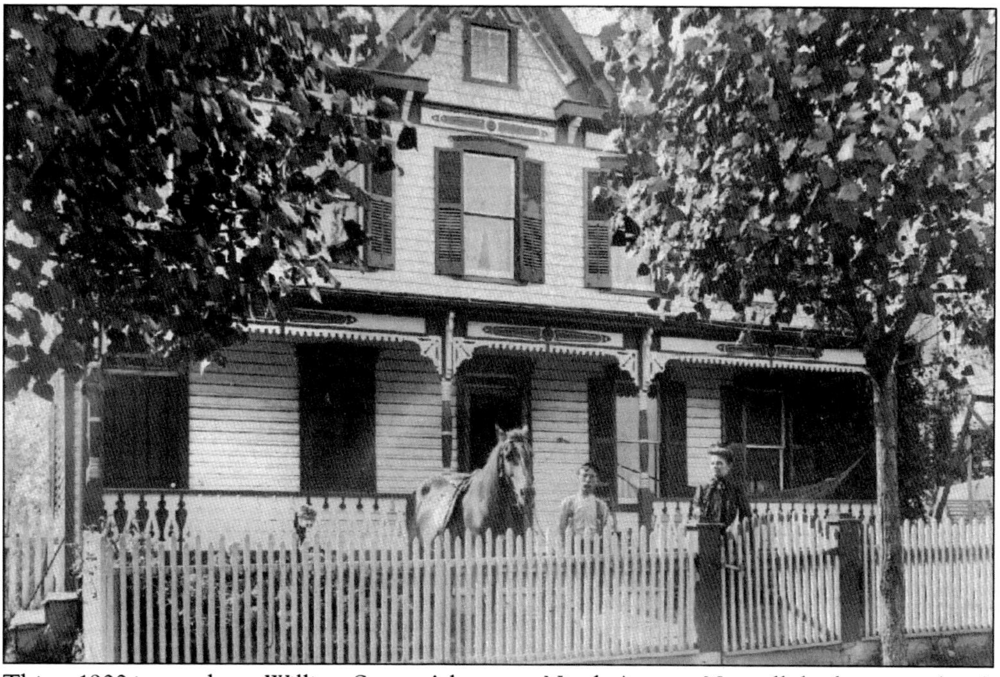

This *c.* 1900 image shows William Stewart's home on Ninth Avenue. Note all the fancy woodwork trim on the house. LeRoy Stewart and his mother are in the photograph, along with Bess, the horse. Bess was used for both work in the garden and for riding. (Courtesy Brunswick History Commission.)

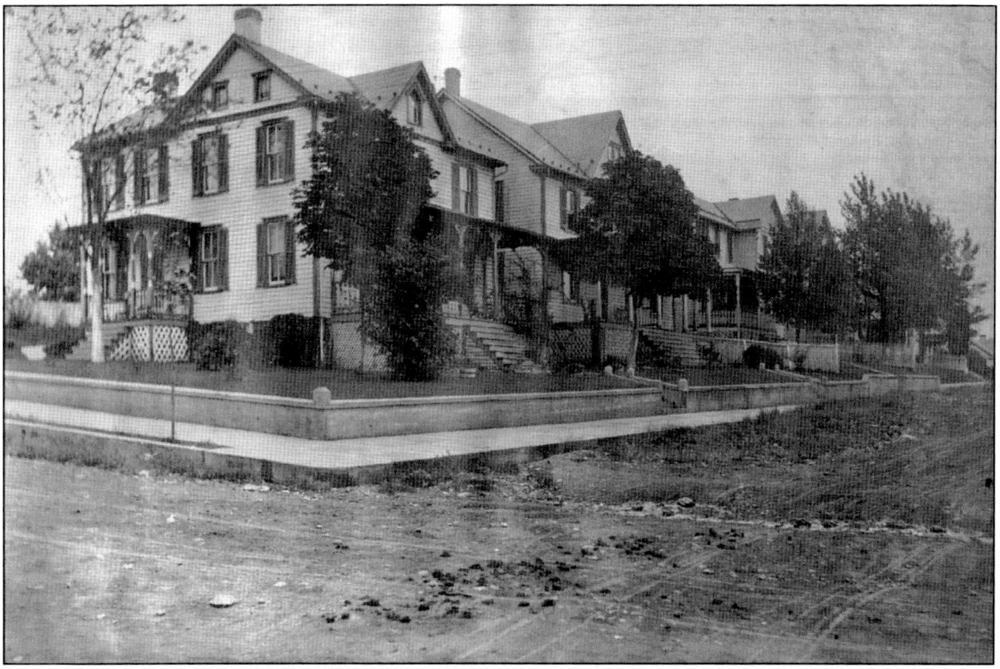

Here's a sight we don't see these days but was commonplace when this photograph was taken—a dirt road full of horse manure. The image shows the Oscar Merriman property on the corner of A Street and First Avenue. (Courtesy Brunswick History Commission.)

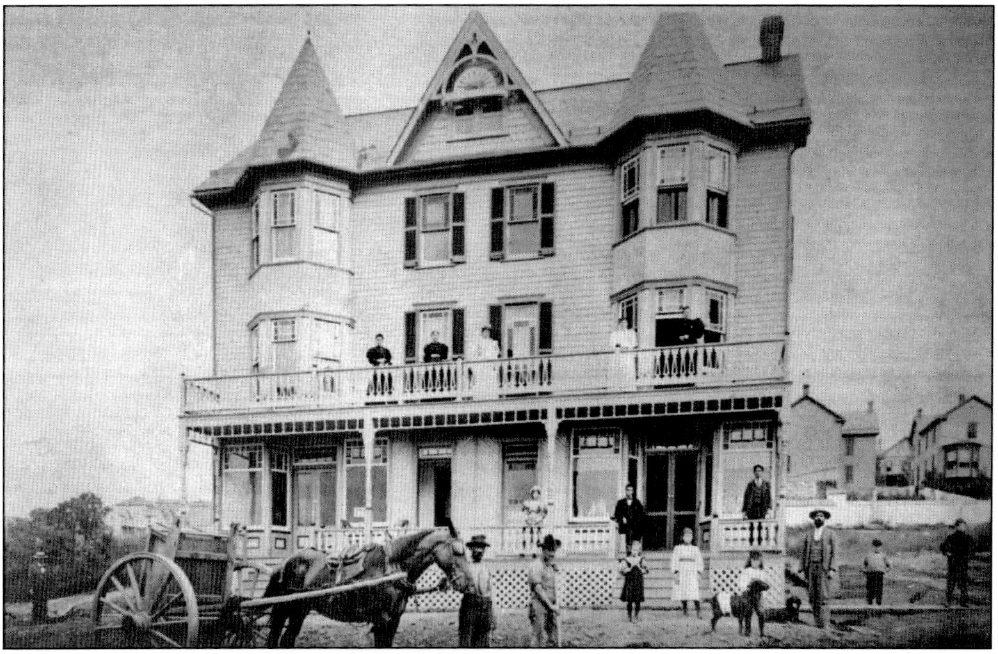

This photograph, taken September 5, 1896, shows another one of the large homes in town, this one an apartment house at 109 East Potomac Street. The man with the horse-drawn cart as well as the dress of the others in the image helps give a good glimpse into the past. (Courtesy Brunswick History Commission.)

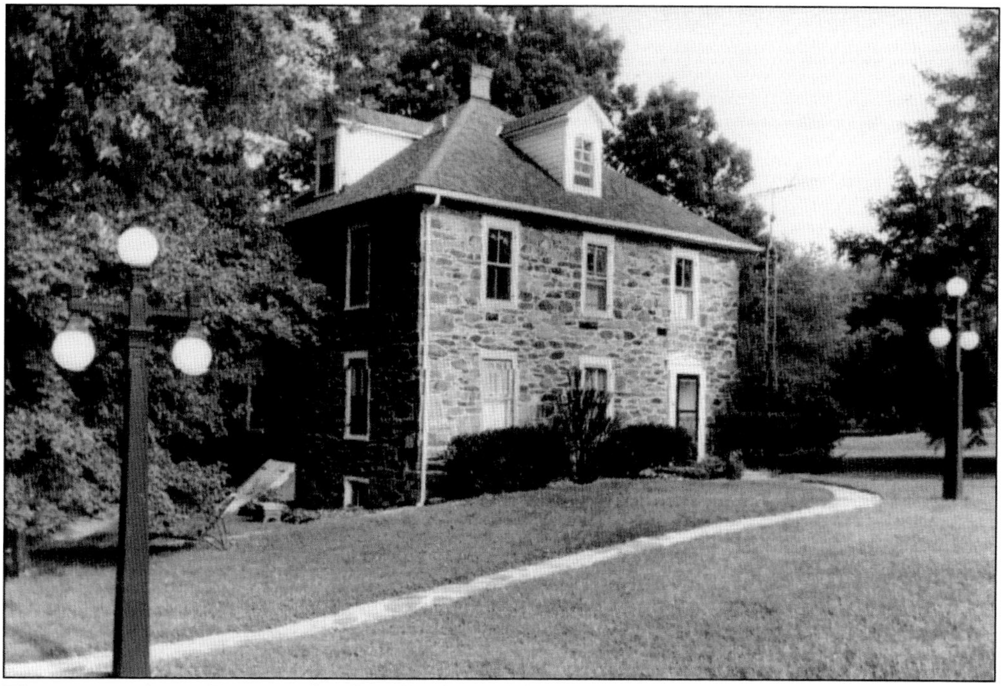

This image shows Brunswick's first (and possibly only) stone house on Sixth Avenue and H Street. The globe streetlights are from Memorial Park on A Street. (Courtesy Brunswick History Commission.)

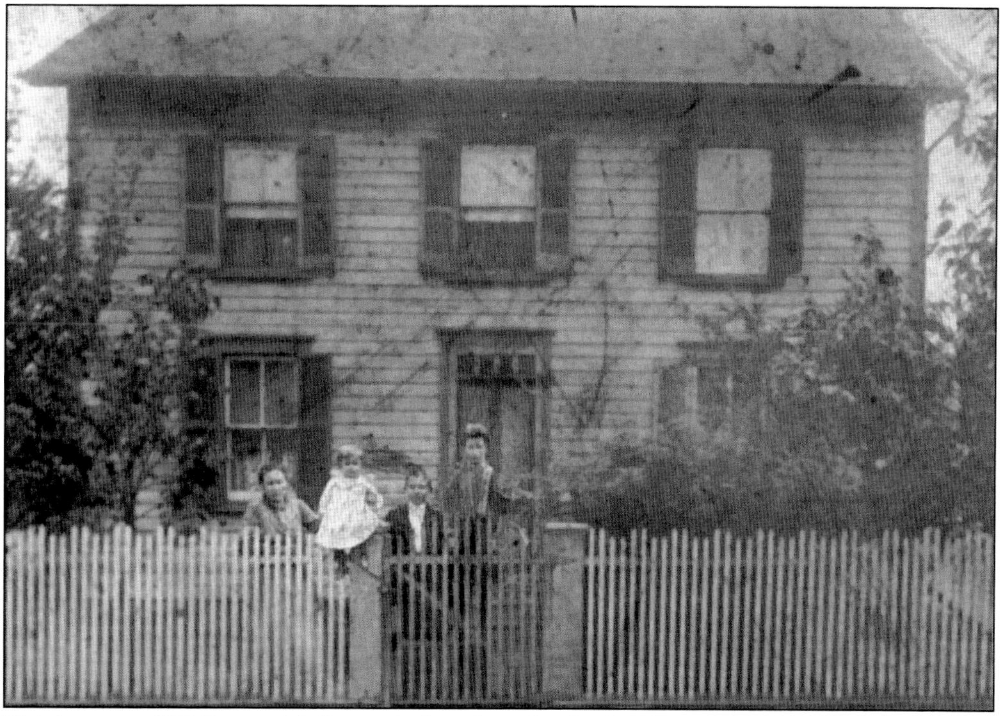

This house, at 308 Brunswick Street, is thought to be the first house constructed west of Berlin. (Courtesy Brunswick History Commission.)

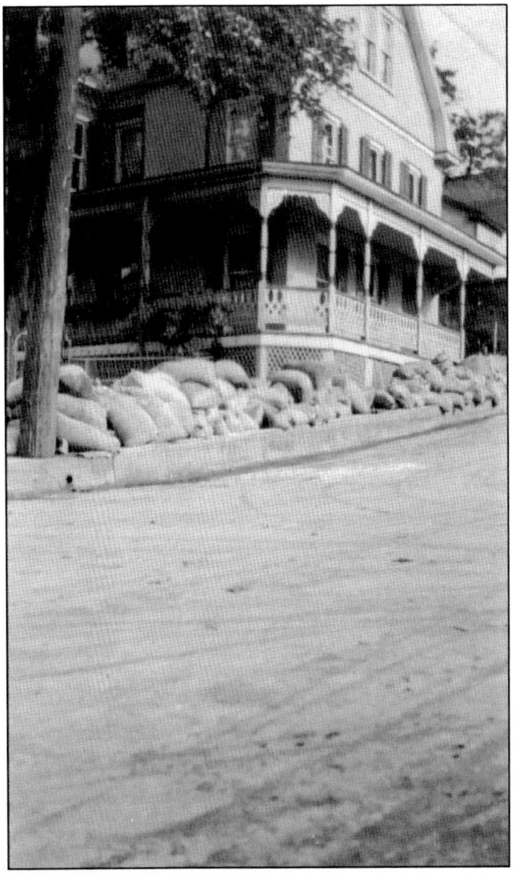

Like many other communities along the river and canal, Brunswick has faced numerous floods through the years. This photograph, taken May 14, 1924, shows salt and feed stacked on the sidewalk along Maryland Avenue. The sacks were removed from flood danger at the mill along the canal at 1:00 a.m. (Courtesy Brunswick History Commission.)

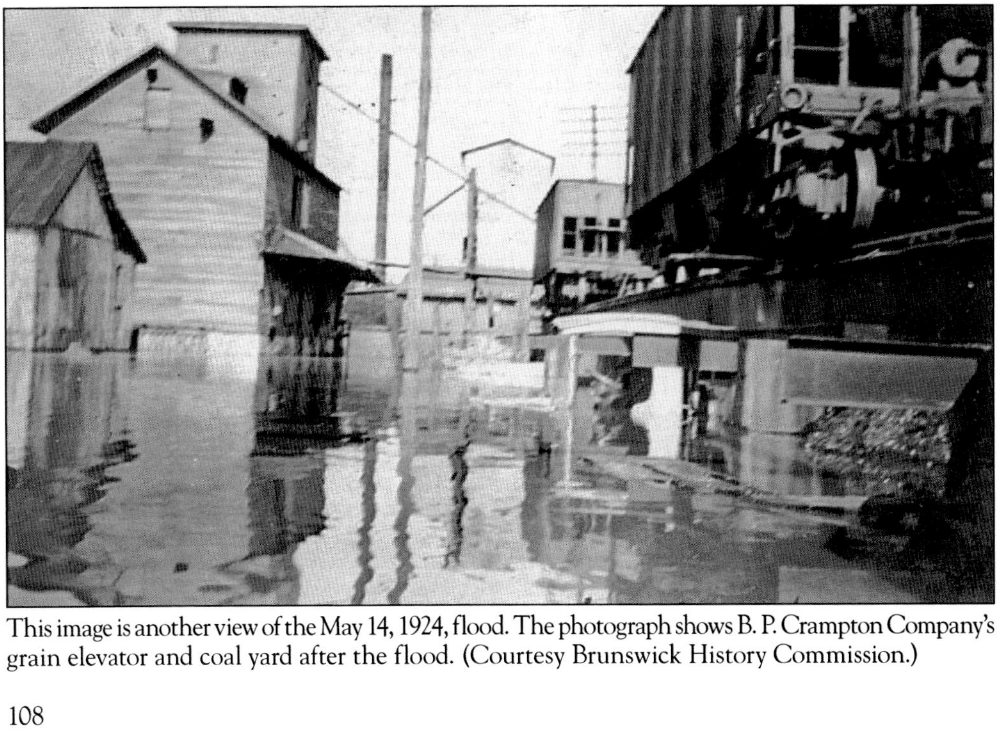

This image is another view of the May 14, 1924, flood. The photograph shows B. P. Crampton Company's grain elevator and coal yard after the flood. (Courtesy Brunswick History Commission.)

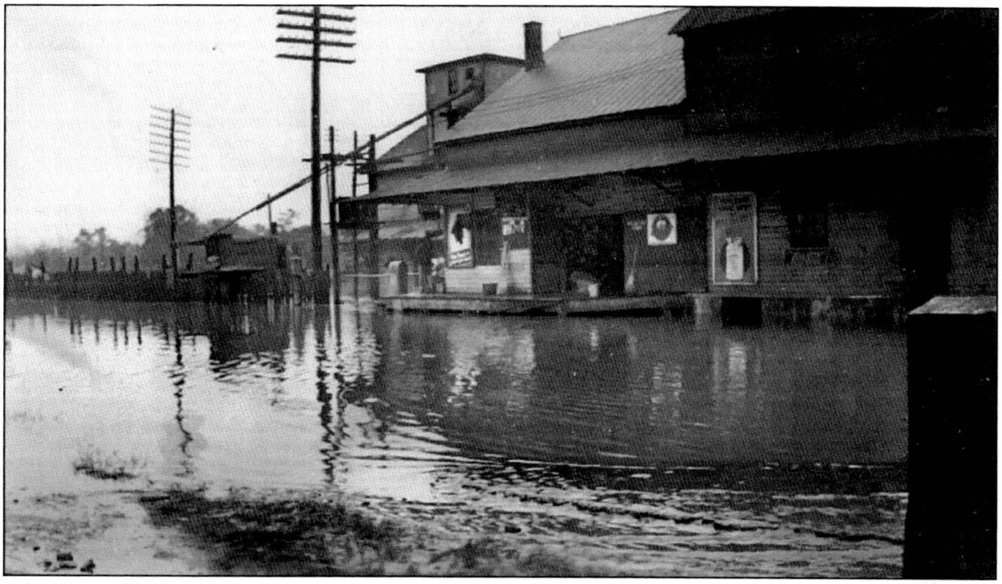

This image shows the Brunswick Mill after another flood, this one on October 16, 1942. (Courtesy Brunswick History Commission.)

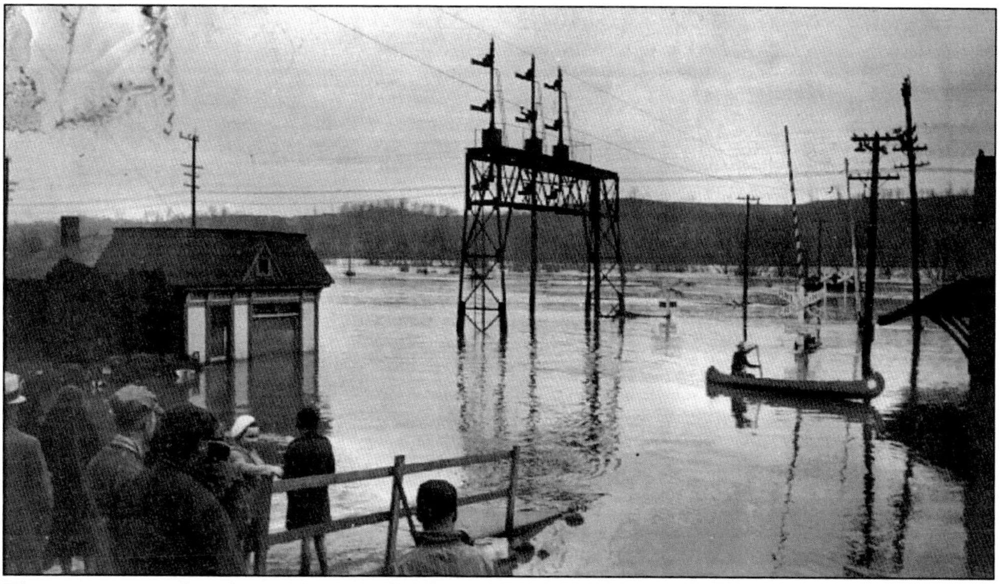

This image was taken during the 1936 flood. The B&O Station can just be seen on the right, and the building on the left was once Flynn's Barbershop. The canoe seems to be the only practical way to move about an area normally traversed by trains. (Courtesy Brunswick History Commission.)

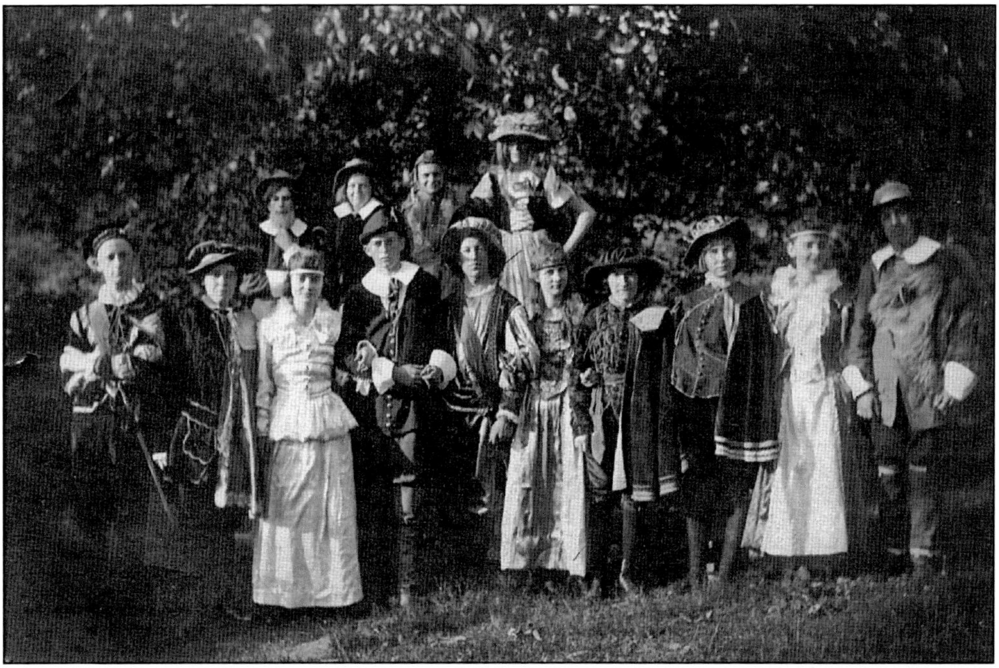

This pre-1917 image shows a group of townsfolk in full costume for one of the many productions staged over the years. (Courtesy Brunswick History Commission.)

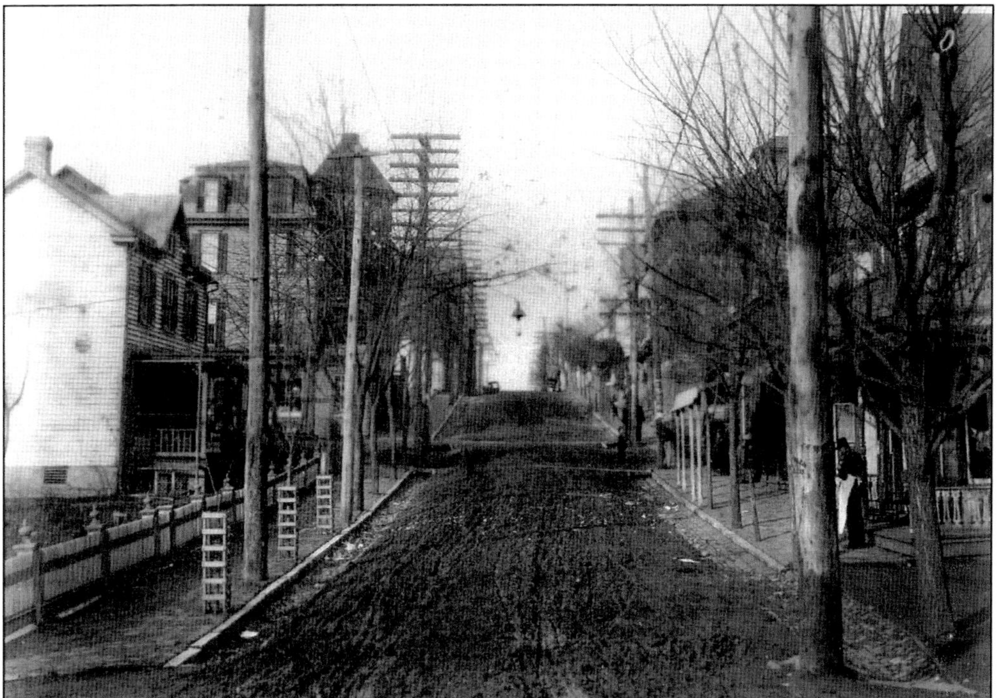

Here is a photograph of East Potomac Street looking toward West Potomac Street taken prior to 1905. The tall building on the left, the Meadows Building, can still be seen today. Note the dirt road and the many telephone poles and wires. (Courtesy Brunswick History Commission.)

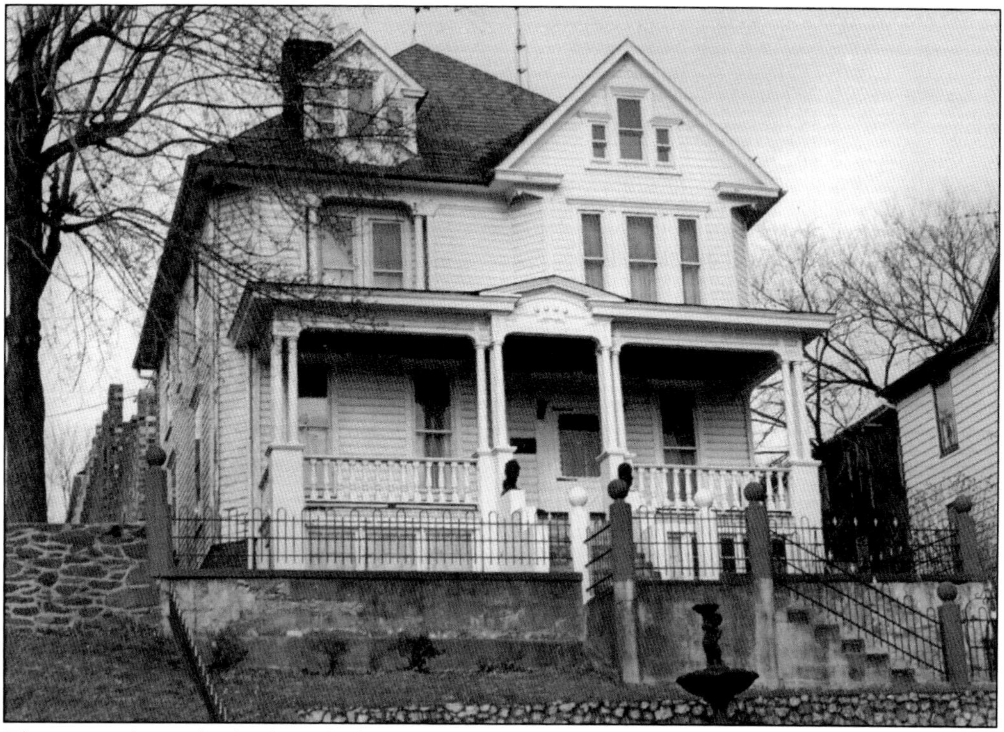

This image shows the finely crafted Victorian Funk House at 13 East A Street in Brunswick. Built in 1905 by Harry B. Funk, it was one of the first homes in town to have gaslight illumination. (Courtesy Brunswick History Commission.)

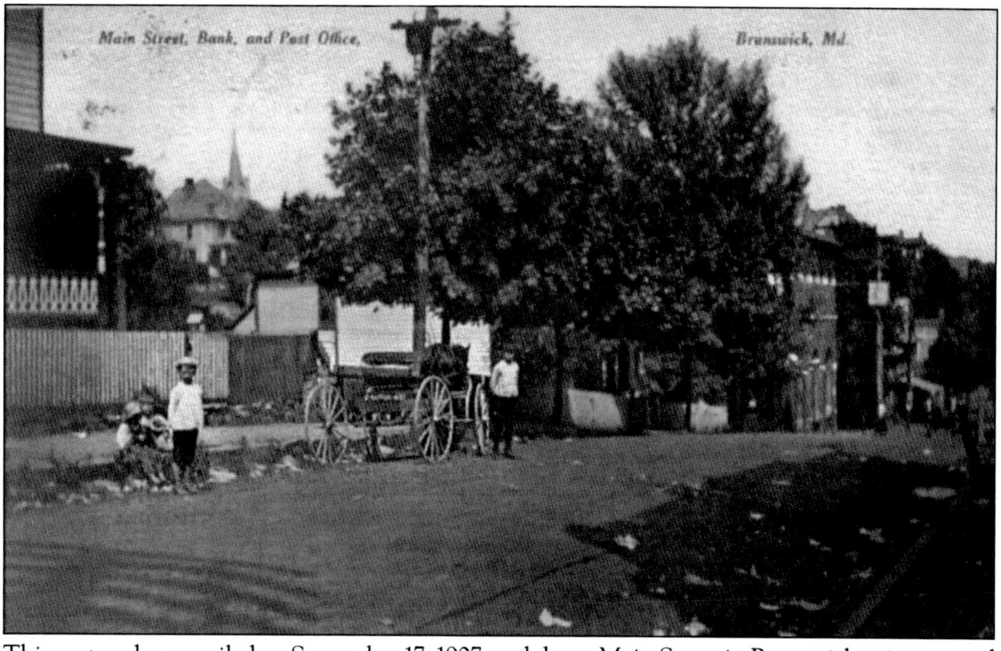

This postcard was mailed on September 17, 1907, and shows Main Street in Brunswick as it appeared at that time. Note the children on the left giving flavor to the quiet street scene. The bank and post office are down the street past the trees. (Courtesy Brunswick History Commission.)

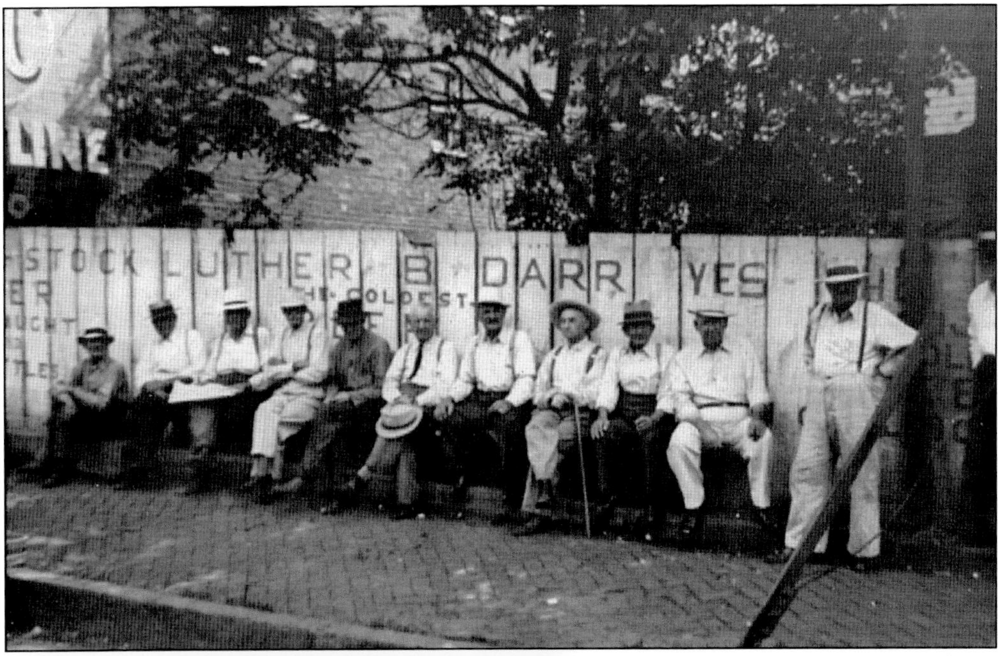

This board fence was constructed by Luther "Lute" Darr for use in advertising on North Maple Avenue. The bench in front was built specifically as a spot for the elderly men around town to gather. The large English walnut tree in the background was planted by Darr in 1901. The painted brick wall to the left is part of a Sinclair gasoline advertisement. (Courtesy Brunswick History Commission.)

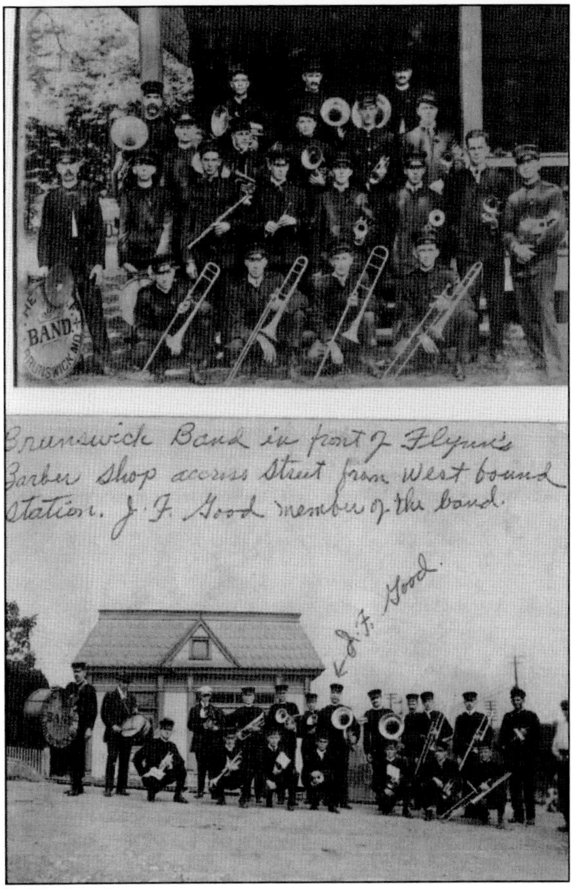

This image shows two views of the Brunswick Town Band. Town bands were once commonplace, and many small towns throughout the region had one. The top image was taken around 1915. The trombone player on the bottom left is Grover "Tops" Stewart. The bottom image shows the band in front of Flynn's Barbershop across the street from the westbound train station. Member J. F. Good is identified in the middle of the photograph. (Courtesy Brunswick History Commission.)

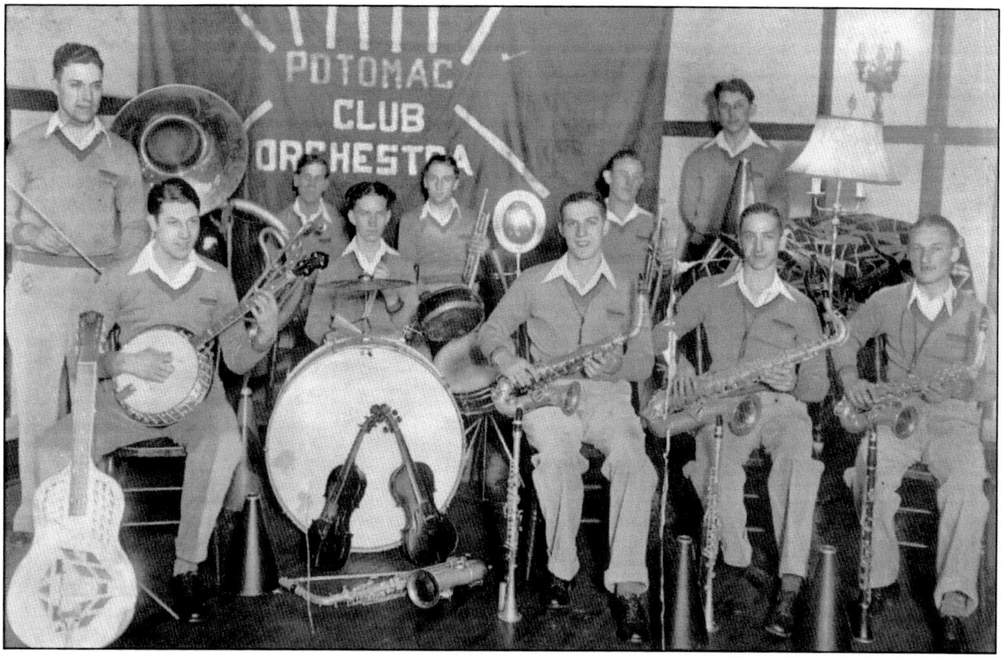

This *c.* 1937 photograph shows the Potomac Club Orchestra. Pictured from left to right are (first row) John Funk (standing), Albert Danner, Bobby Garrison, Don Musgrove, Leo Dean, and Spike Shivers; (second row) Arthur Griffert (seated, position unidentified), two unidentified, and C. Mohler (standing). (Courtesy Brunswick History Commission.)

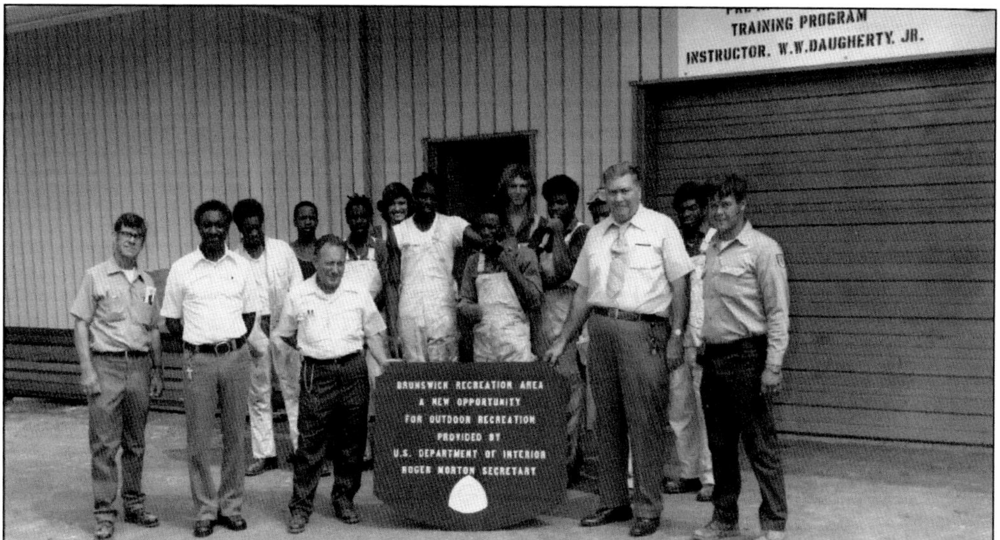

This photograph was taken September 4, 1974, and shows the mayor of Brunswick, Jess D. Orndorff, being presented with a signboard for Brunswick's new outdoor recreation area constructed by the Harpers Ferry Job Corps Union Carpentry and Union Painting corpsmen. Pictured in the foreground are, from left to right, Albert Sanchez (Union Carpentry instructor), Randolph Scott (assistant center director), W. W. Daugherty (Union Painting instructor), Jess Orndorff (Brunswick mayor), and Arthur Izer (Union Carpentry coordinator). In the background are several unidentified carpentry and painting corpsmen. (Courtesy Brunswick History Commission.)

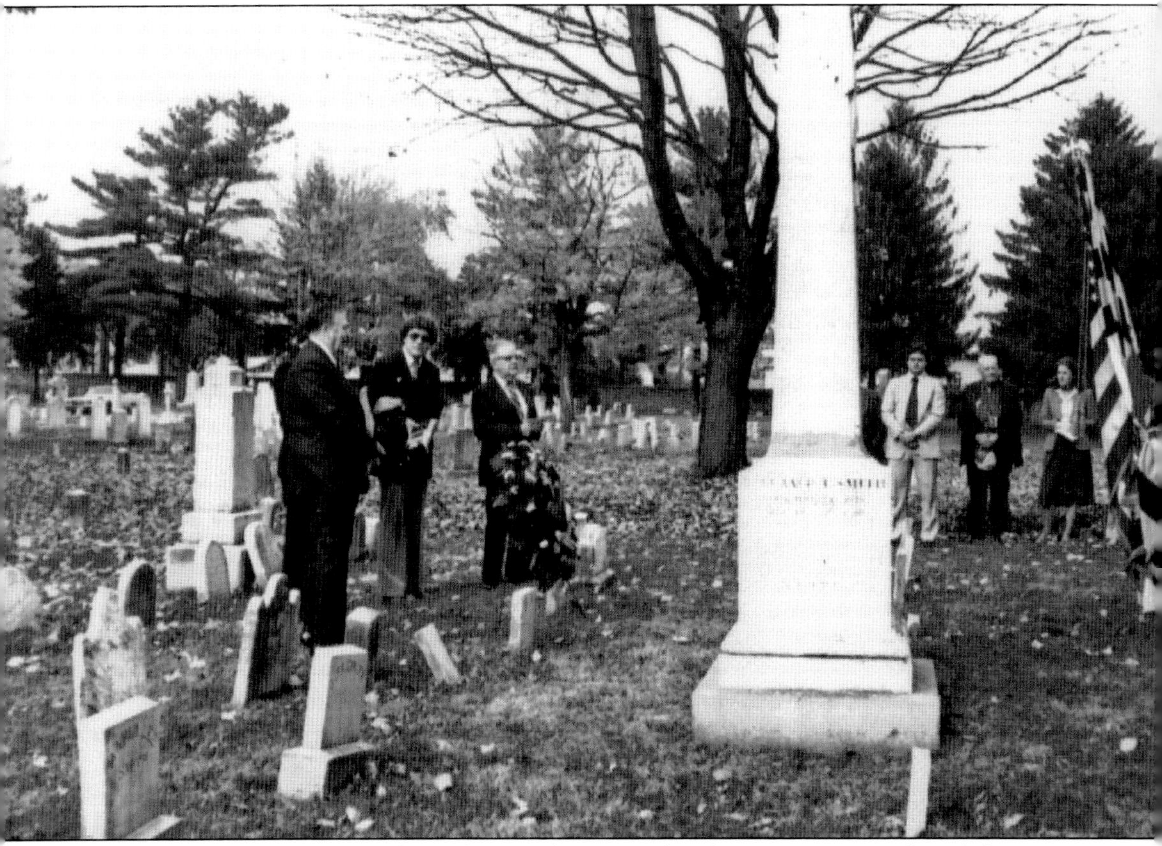

Leonard Smith was one of the earliest settlers in Frederick County. He purchased the western half of John Hawkins's original grant from King George II, known as "Hawkins' Merry-Peep-O-Day," on November 7, 1780, and laid out the town he called Berlin. Two hundred years later, on November 7, 1980, during the town's bicentennial, Brunswick mayor Jess Orndorff, Rev. H. Austin Cooper, and Gary Barkman made a pilgrimage to Leonard Smith's burial site at St. John's Catholic Cemetery on Third Street in Frederick for a ceremony to honor the man credited with creating their town. The Steadman-Keenan American Legion Post provided the color guard shown in the photograph. (Courtesy Brunswick History Commission.)

This image shows the Brunswick telephone exchange and operator Lavetta Irene Kelley Thomas. She was 17 years old when she came to work at the switchboard on April 30, 1917. Early phones in Brunswick were party lines with 12 parties to each line. As in communities across the country, the urge to listen in on their neighbors' conversations was often too great to resist for some Brunswick residents. (Courtesy Brunswick History Commission.)

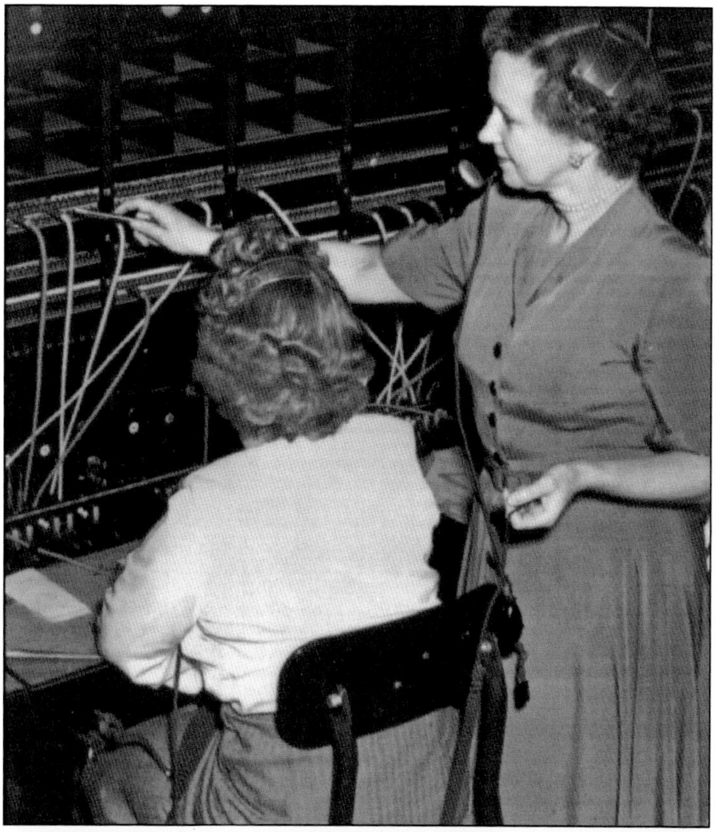

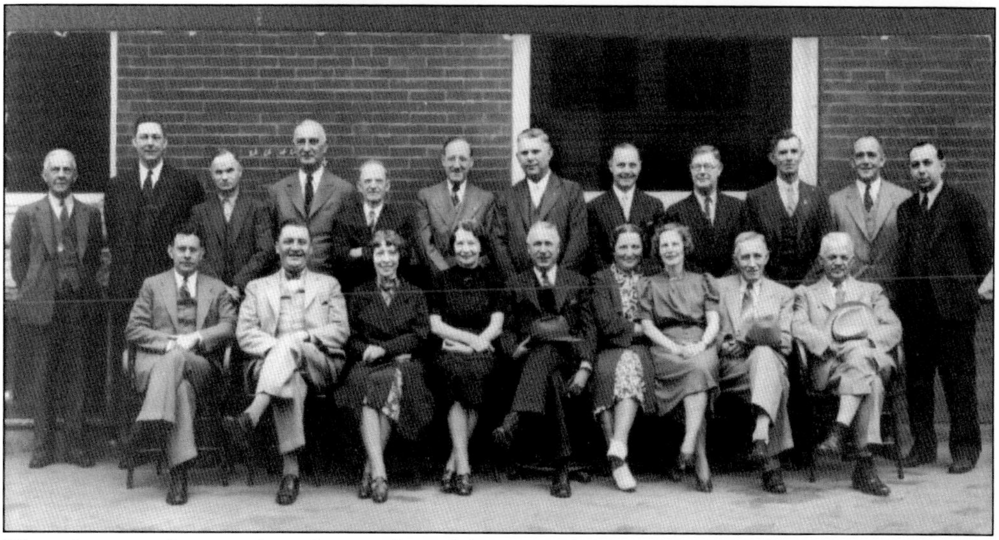

This photograph was taken during the celebration of the conversion of telephone service in Brunswick from operator service to self-dialing service on May 10, 1938. Pictured from left to right are (first row) two unidentified, Nellie Nichols, Bessie Moler, unidentified, Mabel Harrison, Lavetta Kelly Thomas, and two unidentified; (second row) "Willie" Pop Raw, unidentified, Henry Rinker, three unidentified, Harry Mace, unidentified, Pete Dixon, Chester Phillips, and two unidentified. (Courtesy Brunswick History Commission.)

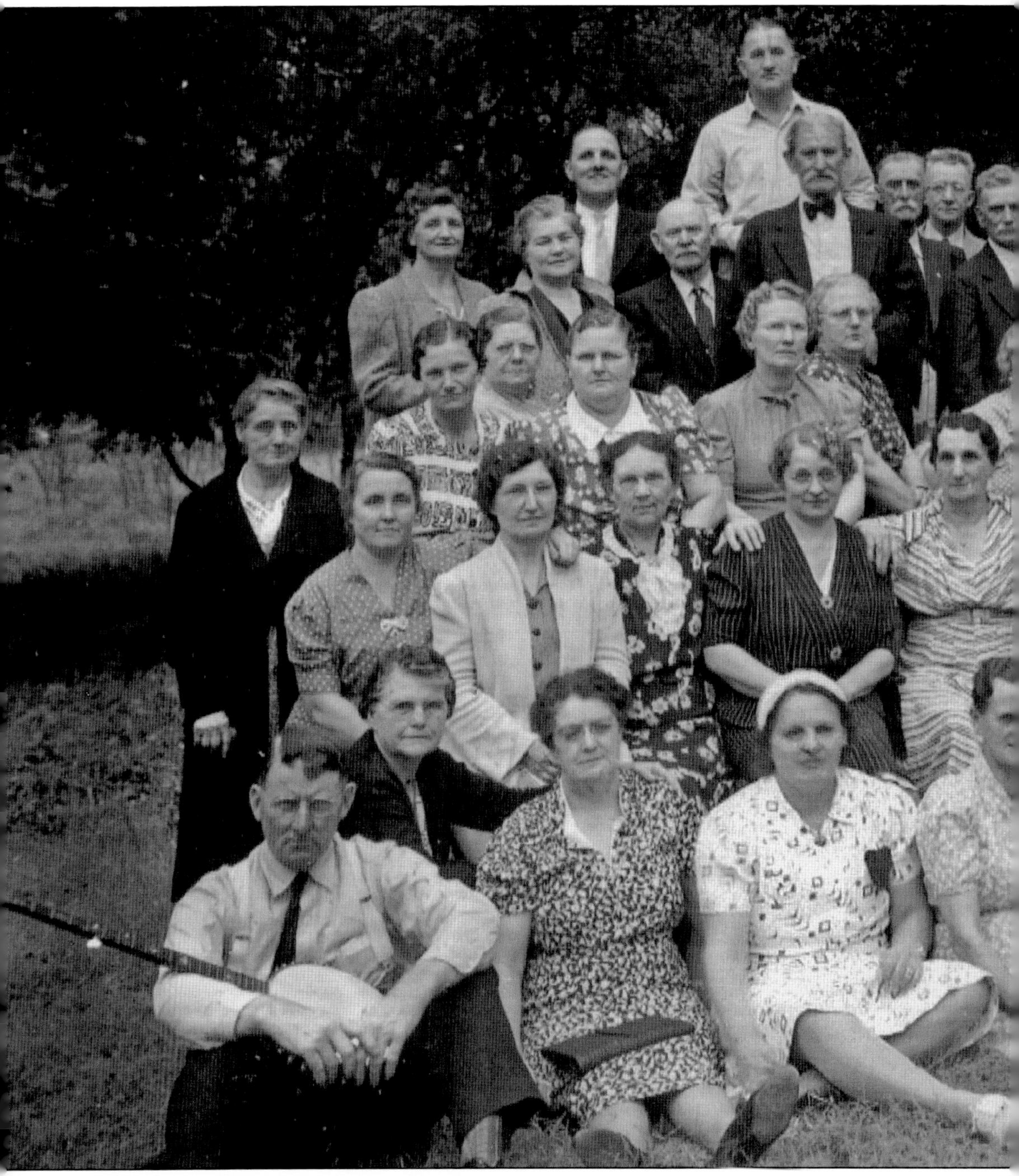

This photograph from September 12, 1939, was taken at the B&O Veterans Picnic held at Lloyd's Wood. This spot was popular, and many church picnics were held there. Pictured are, from left to right, (first row) W. L. Lake, Mrs. Frank Caskey, Mrs. Ira Waltz, Mrs. Frank Caniford, Mrs. James Phillips, Mrs. Leo Carey, Mrs. Emory Nelson, Charles Main, and James Phillips; (second row) Mrs. John Carey, Mrs. W. F. Ayres, Mrs. W. L. Everheart, ? McCoy, Minnie Barker, Mrs. A. B. Sigafoose, Mrs. Harry Allgire, Mrs. Charles Main, Mrs. James Quinn, Mrs. Dennis Cooper, Mrs. John Lloyd, and John Lloyd; (third row) Ella Ruble, Mrs. John Creamer, Mrs. Floyd Strickler, Mrs.

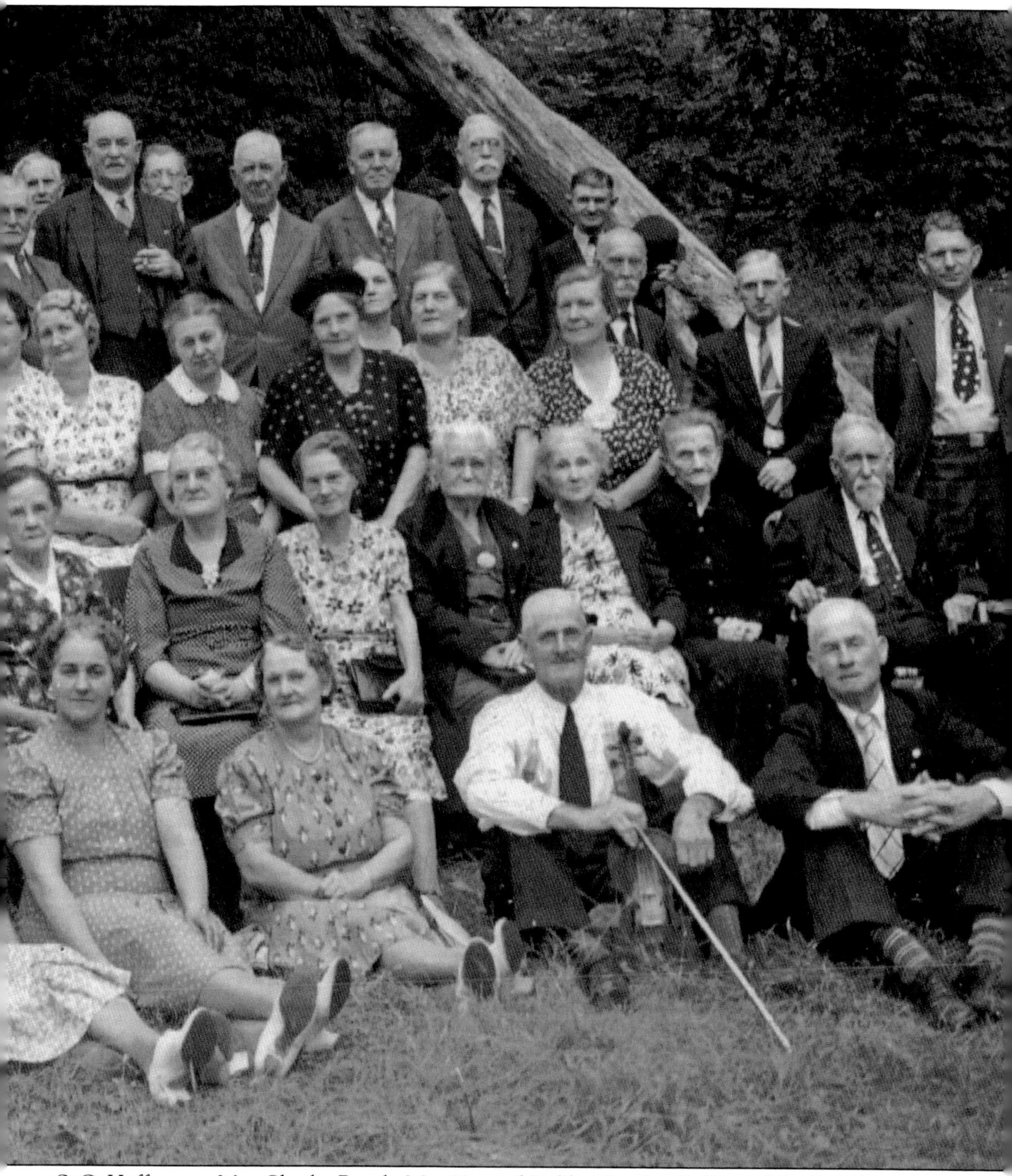

S. G. Hoffmaster, Mrs. Charles Booth, Mrs. Howard Duble, Mrs. Joe Coffman, Mrs. R. T. Foster, Viola Lloyd, Mrs. H. W. Fawver, Mrs. Albert Danner, unidentified (partially hidden), Mrs. H. H. Mitchell, Mrs. William Kline, ? Harrison, ? McCoy, and John Lloyd; (fourth row) Mrs. G. C. Dean, Mrs. L. E. Darr, R. T. Foster, "Bus" Miller, Charles Darr, G. W. Albert, W. L. Delauter, A. B. Sigafoose, W. L. Campbell, H. W. Fawver, W. L. Everheart, J. C. Bowler, and Peter Dietrich; (fifth row) four unidentified. (Courtesy Brunswick History Commission.)

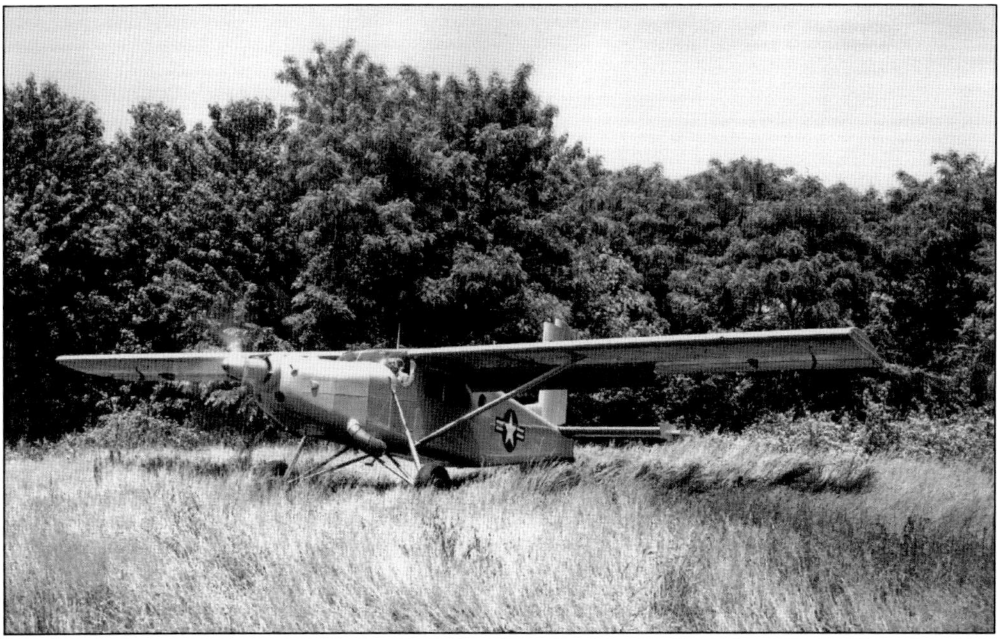

In August 1964, a new STOL (short takeoff and landing) aircraft made a stop in Brunswick at what is the present-day campground site. Built by Fairchild in Hagerstown, Maryland, the Pilatus Turbo Porter plane was being demonstrated to the U.S. Army and Air Force, and was touted for groundbreaking performance, such as needing only 300 feet of runway for takeoff with a full payload. (Courtesy Brunswick History Commission.)

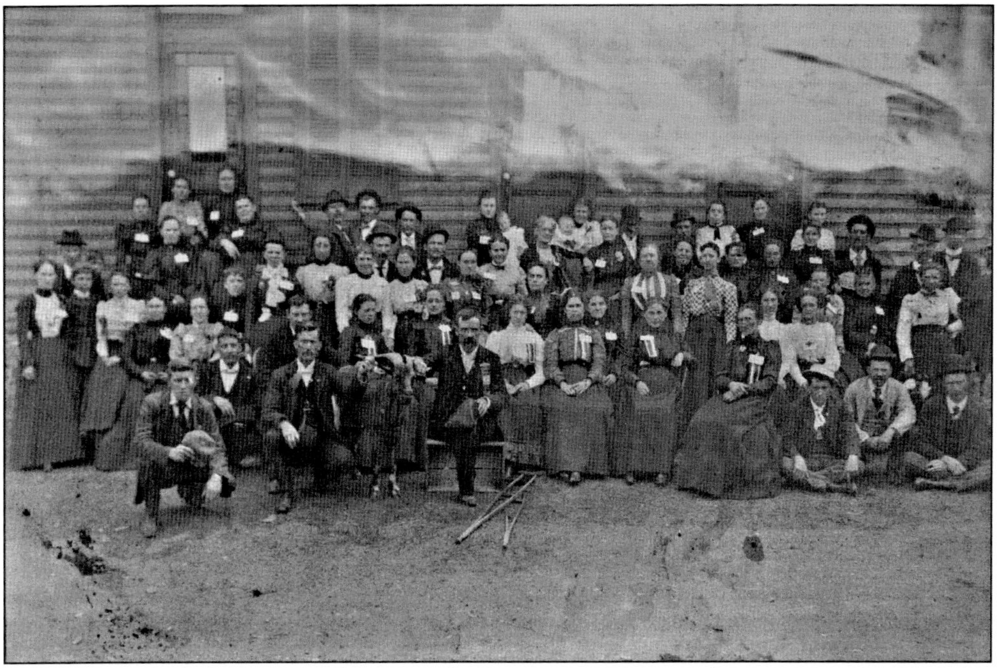

This unidentified photograph of Brunswick citizens was taken, perhaps in Martinsburg, West Virginia, on May 22, 1900. Everyone is wearing some type of ribbon, and the goat certainly leads to more curiosity about the event being documented. (Courtesy Brunswick History Commission.)

There was nothing like a cool dip on a hot day. These two bathing beauties, dressed in the swimwear fashion of the day, posed for the camera c. 1920 prior to diving into the canal. (Courtesy Brunswick History Commission.)

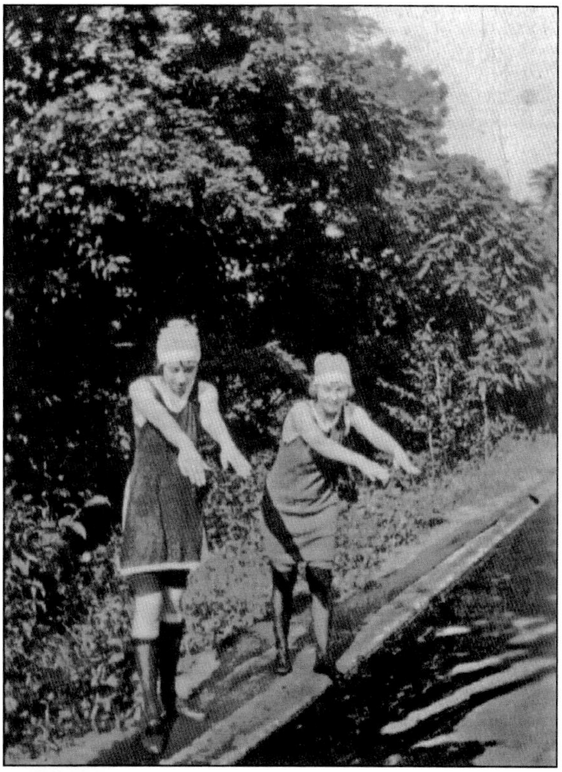

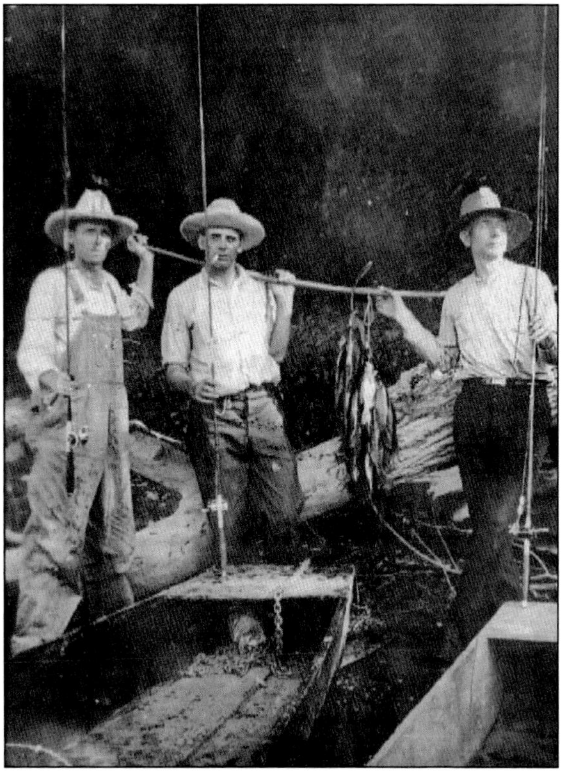

Here is a group of Brunswick men around the mid-1920s sharing one of their favorite pastimes, a day of fishing. Pictured are, from left to right, Jake Keenan, John Austin, and Harvey Moler. (Courtesy Brunswick History Commission.)

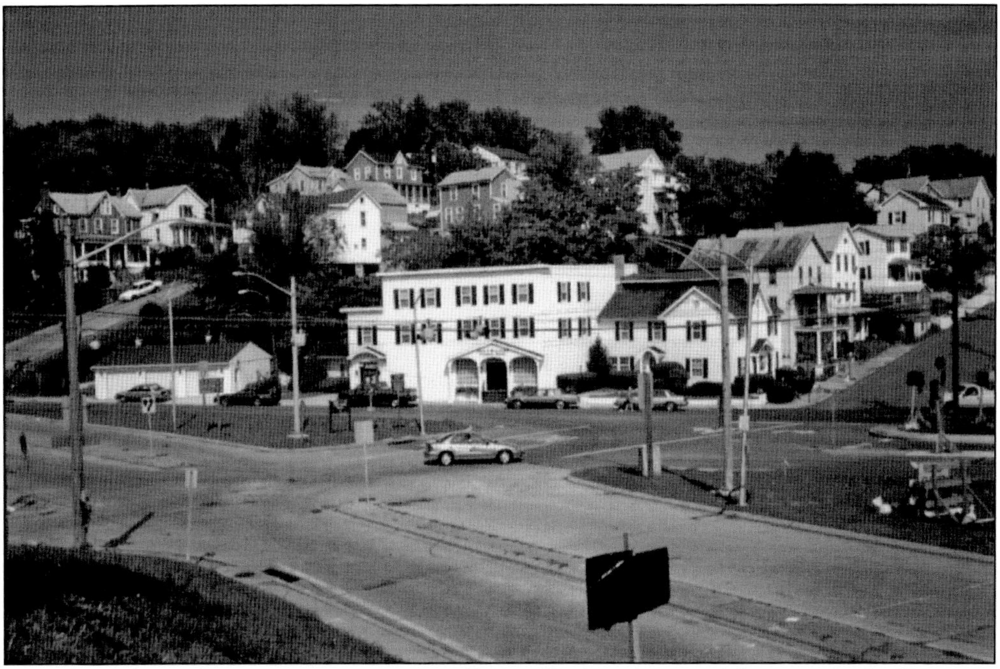

This image shows the intersection as Petersville Road before the roundabout was built. (Courtesy Brunswick History Commission.)

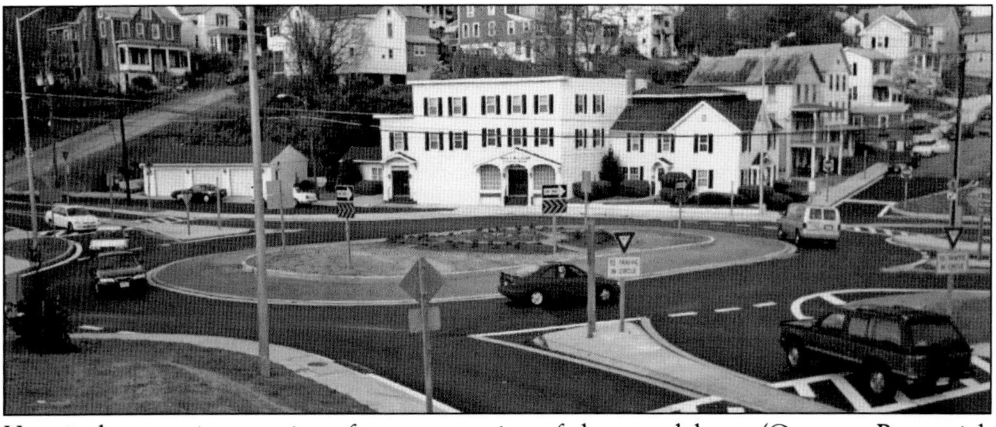

Here is the same intersection after construction of the roundabout. (Courtesy Brunswick History Commission.)

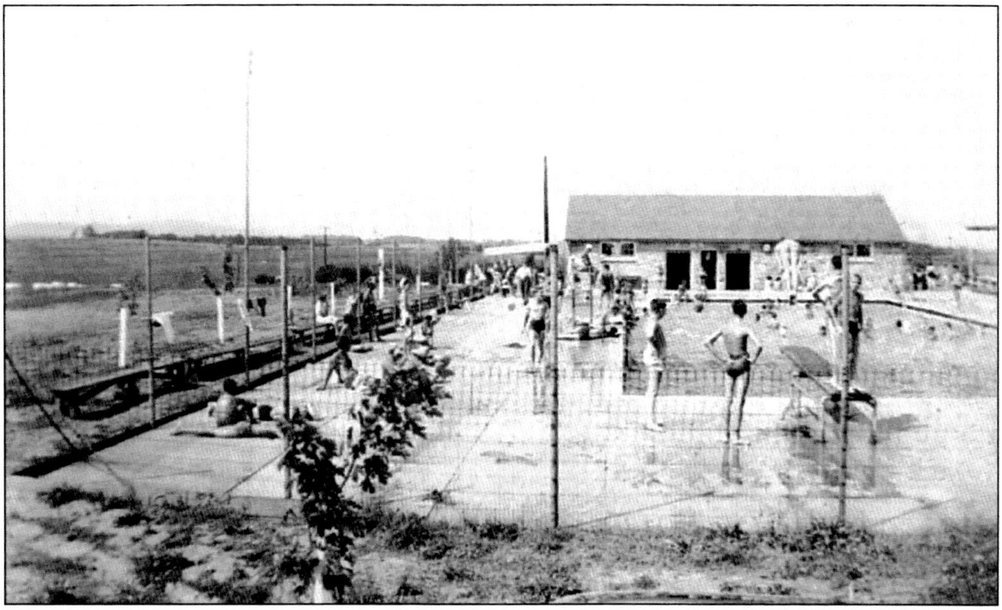

This 1944 image was taken at the Brunswick Pool on Cummings Drive. The pool and the surrounding recreation facilities are on property that was once part of, or adjacent to, Scheer Stadium. (Courtesy Brunswick History Commission.)

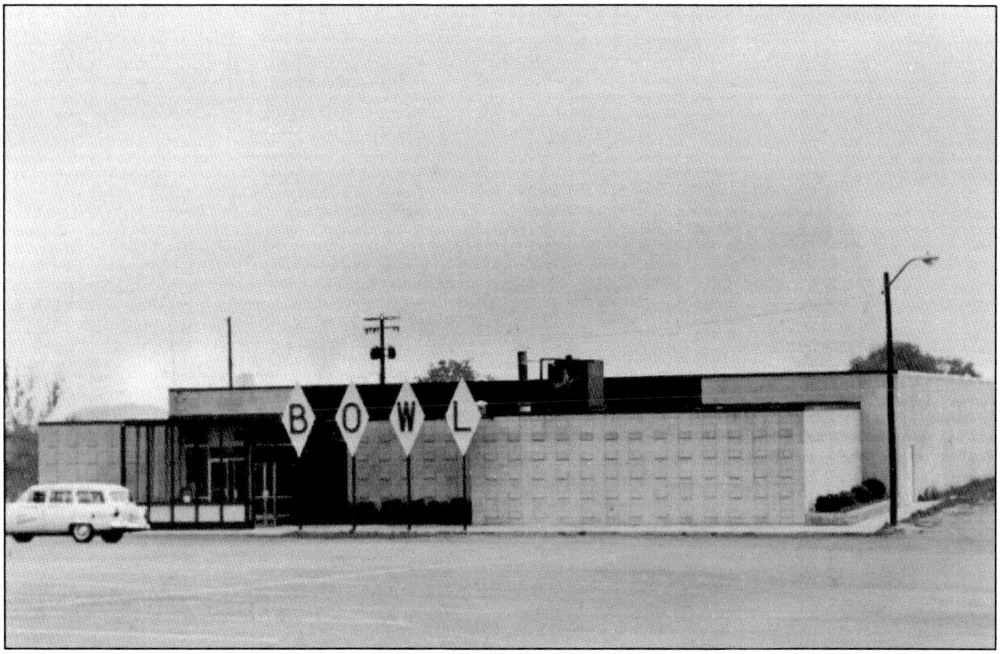

This image shows the old Brunswick Bowling Alley Lanes on Souder Road. This became the site of the new YMCA, which was dedicated on June 28, 1986. The YMCA chapel included a stained-glass window that was salvaged from the wreckage of the first YMCA after the 1980 fire. The YMCA is closed now, and the salvaged window is housed at the town museum. The building on Souder Road is now occupied by the Green Country Inn. (Courtesy Brunswick History Commission.)

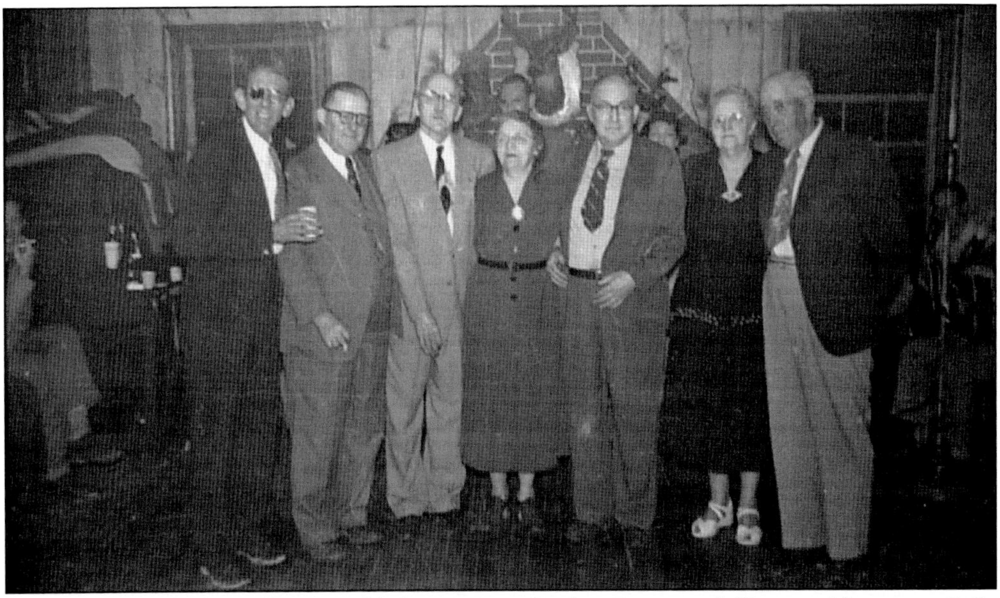

This photograph shows Brunswick's first twins—Luther Brunswick Darr and his sister, Lula Brunswick Darr McMurry—born on April 24, 1891. This picture was taken on the twins' 60th birthday, April 24, 1951, at the Rod and Gun Club in Rosemont, Maryland. Pictured are, from left to right, K. K. Cavalier Sr., Charles Deck, Luther Darr, Lula McMurry, "Brother" Barger, Nell Danner, and Dick Danner. Johnny Norris' band provided the music for the event. (Courtesy Brunswick History Commission.)

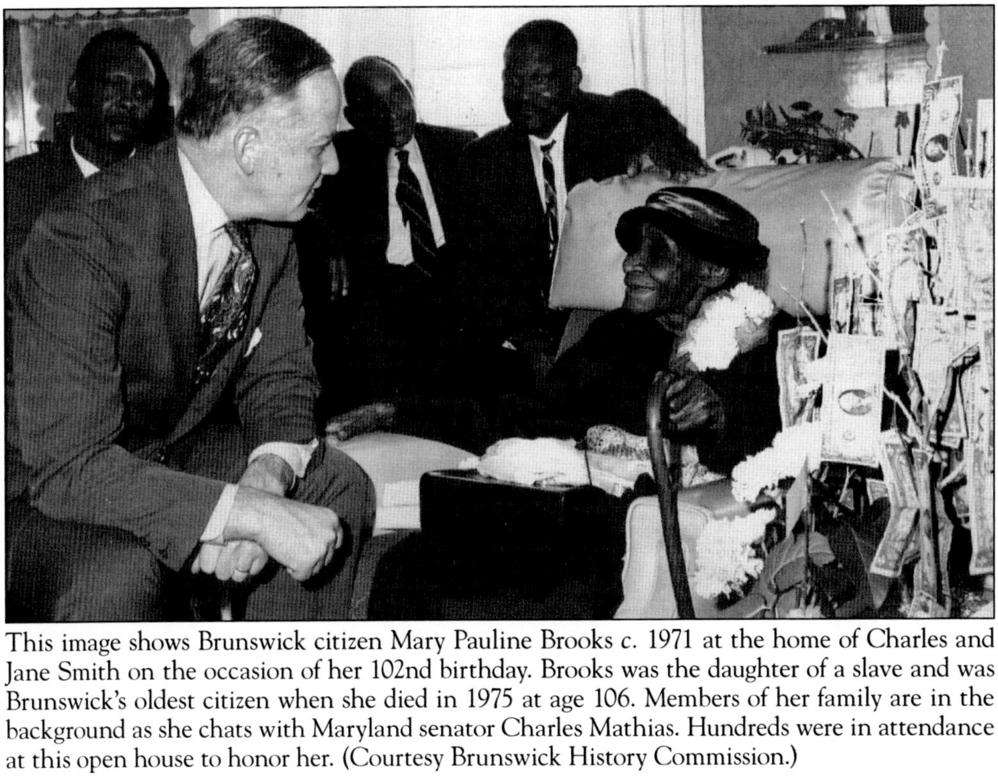

This image shows Brunswick citizen Mary Pauline Brooks c. 1971 at the home of Charles and Jane Smith on the occasion of her 102nd birthday. Brooks was the daughter of a slave and was Brunswick's oldest citizen when she died in 1975 at age 106. Members of her family are in the background as she chats with Maryland senator Charles Mathias. Hundreds were in attendance at this open house to honor her. (Courtesy Brunswick History Commission.)

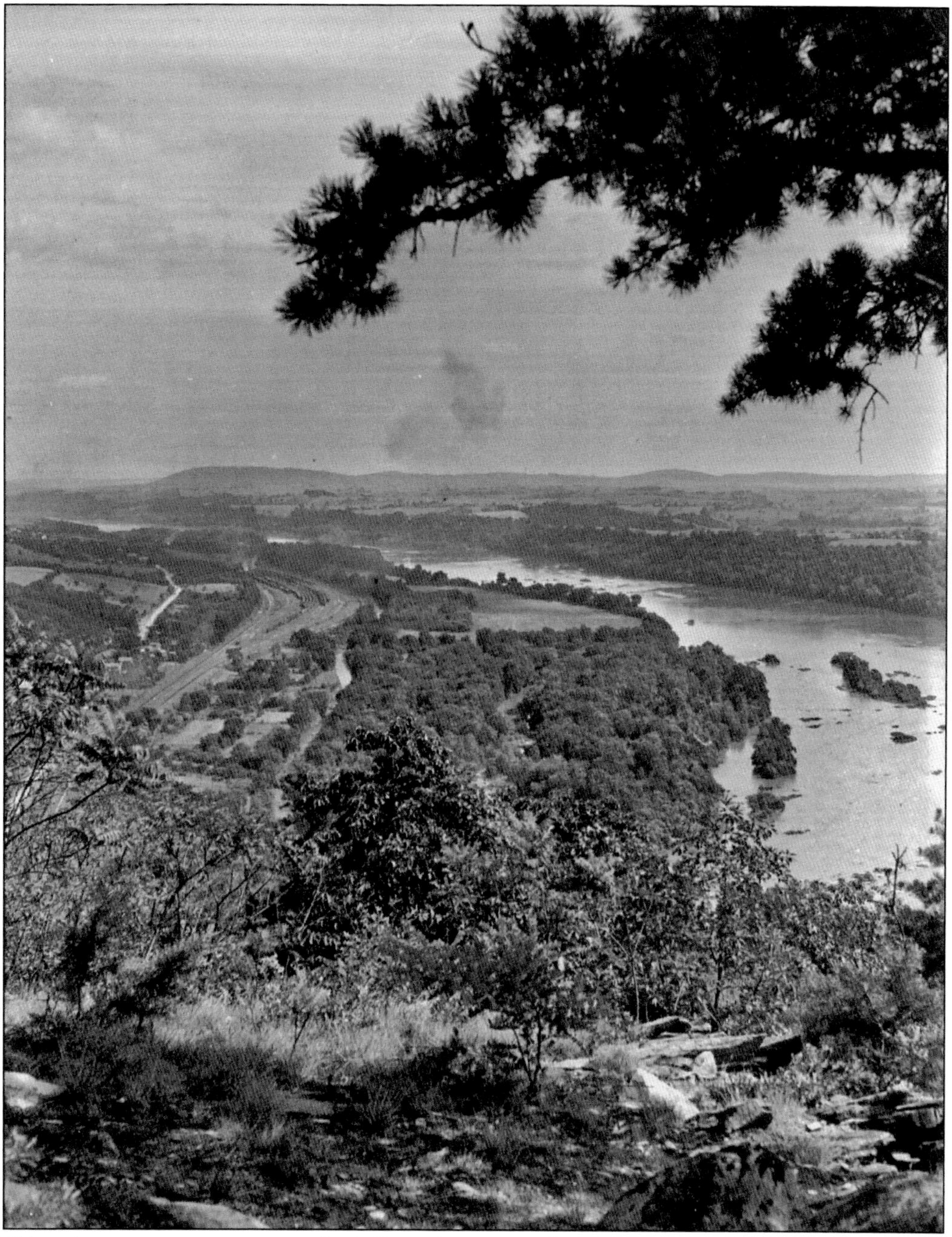

Taken from a vantage point on the hills in the region, this tranquil image shows the Brunswick area. The canal can be seen winding through the trees to the right of the train yards. (Courtesy C&O Canal National Historical Park Headquarters.)

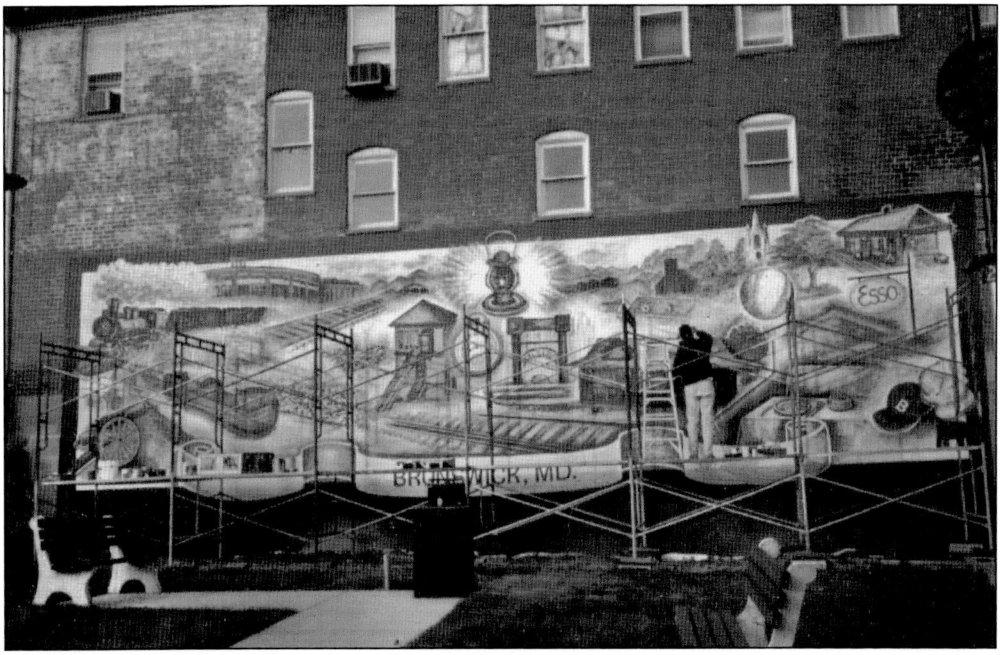

This photograph shows the town mural being painted on the wall of the Daugherty Building. Completed in October 1998, the mural in Square Corner Park is situated on the site of what was once Darr's Confectionery on the corner of Maple Avenue and Potomac Street. (Courtesy Brunswick History Commission.)

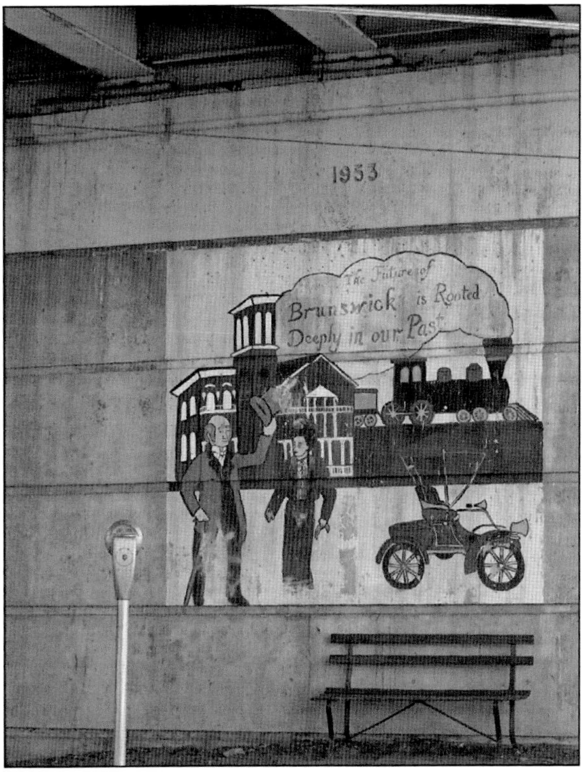

This mural was painted underneath the current Potomac River bridge as a reminder of Brunswick's past. Note the date the bridge construction began, 1953, above the mural. (Courtesy Mary H. Rubin.)

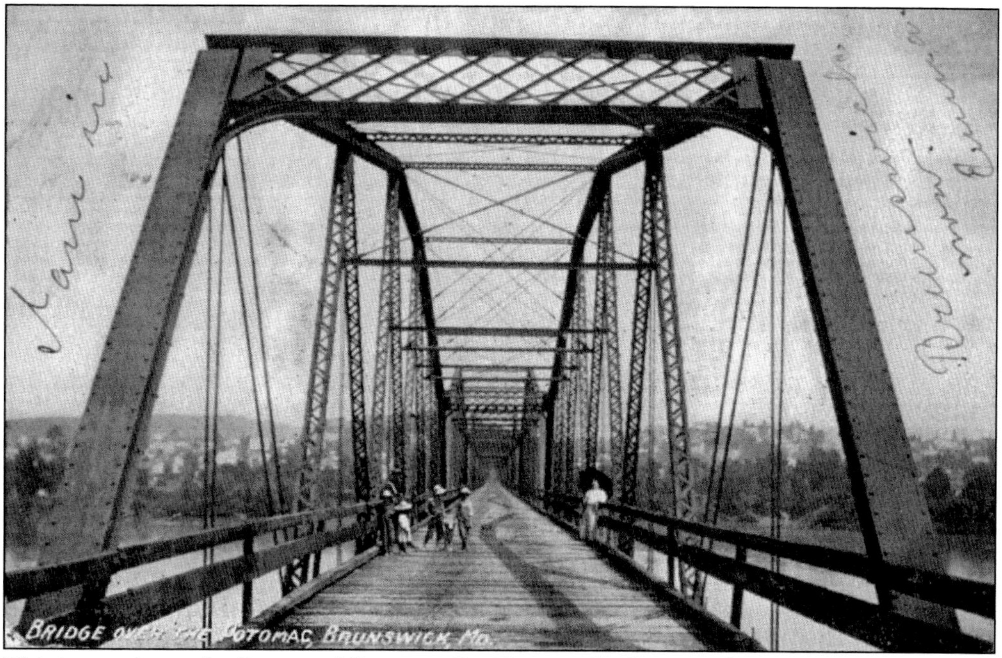

This image shows the Brunswick/Lovettsville, Virginia, bridge over the Potomac River built in 1893. Also known as the Brunswick Lover's Bridge, the old structure was replaced with a new bridge spanning the C&O Canal, railroad tracks, and the Potomac River in 1955. (Courtesy Brunswick History Commission.)

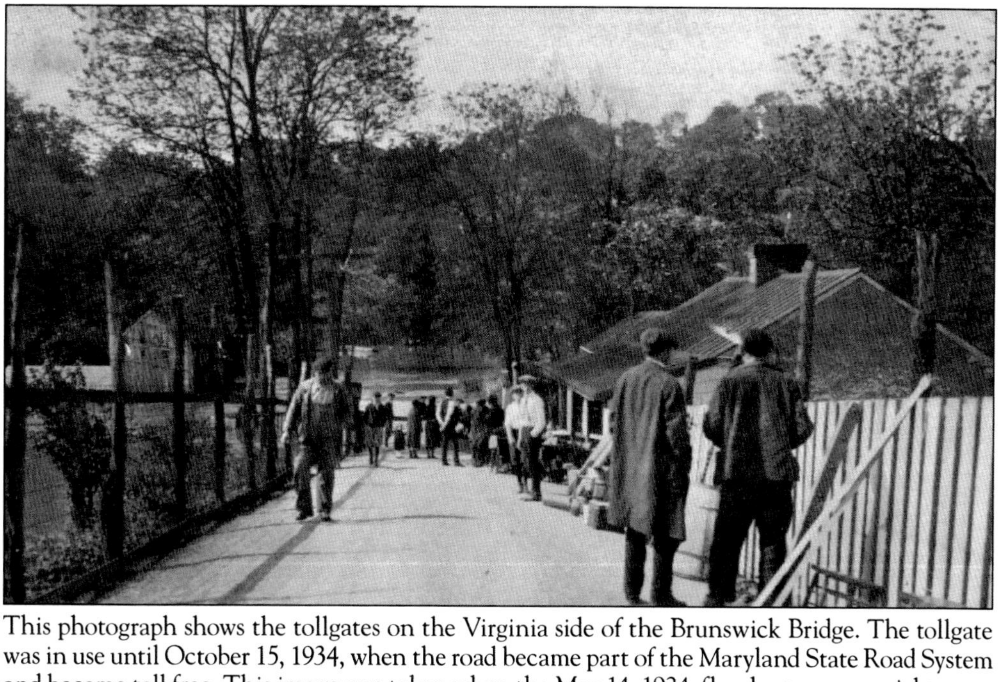

This photograph shows the tollgates on the Virginia side of the Brunswick Bridge. The tollgate was in use until October 15, 1934, when the road became part of the Maryland State Road System and became toll free. This image was taken when the May 14, 1924, floodwaters came right up to the tollgate. The tollhouse was torn down when the new bridge was completed in 1955. (Courtesy Brunswick History Commission.)

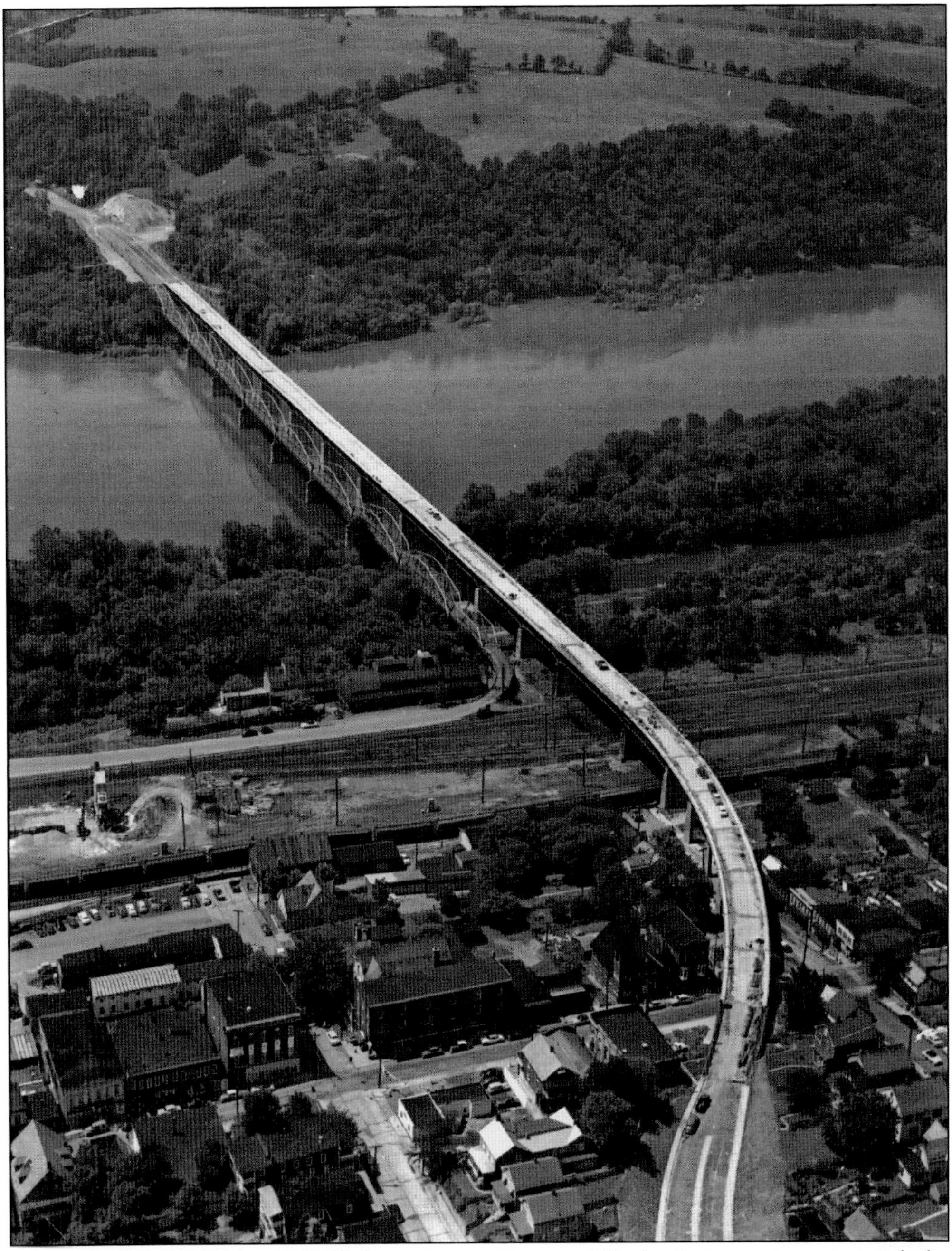

This aerial image from June 29, 1955, shows the new Brunswick Bridge during construction with the old 1893 bridge next to it. The old mill can be seen on the Maryland side of the photograph, as well as many of the buildings of downtown Brunswick. (Courtesy Brunswick History Commission.)

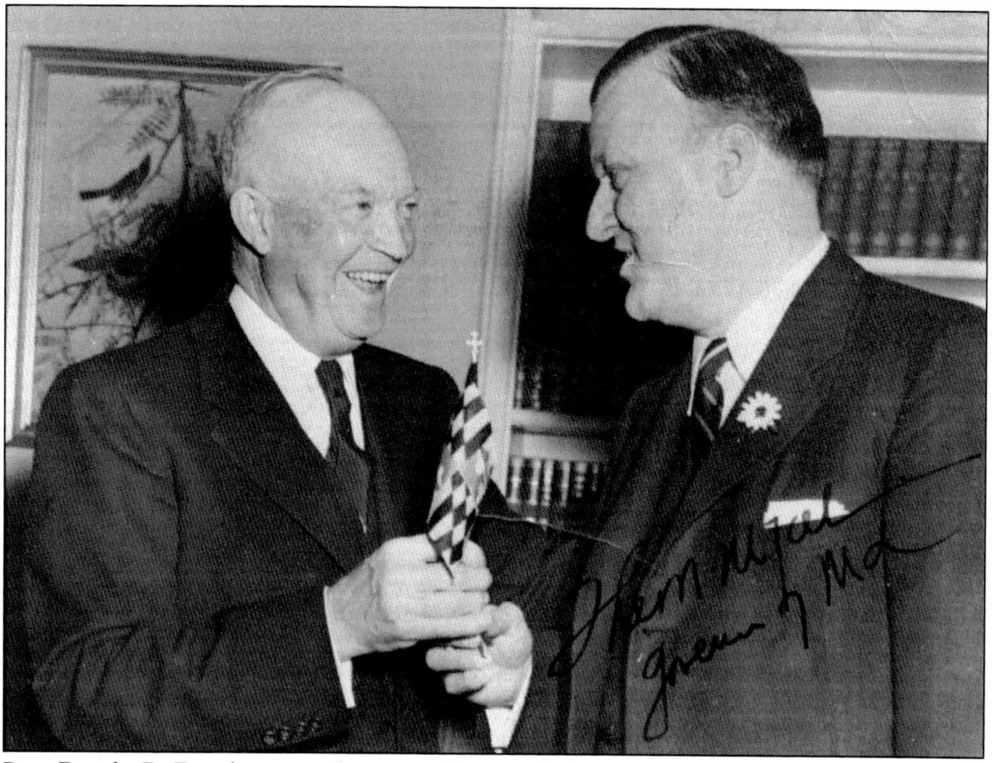

Pres. Dwight D. Eisenhower paid a visit to Brunswick for the opening of the Brunswick Bridge in 1955. He is shown in this image with Theodore McKeldin (right), then governor of Maryland. (Courtesy Brunswick History Commission.)

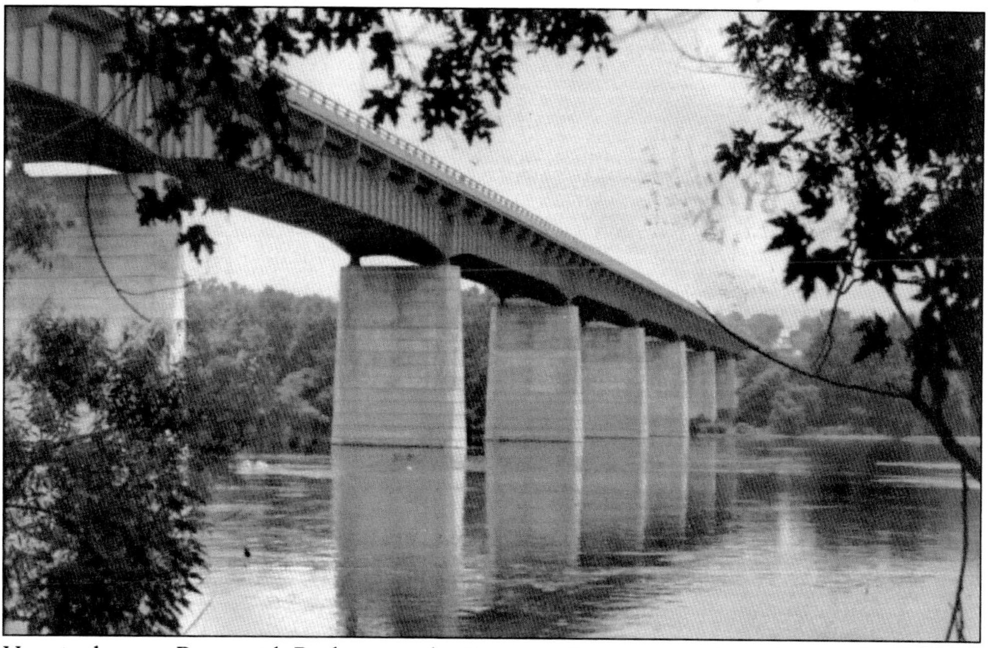

Here is the new Brunswick Bridge over the Potomac River as seen from the Maryland side at water level around August 1970. (Courtesy Brunswick History Commission.)